2013

DISCARDED

Screen Style

COMMERCE AND MASS CULTURE SERIES

Justin Wyatt, Series Editor

Screen Style

FASHION AND FEMININITY IN 1930S HOLLYWOOD

SARAH BERRY

Commerce and Mass Culture   Volume 2
University of Minnesota Press
Minneapolis   London

For information related to this book, go to the University of Minnesota Press web site at http://www.upress.umn.edu.

Published by the University of Minnesota Press
111 Third Avenue South, Suite 290
Minneapolis, MN 55401-2520

Library of Congress Cataloging-in-Publication Data

Berry, Sarah, 1962–
    Screen style : fashion and femininity in 1930s Hollywood /
Sarah Berry
        p.   cm. — (Commerce and mass culture ; v.2)
    Filmography: p.
    Includes index.
    ISBN 0-8166-3312-6 (hc) — ISBN 0-8166-3313-4 (pb)
        1. Costume.   2. Fashion—United States—History—20th century.
    3. Fashion in motion pictures.   I. Title.   II. Series.
PN1995.9.C56 B47 2000
791.43'026 21—dc21   99-040065

Printed in the United States of America on acid-free paper

The University of Minnesota is an equal-opportunity educator and employer.

11 10 09 08 07 06 05 04 03 02 01 00   10 9 8 7 6 5 4 3 2 1

To Cameron

CONTENTS

ACKNOWLEDGMENTS

I would like to thank those who read drafts of this book and whose insight improved it substantially: Richard Allen, Faye Ginsburg, Toby Miller, Andrew Ross, Robert Stam, Chris Straayer, and Jennifer Wicke. They are, of course, in no way responsible for its weaknesses. My research was assisted by the staffs of the Billy Rose Theatre Collection of the New York Public Library; the Elmer Holmes Bobst Library, New York University; the Herrick Library of the Academy of Motion Picture Arts and Sciences; the Gimbel Library, Parson's School of Design; the Baker Business Library, Harvard University; the John W. Hartman Center for Sales, Advertising and Marketing History, Duke University; and the Library of the British Film Institute. I would like to thank Ann Harris and Cathy Holter of the George Amberg Study Center at New York University; the faculty of the Department of Cinema Studies, New York University; the selection committee of the Graduate School of Arts and Sciences Dean's Dissertation Award for their financial support for this project; my colleagues at Murdoch University and the College of Staten Island for their support during my revisions; and Douglas Armato and Micah Kleit for their editing and help in the publication process.

Special thanks go to my friends and family, to Richard W. Fox, who got me started, and to Richard Allen, Frances Goodman, and Toby Miller, who helped me finish.

INTRODUCTION

In 1939, MGM produced a short promotional film called *Hollywood—Style Center of the World,* about the American film industry's gift of fashion to the masses. It tells the story of Mary, a farm girl who has an important date and needs a new dress. She goes to her small-town "Cinema Shop" and sees an ensemble worn by Joan Crawford in her newest film. Mary tries on the outfit, her image intercut with that of Crawford in the original costume. A male voice-over intones:

> And so to this quiet little town, far from the metropolitan areas, the Hollywood influence reaches out to style and gown Mary, just as smartly as Joan Crawford is costumed for her role in [a] new film. . . . The motion picture has annihilated space, blotted out the back woods. . . . today the girl from the country is just as modern and dresses just as smartly as her big city sister.

The Hollywood screen is shown to have bridged the gulf between urban and rural merchandising, acting as a huge, luminous shop window and beacon to the fashion-disadvantaged across the nation. The film represents mass-market fashion as a democratic leveling of social distinctions, suggested in its montage of small-town America and the glowing image of Mary superimposed against billowing wheat fields, happily self-conscious in a chic white ensemble.

The appeal of this fable is hard to evoke in the context of contemporary consumer culture, when we are accustomed to the idea that popular fashion and culture are not only available but also omnipresent throughout the United States due to mass marketing. But this film's representation of the shift from "class" to "mass" fashion marketing celebrates what was still a recent development in the 1930s. In the mid-1920s, American popular culture began to show signs of "fashion madness," stimulated by new methods of production and the opening of department and chain stores across the country. The previous century's time lag between wealthy women's adoption of Paris trends and their gradual uptake by seamstresses, home sewers, and secondhand shoppers was dramatically shortened by these new production and distribution methods.[1] In addition, new media and fan cultures began to erode the authority of traditional society "fashion leaders" in favor of popular celebrities. When a 1929 women's magazine advertisement gushed about a line of "Famous Folks' Frocks," it was referring to styles worn by "popular stars" of Hollywood, not by the socialites traditionally featured in fashion magazines like *Vogue* and *Harper's Bazaar*.[2]

This book explores the relationship between popular fashion and Hollywood films of the 1930s, arguing that both were significant aspects of the decade's shifting definitions of femininity. The 1930s are sometimes viewed as a period of retrenchment for women following the suffrage movement and the rebellious flapper era, a time when the overtly political work of first-wave feminism was diluted by economic struggles and consumer aspirations. But there is another perspective on this era, which takes into account the significance of popular fashion as an aspect of women's negotiation of modernity and post-traditional identity (the shift from hereditary caste systems to capitalist social divisions). Fashion brought the symbolic power of dress into the mass marketplace, an event that epitomized capitalism's shift toward a "symbolic economy" based on the meanings attached to goods and lifestyles rather than on Max Weber's famous Protestant work ethic. The fact that people have come to be identified with what they consume rather than what they produce can be seen as a negative commodification of social identity, as was suggested by the Frankfurt School Marxists and some American sociologists. But because women's domestic labor was never given the same status as other forms of production, the impact of this shift on women's identities is complex.

Male identity and status have, until fairly recently, been defined primarily in relation to work, but women have long been associated with the more symbolic values of beauty, style, and what Pierre Bourdieu calls "physical capital." From Thorstein Veblen onward, this aspect of women's social status has been seen primarily as a way for women to increase their exchange value among men. But women's investment in consumer culture cannot be reduced to husband hunting; it is historically linked to their entry into the service-sector work force, a context in which self-presentation and performance are material issues.[3] In this process, women have not only complied with but also modified the dictates of feminine fashion in relation to their own interests. In other words, women have had to use the performative aspects of modern life (what Erving Goffman called "impression management") in their struggle for greater social mobility and autonomy.[4] Both fashion and film are key indicators of how styles of femininity changed in the early twentieth century, from Clara Bow's youthful sexuality to Greta Garbo's and Marlene Dietrich's Euro-androgyny and Mae West's camp femininity.

The new consumer fashion system promoted stylistic change and mass marketing for purely commercial reasons, but some feminists noted its potentially democratizing effects in the 1930s, particularly in conjunction with the movies. British activist Winifred Holtby, for example, argued in 1935 that "the psychology of clothes is not unimportant. Nowadays, thanks to the true democracy of the talkies, twopenny fashion journals and inexpensive stores, it is possible for one fashion to affect a whole hemisphere with no distinction of class and little of pocket."[5] Consumer fashion certainly did not shatter class barriers in the 1930s, but the introduction of price lines—the production of a single design in a range of prices and qualities—resulted in a relative blurring of the social distinctions that fashion had traditionally served to *accentuate*. Fashion historian Elizabeth Wilson argues that on an "abstract level," post-Victorian women's fashion, "whether made up in precious *crepe de Chine* or cheap rayon, did suggest both modernity and the democracy of urban society," and that the popularity of such clothes may have "contributed to a subjective feeling of emancipation for women."[6]

This view does not imply that consumer fashion in itself had a liberatory effect on women, but that it could represent women's ongoing struggle for visible autonomy in the social sphere. Fashion is a form of communication that, when consciously articulated, can play a significant role in gender politics (Marlene Dietrich, for example, made a calculated fashion statement by refusing to stop wearing men's pants when she arrived in Hollywood).[7] Such gestures by fashion leaders and subcultures have become central to the fashion system's need for the new and the shocking, but historians of fashion and beauty culture, like Kathy Peiss, have pointed out that the very trendiness of early consumer culture was significant because it destabilized older, more essentialist encodings of gender, class, and race.[8] In the 1930s, the effects of consumer culture were felt by women in particular, who were seen as central to the success of the new economy because they bought most goods (even those to be used by men). Similarly, women were seen by Hollywood studios as the primary consumers of cinema— they were thought to outnumber men in theaters and to choose

Marlene Dietrich makes herself comfortable with Maurice Chevalier, circa 1933.

which movies would be seen when attending with men.[9] The resulting overlap in the target markets of the fashion, cosmetics, and film industries gave rise to a culture of cross-promotion that would now be called "synergy": a boom in star endorsements, the merchandising of film costumes through Hollywood "tie-in" labels, product placements in movies, and the extensive use of fashion publicity for upcoming films. The importance of female viewers and fashion consumers during this decade is evident from *Variety*'s review of the film *Fashions of 1934*: "It has color, flash, class, girls and plenty of clothes. It's certainly one of the most saleable pictures extant. . . . The femme appeal is obvious from the billing, so that takes care of the boys also."[10]

In 1930, *Motion Picture* ran a story called "Are You a Screen Shopper?" which opened simply: "The modern woman is a screen shopper. You, being modern, are a screen shopper."[11] But the implications of this campaign to link female film viewing and shopping went beyond the spread of once-elite fashion to the masses; it also made female movie stars central figures in both the film and advertising industries. The number of high-budget films "carried" by female stars (who often earned more than their male costars) was considerable in the 1930s, in stark contrast to contemporary Hollywood filmmaking.[12] According to the *Motion Picture Herald* yearly exhibitors' poll, the most popular stars of the 1930s (male or female) were Marie Dressler and Shirley Temple, and like most female stars of the decade, both endorsed clothing lines.[13] In addition to advertising clothes, cosmetics, and accessories, female stars appeared in film costumes that could be purchased nationwide in department stores through tie-in lines such as "Cinema Fashions," "Studio Styles," and "Hollywood Fashions."

Not surprisingly, then, Hollywood films in this era are marked by a fascination with female power, from the ambitions of gold diggers, working women, and social climbers to the illicit appeal of female androgyny and exoticism. American films of the 1930s certainly promoted specific kinds of gender, racial, and class stereotypes, but they also drew attention to the ways that dress and performance increasingly functioned to define social identity. The economies of consumer fashion and stardom are predicated on the rejection of social position as "ascribed by birth and . . . fixed as part of a cosmological order."[14] Consumer culture thus contributed to the erosion of traditional social categories, replacing them with the aspirational ideal types represented in advertising. But these types must also change in order to renew consumers' motivation to reinvent themselves in a process that raises fundamental questions about these social ideals: if they require constant change, then what are they based on? As Bourdieu has noted, consumer culture promotes a self-referential worldview that values "seeming" over "being," a situation that, I would argue, has had a corrosive effect on older, naturalized hierarchies.[15] Bourdieu refers to such processes as "symbolic struggles," which not only assert new definitions of taste and cultural capital (such as fashionability) but may also improve the social status of those who assert their influence in a particular symbolic field. As Bourdieu suggests:

> Countless social arrangements are designed to regulate the relations between being and seeming. . . . bluff—if it succeeds . . . is one of the few ways of escaping the limits of social condition by playing on the relative autonomy of the symbolic. . . . The reality of the social world is in fact partly determined by the struggles between agents over the representation of their position in the social world.[16]

One way to look at Hollywood films of the 1930s is as a mythology of "bluff," a celebration of symbolic over "real" status. Hollywood cinema was from its inception deeply concerned with issues of social mobility, acculturation, and fantasies of self-transformation. It "appealed to the masses flocking to the urban centers and seeking new national identities to replace the traditional ones" of rural life, and it was produced to a great extent by recent immigrants.[17] As Peter Wollen has pointed out, "the moguls who created Hollywood emerged, for the most part, from the lower reaches of the garment industry." Adolph Zukor began his career as a furrier, Marcus Loew was a fur and cape salesman, Samuel Goldwyn was a glove salesman, Carl Laemmle ran a clothing store, William Fox inspected fabric for garment makers, Louis B. Mayer sold used clothes, and Harry Warner repaired shoes. "It was only natural," Wollen concludes, "that they should want to associate the cinema with extravagant and spectacular clothes."[18]

It is equally clear why such filmmakers would see the significance of clothing to American dreams of self-invention and class transgression. One producer commented that the Jewish studio moguls "felt that they were on the outside of the real power source of the country. They were not members of the power elite." Jesse Lasky once commented, "I yearned to trespass on Quality Street."[19] In their films, fashion was a medium of new beginnings, and the mythology of the "makeover" became synonymous with the Hollywood star's rise from obscurity to fame. Joan Crawford, for example, was widely quoted as saying that "she, too, had her first 'chance' when a friend gave her money to buy 'something decent to wear,'" and in numerous films she played the working girl who made her way to the top, thanks to hard work and a few Adrian outfits.[20]

In the 1930s, tensions around issues of women's social mobility and status intensified due to the depression. In the absence of male breadwinners, many women struggled to keep jobs and reconcile their conflicting positions in the family and the workplace. They were barred from many jobs because of essentialist notions of "women's work" (domestic and service-sector jobs, not industrial or professional ones) and often prevented from continuing to work after marriage (laws were passed to dismiss women from public-sector positions if their husbands were also employed). Women continued to enter wage labor in increasing numbers, however, particularly in service-sector jobs (which grew in number during the depression while traditionally male, industrial jobs disappeared). Such white-collar and retail work placed a heavy emphasis on appearance, and it was not unusual for the ability to act "appropriately" feminine to be included in a job description. But working women could also be blamed for sexual harassment if they appeared *too* feminine on the job (as subjectively defined by their employers).[21] Clearly, this was an era when women were called upon to make numerous calculations about the kind and degree of femininity required by conflicting social, commercial, and domestic spheres.

Marketing discourses of the 1930s placed great emphasis on how "techniques of the self" (such as fashion and etiquette) could help women become more successful both socially and in the workplace.[22] This advertising emphasis on self-improvement contradicted older notions that a woman's social status was defined by her father's or husband's social position. It also challenged the authority of traditional tastemakers by presenting Hollywood stars as a cultural elite worthy of emulation. This shift in taste elites, which was much commented on at the time, granted a solidly nouveau riche social group the cultural status once reserved for a more aristocratic "smart set." This process typifies the way that modern social relations are partially defined in the symbolic realm—as Chris Schilling points out, modern class status is defined according to "the ability of dominant groupings to define their bodies and lifestyles as superior, worthy of reward, and as, metaphorically and literally, the embodiment of class."[23]

Social status was often depicted in Hollywood films of the 1930s as a matter of economic resources, dress, and acquired social protocols. This emphasis on the idea that upper-class glamour is a matter of appearances rather than "breeding" (and can therefore be emulated) does not imply that viewers were interested in adopting the *values* of the upper class. On the contrary, I would argue that Hollywood films and popular fashion discourses of this decade emphasized the demystification of upper-class glamour in ways that underscored the economic basis, rather than inherent social superiority, of upper-class culture. For example, Joan Crawford continually enacted a rise from the working class to the bourgeoisie but usually with an emphasis on her moral superiority to those whose lifestyle she appropriated. Crawford was most likely admired and imitated because of her characters' determination not to be trapped in predetermined social roles, not just because they escaped the working class.

Similarly, the cross-promotional relationship between the film and fashion industries does not represent the mass dictation of clothing style by U.S. culture industries to the American public. In fact, it marks a point of diversification in American commercial style cultures based on the expansion of markets and use of popular celebrities as fashion leaders. As Angela Partington suggests, multiclass marketing can be seen as more compatible with fashion subcultures (such as immigrant, ethnic, regional, and working-class style affiliations) than earlier, more "top-down" models of fashion conformity.[24] Unlike the couture fashion system, which is predicated on exclusivity, consumer fashion is about popularity. The middle- and working-class fashion market has tended to value "smartness," defined primarily as "what everyone else in one's social class is wearing."[25] Since the end of the silent-film era (when female stars often chose their own contemporary costumes), Hollywood costume has rarely been avant-garde by high-fashion standards. Studio designers could not afford to innovate or anticipate major changes in fashion because they could never be sure exactly when a film would be released and how it would correspond to the fashion cycle. As a result, Hollywood costume design often represented a kind of stylistic mannerism: it took a familiar line and made it spectacular. Fashion spin-offs could then be made that simply recut the style in its most conventional forms. What is significant about this process is that Hollywood costumes could be outrageous on-screen and still be compatible with popular taste.[26]

Hollywood costumes of this era were designed to be both dramatic and familiar, and their fashion influence had more to do with the dissemination, stylization, and revival of particular styles than with radical design innovation. But costumes of this era also incorporated dress trends prevalent in Hollywood itself, a style culture that became increasingly independent from Paris and New York as the decade went on. The offscreen style of particular stars, for example, is credited with popularizing fads that were then taken up nationwide (Crawford's suntan and overpainted mouth, Dietrich's pantsuits). Some of these fads represented the incorporation of popular "street style" into Hollywood chic: Crawford's daring use of colored nail polish (painted red down to the cuticle, not just tinted an acceptably "natural" pink above the moon), for example, was picked up from a popular trend among young urban women.[27] As sportswear and casual ready-to-wear became an increasingly visible segment of the American garment market, the traditional flow of design innovation from Paris to New York was countered by both Hollywood's influence and the increasing autonomy of American designers.[28] As the *Vogue History of Twentieth-Century Fashion* notes, "New York and California were the two American sources of ready-to-wear fashion. New York concentrated on cosmopolitan styles of urban dress, while Californian firms such as White Stag, Catalina and Jantzen specialized in sports and casual wear."[29]

The glamour of 1930s Hollywood star culture has often been dismissed as a symptomatic form of escapism or fantasy, particularly when compared to the decade's populist social-problem films. It may, indeed, have been a vehicle of fantasy, but I would argue that notions of the carnivalesque may be more relevant to its popularity than escapism (which implies a glossing over of social conditions). The use of costume to parody, invert, and denaturalize social distinctions may have been a significant part of Hollywood cinema's entertainment value, along with its demystification of specific codes of behavior, dress, and social entitlement. It also marked a turn toward the proliferation of styles and consumer subcultures that has made it increasingly difficult for taste to be determined by a single, unchallenged elite.[30] Contemporary style cultures are heavily influenced by marketing and the media, but they represent a more diverse and contested arena of social communication than has often been acknowledged. Hollywood cinema of the 1930s idealized self-invention, emphasizing the pleasures of consumerism and social performance. This consumer ethic contributed to significant changes in the fashion and gender norms of that decade. Fashion and fan cultures are often seen as trivial or suspect, but it is clear that they have played a role in women's quest to maximize access to a greater range of social worlds. In addition to stimulating consumption, the utopian premises of late capitalism—its "fables of abundance" and credit-based inclusiveness—have also contradicted traditional assumptions about social identity. If consumerism has functioned as capitalism's panacea, it is one that may also have raised serious questions about the legitimacy of social divisions and gender norms.

The following chapters are organized thematically around different aspects of femininity and fashion: class and social status, spectacle and masquerade, exoticism and cosmetics, and women's adoption of menswear. Chapter 1 examines the relationship between cinema, consumer fashion, advertising, and discourses of class and social status. An editor of *Vogue* noted that beginning in the 1930s, fashion models were often "recognizable copies" of film stars, and costume historian James Laver wrote of a concurrent trend toward the creation of fashion "types" that copied specific female movie stars.[31] Elizabeth Wilson notes that in this period, "Bullock's department store in Los Angeles had divided customers into six personality types. . . . The store's promotional material attempted a description of each, trying to match them to the kinds of clothes they were likely to buy."[32]

The use of stars as fashion types was a key aspect of the mass marketing of fashion in the United States; stars offered female consumers a way of personalizing particular types of femininity, which were then symbolically appropriated through fashion. But in Hollywood films this kind of style appropriation was often featured in Cinderella stories in which fashion also facilitated class "passing" and the transgression of social divisions. These films promoted the idea that fashion consumerism could facilitate upward mobility, but they often included a populist critique of social elites. By foregrounding the performative aspects of social status, they demystified class by presenting it as a question of style and money rather than a WASP pedigree.

Chapter 2 looks at Hollywood's use of fashion as cinematic spectacle and as a central element of the self-stylization of female Hollywood stars. Traditions of fashion spectacle such as the stage revue, beauty contest, and fashion show are examined in relation to Hollywood genres like the musical, the fashion film, and the costume drama. The relationship between these genres and the marketing of consumer fashion are explored in terms of the way costume films often celebrate the popular appropriation of "high" fashion or the rendering of historical opulence in popular forms of spectacle, melodrama, and masquerade. In the 1930s, studios used fashion films and costume drama to capitalize on the popularity of charismatic actresses such as Greta Garbo, Norma Shearer, Bette Davis, and Katharine Hepburn, who could "carry" high-budget productions. These films' use of costume as artifice supported discourses of consumer fashion and underscored connections between performance and gender.

Chapter 3 deals with the popularization of cosmetics following a century of taboo. Max Factor, who created much early cinematic makeup, made Hollywood glamour the main selling point of his retail products, as did the countless manufacturers who used stars to endorse their products. The degree of artifice employed by Hollywood makeup artists was emphasized in fan magazines, and cosmetics were often described in terms of the democratization of beauty. At the same time, actresses like Dolores Del Rio, Raquel Torres, Lupe Velez, Dorothy Lamour, and Hedy Lamarr turned Latin and tropical beauty into an alluring beauty "type" rather than its ethnic antithesis. This Hollywood exoticism maintained what Ella Shohat has called "the spectacle of difference" in order to provide a consumable exoticism, but it also ushered in a commodified multiculturalism that significantly challenged nativist beauty norms.[33]

Chapter 4 takes up the representation of working women

and the popularization of menswear. The Hollywood "career girl" dates back to early silent films and the working heroines of serial melodrama. The fact that working women made up a sizable portion of the American cinema audience throughout the 1930s makes it unsurprising that positive characterizations of career women were prevalent. This chapter looks at earlier attempts by feminists to challenge taboos against women's pants, and examines the role of Hollywood stars in popularizing menswear. Women's adoption of pants in the 1930s foregrounded issues of women's social mobility, their presence in traditionally male workplaces, and the popular appeal of Hollywood androgyny.[34]

CONSUMER FASHION AND CLASS

In 1908, the new popularity of ready-made lingerie prompted a Chicago man to seek a restraining order against his own eighteen-year-old daughter, who wanted to buy a nightgown. "She never wore a nightgown in her life," he testified, "and neither did her parents. She's been associating with nifty people, that's the trouble with her. The first thing we know, she'll be buying an automobile."[1] Such paternal anxiety about women's desire to "suit themselves" accompanied the shift to a mass market for fashion. As women entered the workforce in increasing numbers, attempts to control their behavior often focused on the issue of clothing, and employers sometimes tried to assert authority through dress codes. In 1907, such an attempt was a "major issue" in the first large strike organized by a union of female telephone operators.[2] In this context, the wearing of a nightgown could be part of a significant power struggle.

The widespread availability of mass-produced fashion by the end of the 1920s initially provoked the same bourgeois disapproval that had accompanied the rise of ready-to-wear clothing in the nineteenth century. In the 1929 book *Middletown,* a path-breaking sociological study of midwestern American values and habits, a businessman complained, "I used to be able to tell something about the background of a girl applying for a job as stenographer by her clothes, but today I often have to wait till she speaks, shows a gold tooth, or otherwise gives me a second clew [sic]."[3]

But along with snobbish anxiety about mistaking shop girls for ladies, criticism of "fashion madness" within rural and working-class communities was part of a larger debate between consumers who prioritized product durability and utility and those who considered style a valid reason to replace goods. The debate was surprisingly short-lived. A variety of cultural and economic interests contributed to the rapid embrace of consumer fashion by the 1930s—not only in clothing but in product styling that was applied to a remarkable variety of objects. Fashion was suddenly seen as the marketing concept that would fuel a new consumer economy. Along the way, worries that popular fashion might disrupt social class distinctions were replaced by new rationales for fashion as a means of self-articulation, improvement, and upward mobility.

Selling Style

In the late 1920s, advertising trade journals began to register anxiety that the economy was slowing due to market saturation. The specter of overproduction made consumer demand an increasingly central part of the capitalist equation. The automobile industry foresaw that soon all families with enough income to buy a car would already own one; the textile industry suffered losses in such staple goods as cotton because consumers preferred "fancy novelties made of cheaper materials" like rayon, which could be purchased at new "mass production chain stores" like Woolworth and A&P.[4] The problem of industrial overproduction was met with a dramatic expansion of consumer credit and marketing strategies; these were aimed at making large purchases more accessible and at making it

2

easier to replace goods that were still functional but seen to be "old fashioned." By 1930 it could be proclaimed that "just as credit and its availability [supported] the entire productive machinery of the nation . . . [consumer] credit sustains the whole system of distribution."[5] Household appliances like radios and phonographs, which had once been upgraded for technical improvements, came to be replaced because of styling changes.

By 1910, every standard item of women's clothing had become available ready-to-wear. New ensembles like the "Gibson Girl" skirt-and-shirtwaist and the "man-tailored" suit (featuring a fitted jacket and narrower skirt) were available at relatively low cost, catering to women in white-collar and service-sector work. The ready-made clothing industry was marked by a "leveling up of expectations"[6]; the combined effects of new media, faster distribution, and a retailing emphasis on window display made the idea of constant change in clothing design and detail a widespread aspect of consumer demand. Capitalizing on this, wholesalers found that a rapid turnover in styles could be highly profitable as long as production was divided between many small contractors who used underpaid, "sweated" labor. In 1909, the *Dry Goods Economist* suggested that "the way out of overproduction must lie in finding out what the woman at the counter is going to want; *make it; then* promptly drop it and go on to something else to which fickle fashion is turning her attention."[7] The use of subcontracting to produce variety in clothing perpetuated horrific labor conditions for garment workers by maintaining nineteenth-century piecework as a standard mode of production even after the tools of continuous, large-scale manufacture became available. By the mid-1920s, labor unions and the adoption of new equipment made assembly-line techniques more common, but with industrialization male workers increasingly replaced women in all but the most ill-paid and labor-intensive positions. The "fashion system" reached maturity by the end of that decade, and its use of style as a mechanism of planned obsolescence became an inspirational model for other once utilitarian goods.[8] As Roland Marchand has pointed out, the concept of style gave the burgeoning advertising profession a way to "virtually create business" for itself by applying fashion value to a whole range of consumer products.[9]

But the new consumer economy needed a key participant for its promotion of style value to be effective: the American housewife, who had "billions to spend—the greatest surplus money value ever given to woman to spend in all history." A 1928 study found that women made 80 to 90 percent of all consumer purchases, which may have prompted the advertising trade journal *Printer's Ink* to remark that although "the proper study of mankind is *man* . . . the proper study of markets is *woman.*"[10] Since the turn of the century, cheaper retail commodities had made women's domestic production unnecessary, and the chore of manufacturing provisions (or overseeing their production) was replaced by that of shopping for them. The growth of department stores in the 1880s created a space devoted to domestic goods with an emphasis on display that made shopping more pleasurable, with amenities like cafés and lounges that fostered a commercial female public sphere. In New York, department stores were clustered along Broadway and Sixth Avenue in an area referred to as "the ladies' mile."[11] Women's shopping activity was controversial from the beginning, however, provoking both condescension and alarm. In 1882, William Dean Howells sneered at the activity of female shoppers "intent upon spending the money of their natural protectors." But by the end of the nineteenth century, it was clear that female consumption was to be an important engine of commerce, and criticism on the part of business professionals was most often concerned with the problem of "fickle demand, as represented by the female consumer."[12]

Women's responsibility for household purchases made them highly visible representatives of the new economy, stand-ins for the irrationality of market and manufacturing activity under commodity capitalism. The notion that consumerism was a feminine "weakness" had become commonplace by 1929, when Christine Frederick, author of *Scientific Management in the Home* (1915), published a large volume on marketing called *Selling Mrs. Consumer.* In the section on "Feminine Instincts and Buying Psychology," Frederick asserted that "as a sex, woman is predominantly emotional":

> Doubtless this is why Mrs. Consumer is the heart and center of the merchandising world, the great family purchasing agent, who spends most of the money men earn and who is deeply concerned with all the details of ten thousand little items of merchandise, which can be more thrilling to her than men usually realize.[13]

Frederick's husband, J. George Frederick, had written in 1925 of the need for advertising copy to be "so planned that [consumers'] unconscious judgment and not their conscious judgment be obtained."[14] Christine Frederick obligingly compiled a list of women's "primary instincts" to be appealed to by copywriters, since she observed that women have an "especially unconscious mind." In addition, she cited a widely circulated statistic that an average woman has the intellect of a fourteen-year-old. By the end of the 1920s, the female consumer epitomized resistance to "rational" selling techniques. She was said to require appeals without too much copy, since "women will read anything which is broken into short paragraphs and personalized." For many marketing professionals, advertising that flattered the housewife was, like the broader notion of consumer sovereignty, "a veneer over a deeper structure of belief that equated the consumer audience with a mass of doltish dupes."[15]

Personal Style and the Fashion Type

Style became a means of product differentiation that was quickly aligned with the concept of personalization. Neil Harris has argued that this emphasis arose because new commodities generated a fear of mass-produced uniformity as well as a sense of moral confusion: "In the 1920s, the flood of goods seemed impossible to dam; corruption could be avoided not by a refusal to participate in the great consumer drama but by the exercise of choice and the determination of particular relationships between objects and individuals."[16]

While I doubt that most new consumers felt in danger of material corruption (an anxiety more common among elites who feared that "overabundance" might make the working class lazy),[17] the "flood of goods" did pose a challenge to both consumers and marketers in terms of product classification. Women's clothes had previously been available with a variety of detail but relatively few generic categories. They were defined by social occasion (the tea frock, the traveling suit), and such styles were in turn delimited by class. Following industrialization and World War I, women's activities changed radically, and varieties of dress were designed to accommodate new activities (white-collar suits, shorter skirts, sportswear, etc.). By the 1920s, the range of styles available was potentially disorienting, and marketers sought to define new, workable fashion categories. The most successful new merchandising strategy was the concept of the fashion type, whereby clothing was categorized according to certain kinds of feminine personality.

Fashion guides of the 1930s emphasize the importance of choosing the right clothes based on the wearer's personality, but as Frieda Wiegand McFarland points out in *Good Taste in Dress* under the heading "How to Discover Your Style," "Many girls have a style of their own, but are unconscious or indifferent to it. Are you one of these girls? If so learn about yourself. That is how movie celebrities turn into personalities. They get acquainted with their own style, and then play it."[18]

Analyzing one's own personality in order to discover "its" style was, for many, an unfamiliar process; the very concept of being able to evaluate personality as opposed to taking an audit of moral character was relatively new. In most cases, fashion guides advised the identification and cultivation of personal qualities that were already present; some, however, like *Designing Women* (1938), recommended total performativity, and urged the reader to

> cast yourself in a certain role and dress the part. This is the subtlest aspect of taste, the greatest aid in achieving distinction and incidentally the most fun. . . . you must *decide* on your temperament so that you can express it in every line, shade, and fabric of your wardrobe. (emphasis added)

Designing Women went on to explain that "in the following pages we shall attempt brief character sketches of six fundamental temperaments. And you must decide which one is yours. Then study the wardrobes suggested for that type and see how you can make them fit in with your requirements."[19]

Fashion types were marketing tools for classifying customers and organizing demand by linking new goods to preexisting popular style genres. The concept appeared frequently in discussions of fashion beginning in the 1920s and was enacted in the first film costumed by MGM's designer Adrian, *What Price Beauty?* (1924), in which "the heroine wanders through a highly modernistic beauty parlor and sees models on pedestals, all wearing clothes illustrating different 'looks.'" In 1925, a *Screen News* article advised the reader to "Adhere to Your Type Religiously If You Would Be Smartly Gowned," and retail experts, department stores, and home economists used lists of fashion types to define and predict consumer behavior.[20] In *The Economics of Fashion* (1928), an early marketing textbook by Paul H. Nystrom, fashion types were included in a chapter on "Standardization of Sizes and Types," indicating that standardized classes of consumer were as important to mass production as consistent product sizing. The most basic classifications of women began with three "fundamental" types: dramatic, ingenue, and athletic. Nystrom noted that complexion types were one possible way of coordinating consumers with appropriate products, but that individual color preferences tended to overrule guidelines matching clothes to hair, skin, and eye color (this strategy was successfully taken up, however, by the cosmetics industry).[21]

In *Selling Mrs. Consumer* (1929), Frederick offered a list of nine types, while in *Individuality and Clothes* (1930), Margaret Story offered a list of "Women of the Ages," including Cleopatra ("the exotic"), Theodora ("the romantic"), and Joan of Arc ("the leader").[22] However, Story's use of historical fashion archetypes was quickly replaced by references to contemporary figures, particularly Hollywood movie stars. In *Good Taste in Dress* (1936), the "athletic type" was associated with Ginger Rogers, the "boyish type" with Katharine Hepburn, the "sophisticated type" with Kay Francis, the "ingenue" with Janet Gaynor, and the "romantic type" with Norma Shearer and Marlene Dietrich. Costume historian James Laver commented in British *Vogue* that the movies had become an "engine for imposing types of beauty," and that "one curious result of the power of the film has been the spread of type-consciousness to classes which have previously known nothing of such conceptions."[23]

The use of the personality type for fashion marketing is part of the cultural shift from a valorization of character to the cultivation of personality, which historian Warren Susman finds evident in popular literature around the turn of the century.[24] Susman suggests that in the early twentieth century, Protestant imperatives to monitor one's moral character were increasingly modified into a general requirement to improve one's social skills.[25] The popularity of personality-based self-help culminated in 1937 with the runaway best-seller by Dale Carnegie, *How to Win Friends and Influence People*, a book that remained popular well into the 1950s. The discussion of personality was not limited to popular literature, however. It had been a focus of the emerging field of social psychology for some time, particularly among followers of George Herbert Mead. A philosophical pragmatist, Mead described the human self as a product of ongoing negotiations between subjective acts and conscious adaptation to external conditions; these ne-

From the article "Eye Make-Up Styles for Types," *Photoplay*, April 1933, p. 71.

gotiations allowed humans to modify their own behavior based on experience. Unlike behaviorism, a mode of psychology that was influencing the advertising profession, Mead's theory emphasized conscious change over conditioning.[26] In 1937, a psychologist attempted to summarize this concept of personality in *Scientific American*: "It would seem, from the results of psychology, that the familiar thing called personality is not a thing but a bundle of things. . . . the unity that is personality is the unity produced by parts existing together in functional relationships."[27]

Throughout the decade, self-help and fashion guides explored new concepts of personality in works such as *Cultivating Personality* (1930), *How to Develop Your Personality* (1932), *Building Personality* (1934), *Your Clothes and Personality* (1937), and *Designs for Personality* (1938).[28] Such guides offered chapters on matching clothing to one's desired personality, and identified the designs and colors that corresponded to a taxonomy of personality types. The trend was parodied in *A Star Is Born* (1937) when a dowdy, middle-aged woman exits the preview of Vicky Lester's new film saying, "Ain't she cute? You know, I think she's the same type I am, don't you?" In 1938, one fashion writer quipped:

> "Personality" has been the catchword of the public opinion formers these last few years. . . . I don't want to labor the point, but it seems much more important . . . to get one's hair done in the most flattering fashion, and to disregard the fact that one may possibly be honest or kind to stray animals.[29]

Such skepticism about marketing emphases on fashion and personality types indicates that this strategy was not necessarily taken at face value. Such generic types may have been utilized to form localized "mix and match" references to commercial style categories. What is significant, however, is the way that fashion types were linked to Hollywood stars and their representation of social identity as a conscious construction.

Screening the Fashion System

Fashion types began as a marketing tool for the clothing industry, but their translation into a style spectrum of Hollywood stars highlighted the function that theater and film stars had begun to have as fashion leaders. Dating back to Sarah Bernhardt's daring use of kohl and lip rouge and articles like Lillian Russell's 1910 "Beauty as a Factor in Success on the Stage," actresses became representatives for a newly legitimized commercial beauty culture.[30] In 1893, Macy's department store promoted itself with an early fashion "tie-up" by supplying the gowns for a new Edgar Rice play, and early film producers followed suit. In 1912, the adventure serial *What Happened to Mary?* (starring Mary Fuller) appeared both on film and serialized in *The Ladies' World,* with ads inviting its middle- and working-class readers to inquire about " 'Mary' hats and gowns"; and in 1916, one of Pearl White's elegantly functional outfits—a black suit with a white blouse, loose tie, and velour beret—"became almost a uniform dress for New York typists."[31]

Along with fashion newsreels, film serials were the first genres to advertise fashion as a significant feature. Essanay advertised the serial *The Strange Case of Mary Page* (1916) with reference to its "33 specially designed gowns by Lady Duff Gordon," the British couturiere whose "Lucile Ltd." line was the training ground for several Hollywood studio designers. Women were encouraged to view the movies as guides to fashions that could be assimilated into their own wardrobes, and to regard fashion interest as a reasonable motivation to go to the movies. In 1915, *Photoplay* ran an article emphasizing the new opportunities for women in small towns to try out recent fashions by sewing their own copies of film costumes, and in 1925, *Photoplay*'s article "Screen Inspired Readymades" included prices and information on how to purchase copies of film costumes through the magazine.[32]

The movies also played an important role in the promotion of style and "modernistic" material culture. In 1925 Cedric Gibbons, the art director who had "put the glove on the mantelpiece" of Hollywood film (by building sets instead of painting them), went to Paris to see the *Exposition des Art Décoratifs et Industriels Modernes.* On his return, he designed

Our Dancing Daughters (1928) at the newly formed MGM. The film was a huge success, launching both the career of Joan Crawford and the popularity of Art Deco design in the United States: "The decorating craze touched off by *Our Dancing Daughters* was unprecedented. Households began aping Gibbon's use of such elements as venetian blinds, dancing figurines, and indirect lighting. Those with money and relatively adventurous tastes were soon having their homes redecorated in the 'modern' style."[33]

In spite of Gibbons's penchant for white sets, Art Deco found access to the American home primarily through its emphasis on color, which was popularized in the vivid Orientalist set designs of Joseph Urban for the Ziegfeld Follies, making color an American decorating craze following the European one.[34] A number of films of the 1920s and early 1930s featured two-strip Technicolor sequences that highlighted vivid sets and costumes. Films like *The Merry Widow* (1925), *Irene* (1926), *The Black Pirate* (1926), *Fig Leaves* (1926), *The Wedding March* (1928), *Glorifying the American Girl* (1929), *Rio Rita* (1929), and *Gold Diggers of Broadway* (1929), among others, used color to emphasize stage spectacles, elaborate costumes, or fashion show sequences (featured in *Irene* and *Fig Leaves*).[35]

The film industry was often seen as a partner to advertising in the promotion of style-conscious consumerism, as Will Hays, president of the Motion Picture Producers and Distributors of America, Inc. (MPPDA), acknowledged to a meeting of advertising executives in 1930:

> we are accused abroad of selling American goods and it is true that every foot of American film sells $1.00 worth of manufactured products some place in the world; the trade follows the film, not the flag, and there is definite advertising value in every foot of American film. . . . there are no hick towns anymore, the styles are out in Sullivan as quick as Fifth Avenue.[36]

The same year, the *Motion Picture* article "Are You a Screen Shopper?" gloated that "Hollywood movies are not only selling American bathtubs to the heathen Chinee [sic], but they are selling clothes, haircuts, and cosmetics to women in . . . your own home town."[37]

The article praised the producers of the fashion newsreel series *Fashion Features* (screened in "natural colors") for bringing "the latest fashion trends directly to the attention of women" even before they had begun to appear in fashion magazines. The series did not, however, disguise its advertising function, since it listed department stores carrying the clothing displayed. At the same time, however, the presence of brand-name products within the mise-en-scène of Hollywood films began to increase dramatically following the Wall Street crash and its eventual impact on the film industry. As Charles Eckert has vividly detailed, product placement joined overt merchandising tie-ins in the 1930s as a significant source of studio revenue. In 1933, the Warner Bros. studio created "a special department of tie-ups," and its movies featured General Electric kitchen equipment and General Motors cars; the same year, MGM signed a $500,000 contract with Coca-Cola. By the end of the 1930s, the major studios sent scripts to their "exploitation" departments as a matter of course, to be broken down into categories of sponsored products.[38] Similarly, by 1929 the importance of the female audience had "generated an industry-wide emphasis on star costume," evidenced by the distribution of fashion stills and copy designed for newspapers and magazines: "In every major studio, one publicist, always a woman, was the fan magazine contact whose job was to ensure that star publicity material was converted to make-up, hair style, wardrobe or figure care articles."[39]

In the late teens and twenties, Hollywood's relationship to costume design was eclectic and fairly personalized; in the frequent absence of an in-house designer, many actresses favored a particular couturier or "modiste," and some even designed their own costumes.[40] Fashion designers quickly saw

In Warner Bros.' "GOLD DIGGERS OF 1935," Buick is featured with Dick Powell and the Berkeley Girls. Warner Bros. consistently choose Buick for shots of lavish musical revue display, and for those depicting people in the modern manner.

Hollywood—*Creator of Style*— *Chooses* BUICK *for Its Own*

In brilliant Hollywood—where picture directors and stars create the styles for a nation—Buick plays the star style part. A world once ruled by Paris now looks to Hollywood; and there Buick is the featured car. In production after production, for the hit pictures of the year, Buick is chosen . . . just as it is favored by those who value the prestige of modish, modern design. ¶ All you have ever known or heard of Buick size and roominess . . . of Buick quality and dependability . . . luxury, performance and

$795
and up, list prices at Flint.

economy . . . is now surpassed. To see Buick today is to feast your eyes upon aristocratic, sparkling style. To drive it is to gratify your enthusiasm for unsurpassed performance and to enjoy the unprecedented ease and simplicity of the newest automatic operating features. To ride is to know the finest of all fine motoring. ¶ Twenty-five beautiful models, in four series. Four popular price groups, $795 to $2175, list prices at Flint, Michigan. Prices subject to change without notice. Special equipment extra. Favorable G. M. A. C. terms.

BODY   BY   FISHER . . . A   GENERAL   MOTORS   PRODUCT

A Buick/Warner Bros. tie-in advertisement, *Vogue,* March 15, 1935.

the publicity advantages of having their gowns displayed in feature films, but Hollywood was still considered vulgar, on the whole, by fashionable elites. Until the late 1920s, *Vogue* magazine's use of the description "pretty Hollywood" would have suggested a style that was lavish or exaggerated beyond the bounds of good taste; in 1931 Cecil Beaton commented in *Vogue* that silent-era Hollywood had been considered "a wilderness of vulgarians."[41] A 1924 article in *Motion Picture Magazine,* "The Verdict of the Vanderbilts," offered the comments of "a genuine 'society woman'" on "an alleged 'society picture.'" She was adamant that "none of us would ever dream of including in our wardrobes such details as seem essential to 'society women' in pictures. . . . Modistes may carry such goods, but they certainly never show them to their Fifth Avenue clientele."[42]

By the early 1930s, however, two designers who had worked with the couturiere Lucile, Howard Greer and Robert Kalloch, were in Hollywood, as well as Bernard Newman, who had been head designer at Bergdorf Goodman. In 1935 Omar Kiam, who had been a New York designer before moving to Hollywood, reproduced some of his *Folies Bergère* (1934) costumes for Saks Fifth Avenue. The reproductions were modeled in *Harper's Bazaar,* proving that Hollywood design had finally entered the world of elite fashion, as well as Macy's and Bloomingdale's.[43] These and other designers gave female Hollywood stars a more soignée, sophisticated look. In 1929, Howard Greer noted the passing of the era when female stars like Jetta Goudal appeared on screen in completely unique gowns, saying that "the day of individuality and eccentricity in line is done. . . . The smart woman is a pattern. Her frocks follow the accepted vogue."[44]

Hollywood's improved fashion status thus amounted to an increasing adherence to mainstream trends, but as in the American ready-to-wear market, this did not necessarily mean strictly following Paris designers. In 1934, for the first time in nine years, Travis Banton said that he would not make his seasonal visit to Paris; instead, he planned to travel to New York and Palm Beach to see what stylish women were wearing. He also claimed that the influence of Hollywood on the fashions worn in New York was now greater than that of Paris.[45] This may not have been true of New York's fashion elite, but it was probably an accurate assessment of the impact of Hollywood costume on the majority of "smart" American women. What Banton's comments point out is that ready-to-wear fashion culture was more significant to his design plans than the Paris fashion shows.

By the early 1930s, it had become clear that fashion display was a significant aspect of female box office appeal, and Hollywood costume publicity began to emphasize films' display of "wearable" styles, in addition to the ongoing use of costume for characterization, spectacle, or drama.[46] In "Your Clothes Come from Hollywood" (*Photoplay*, 1929), readers were told that

> a radical change has come to the screen in the last few years. It is due to the efforts of such designers as Max Ree, Howard Greer, Travis Banton, Sophie Wachner, and Gilbert Clark. These people have banded together to set aside the old school of motion picture dressing; to make women as smartly gowned on the screen as they would be in a civilized drawing room.[47]

The article concluded with a warning that the appropriation of screen styles must differentiate between "gowns that are made for character" and those that are more generically fashionable. However, this issue also featured "Costumes with the Dramatic Instinct," in which "drama" was seen as an appropriable aspect of Hollywood style, making average women appear more exciting. A 1936 article noted that Hollywood costume became a fashion influence when "girls began asking themselves . . . 'If clothes can accent a character in the movies like that, why can't they do that for me?'" Another magazine drew an analogy between the performance of the screen actress and the skills needed by the average girl for social success: "First, there's a 'test,' then one has to learn the 'make-up' and 'lighting effects' for colors. One must learn her 'lines,' and most important of all, one has to put dramatic value into dressing."[48]

When *Photoplay* introduced a new fashion columnist in 1931, known simply as "Seymour," the magazine's fashion section took on a distinctly consumer-guide-like tone. Five months later, *Photoplay* introduced "Hollywood Fashions," a chain of costume retailing franchises "sponsored by Photoplay Magazine." In this and subsequent issues of *Photoplay*, the usual fashion spread in the middle of the magazine featured ten outfits identical to those being distributed that month to "Hollywood Fashions" retail boutiques in major department stores nationwide. These outfits were advertised under the heading "Now at Modest Prices: Styles of the Stars!" The emphasis on affordability may have been to differentiate Hollywood Fashions from the existing Cinema Shops, a chain of department store boutiques begun by Bernard Waldman for his Cinema Fashions label in 1930. According to *Modern Screen*, the Cinema Shops carried medium- to high-priced dresses ($15–$35).[49] A 1934 press book for *Imitation of Life* cites "special co-operation from the 400 Cinema Shops scattered throughout the United States," and according to a 1937 story in *Fortune* magazine, Waldman's franchise also sold individual licensed designs through fourteen hundred other retail outlets at a price range of $14 to $40 per dress.[50] Warner Bros. also began licensing costumes in 1934 under the label Studio Styles, which featured the designs of Orry-Kelly. *Photoplay*'s "Hollywood Fashions" franchise was, like Waldman's Modern Merchandising Bureau, a non–studio-specific organization that mass-produced a range of designers' work. Advertisements for "Hollywood Fashions" credited Josette de Lima (RKO), Robert Kalloch (Columbia), Walter Plunkett (RKO), Rose Crowley (RKO), Earl Luick (Warner Bros.), Travis Banton (Paramount), William Lambert (Fox), Howard Greer (RKO), and Orry-Kelly (Warner Bros.).[51]

Advertisement for Studio Styles in *Vogue,* March 15, 1935.

Fashion publicity increasingly emphasized dual aspects of Hollywood costume: its on-screen appeal as dramatic spectacle, and its value as a consumer guide to new fashions. In response to mainstream fears that studio designs were too "theatrical" for the average woman, the *Saturday Evening Post* ran an article arguing that Hollywood now consciously addressed the needs of the consumer: "'Right,' Hollywood agrees now. . . . 'We shall continue to make theatrical clothes for the stars who can wear them and the sets which demand them. But from now on the little woman shall be increasingly in our thoughts.'"[52] But these two aspects of screen style were not always differentiated. For example, Paramount designer Travis Banton commented in a 1938 press release for *Bluebeard's Eighth Wife* that

> the clothes I have designed for Miss Colbert in this production are an ideal example of what I consider the current style philosophy for women in every class. By that I mean, clothes which are used to tell a story, further an impulse or stress a desired purpose in the life of the woman in question.[53]

Banton encouraged women to use the theatrical potential of clothing, rather than to downplay it, but he also counseled women to avoid fads and plan their wardrobes carefully. Clothing could "further an impulse," but it should also be selected deliberately, rather than impulsively, in order to tell the right kind of "story" about the wearer.

Banton's concern to dissociate himself from fashion fads may have been due to studio designers' lack of control over the circulation of their designs. Woody Feurt, the former merchandise manager of Bullocks Wilshire, described in an interview how costume merchandising often ran counter to the interests of studio designers. The MGM designer Adrian, for example, turned down a New York sportswear manufacturer's proposal to market clothing with Adrian's name. MGM supported the deal, but Feurt counseled Adrian against it, arguing that "they will never faithfully reproduce your clothes. They

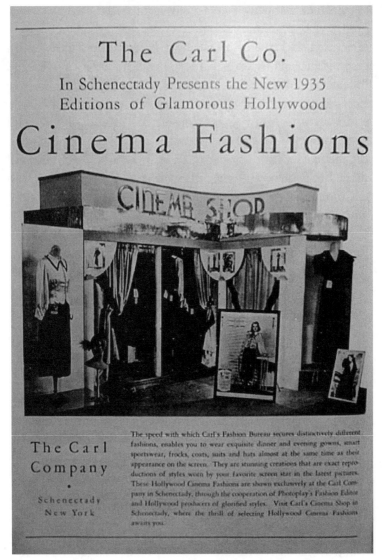

The speed with which Carl's Fashion Bureau secures distinctively different fashions, enables you to wear exquisite dinner and evening gowns, smart sportswear, frocks, coats, suits and hats almost at the same time as their appearance on the screen. They are stunning creations that are exact reproductions of styles worn by your favorite screen star in the latest pictures. These Hollywood Cinema Fashions are shown exclusively at the Carl Company in Schenectady, through the cooperation of Photoplay's Fashion Editor and Hollywood producers of glorified styles. Visit Carl's Cinema Shop in Schenectady, where the thrill of selecting Hollywood Cinema Fashions awaits you.

Advertisement for Cinema Fashions in *Photoplay*, December 1934, p. 54.

just take the idea and make several dresses out of one. . . . They'll probably only pay you royalties on what they faithfully copy, which they won't do at all." Adrian rejected the offer and waited until 1942 to open his own couture salon, Adrian

Ltd., in Beverly Hills. In the meantime, however, MGM was free to send Adrian's costume designs for films like *Letty Lynton* (1932) and *Queen Christina* (1933) to New York manufacturers to be copied for tie-in labels.[54]

Five costume designers (Edith Head, Orry-Kelly, Walter Plunkett, Travis Banton, and Howard Greer) joined "Carolyn Modes" in 1938 in order to design retail fashions, but it is unclear what relationship these garments bore to the designers' studio costumes. For the studios, any association between costume designers and retail fashion was good publicity because it linked Hollywood style to the growing support for American ready-to-wear and wholesale designers like Hattie Carnegie. Fan and popular magazines in this period differed from upmarket fashion magazines like *Vogue* and *Harper's Bazaar* in their conviction that Hollywood design was more innovative than Paris (a claim not supported by studio designers themselves).[55] This claim was, in part, due to a depression-era "Buy American" campaign promoting the U.S. garment industry, which used socialites and fashion journalists to promote Hollywood design and American production over imports. A typical newspaper story on the campaign announced that "Miss Jean Stevens, Chicago society leader . . . is here to study and take back Hollywood styles to Chicago. . . . Miss Stevens believes styles here are superior to those of Paris and other European centers."[56] American sportswear labels increasingly capitalized on the stylish connotation of "California" and "Hollywood" brand-names.[57]

Just as on-screen product placement went from the ad hoc search for paid props to the organization of large, cross-promotional merchandising agreements, the retailing of Hollywood costumes became increasingly organized over time. By the mid-1930s, Hollywood-endorsed fashions were available everywhere, from Saks to Sears, Roebuck; in addition, the deepening economic depression meant that the tradition of home sewing continued as significant source of clothing for middle- and working-class women. Butterick offered costume-related "Starred Patterns," and costume patterns were regularly available in *Silver Screen, Movie Mirror,* and *Modern Screen.* As Charlotte Herzog and Jane Gaines have noted, home sewing discourses tended to emphasize the modification and personalization of Hollywood styles to make them "wearable." In addition, sewing competence was assumed in many fan magazine captions and articles describing costume designs, which used a detailed descriptive and technical language.[58] Much fashion discourse from this period would be inaccessible to most readers today because it assumed an understanding of the rules of basic clothing construction—the implications of using certain fabrics, lines, and techniques. Such skills were also advertised by Singer Sewing Schools during the depression (often in Hollywood fan magazines), which promoted home sewing as a means of gaining access to a world of fashion and self-invention in spite of a limited income.

"That's Individuality": Stars and Emulation

Style adaptation also became the watchword of fan magazines' fashion advice about emulating Hollywood stars.[59] In "The Most Copied Girl in the World," Joan Crawford was credited with innovating numerous fashion fads: "You will know what we mean if you have battled your way through huge puffed sleeves . . . brightly daubed lips, Zulu sun-tan, slacks, gardenias, wide-lapeled polo-coats [and] unplucked eyebrows."[60] At times advice columnists were more cautionary: Madame Sylvia, one of the first diet and fitness gurus of Hollywood, advised a winner of the Jean Harlow look-alike contest,

> just because you look like her—don't imitate Jean Harlow's mannerisms. . . . Be yourself! You are basically the Jean Harlow type, yes—but, that doesn't mean you should try to make yourself a carbon copy of her. . . . you see, there are just a certain number of basic types in women. In all literature there are just 36 basic plots. Yet millions of stories are written. . . . That's individuality, girls![61]

22

Madam Sylvia's description of individual style as the result of exploring one's options within a specific genre (here the "Jean Harlow type") is typical of the marketing use of stars as fashion types; this "variations on a theme" approach to style was said to allow for the safe emulation of Hollywood stars without looking like a "carbon copy." Fan magazine advice offered encouragement tempered with pragmatism about real-life limitations: as *Modern Screen* noted, "we'd all love to be glamorous. And yet most of us must be practical."[62]

The 1930s also saw the greatest use of testimonial and endorsement advertising in history, much of it by Hollywood stars. It amounted to roughly twice the percentage of testimonial use in any other decade between 1900 and 1980. The Lucky Strike cigarette campaign is perhaps the most infamous, because of its scale and the fact that several personalities later admitted to having been paid for an insincere endorsement. But movie stars were a source of ongoing testimonial advertising, even after a backlash began in the late 1920s and the Federal Trade Commission established regulations concerning paid endorsements.[63] In 1927, Constance Talmadge was found to have endorsed "eleven different advertisements of eleven different products" in a single issue of *Liberty* magazine, and Queen Marie of Romania endorsed so many products, following her first appearance for Pond's facial creams in 1924, that she became both a joke in the trade press and a popular synonym for phoniness (she is the butt of jokes in *By Candlelight* [1933] and *Roberta* [1935]).[64]

The question of whether the success of testimonial advertising could be attributed to a literal belief and emulation on the part of the consumer was open to debate, however. In "Are You a Screen Shopper?" the effectiveness of Hollywood stars as fashion models was attributed to the sense of intimacy they inspired in viewers:

> The stage stars could not have changed the public attitude toward make-up. They have always seemed . . . "different,"

23

a race apart. . . . But the screen actresses have been personal friends of their fans from the beginning. And their generous praise of face powders and cosmetics has done much to make their use at first respectable, then universal, and now skillful.[65]

The backlash against paid testimonials was based on similar assumptions about women's trust in and identification with celebrity endorsers. This assumption was considered naive by some commentators, however. In 1931, *Advertising and Selling* ran "The Inside of the Testimonial Racket," which commented:

> I really don't think the public swallows much of the actual testimonial stuff anyway. I think the main value of endorsements is not the fact so-and-so uses such-and-such a product, but rather lies in the name and photograph of the person featured, a person in whom the public is interested. People will always be more exciting than products.[66]

The 1932 film *What Price Hollywood?* opens with a sequence of images that directly addresses the popularity of star endorsements but with an element of self-parody that presents star emulation as more playful than naive. Fan discourse is related in this sequence to pleasure, self-adornment, and employment, since the film narrates the heroine's rise from a waitressing job at the Brown Derby to fame as the newest Hollywood star, dubbed "America's Pal."

Mary Evans (Constance Bennett) is introduced in a montage sequence that begins with a fade-in on the pages of an open fan magazine (its layout is identical to that of *Photoplay*). The pages are flipped as we watch from the point of view of the reader, who stops at an advertisement featuring "Glenda Golden, Frolic Beauty and Screen Star," wearing "Sheer Silk" hose.[67] The magazine image is followed by a dissolve to a pair of woman's legs as she pulls on her stockings. Another dissolve back to the magazine shows its pages flipped to a two-page fashion spread captioned, "Follow Hollywood Star Styles";

this image is followed by a dissolve to a medium shot of a woman from the waist down as a stylishly long skirt slides down over her slip. There is another dissolve back to the magazine and a photograph of a woman applying lipstick, with the caption, "Hollywood stars prefer . . . Kissable Lipstick."[68] This advertisement is followed by a dissolve to an extreme close-up of a pair of rosebud lips, iconically famous as those of Bennett, to which she is carefully applying lipstick.

The camera pulls back to a medium shot, as Bennett's Mary Evans looks from the mirror in her left hand and picks up the magazine in her right. Satisfied with the comparison, Mary holds up the mirror and smiles, then corrects her expression to an exaggerated, disdainful pout, chin held up and eyes narrowed. There is a final dissolve to a shot showing Mary reading the magazine with the pages folded back, revealing a photograph of Clark Gable and Greta Garbo embracing. As she turns the magazine over and sees this picture, she smiles and murmurs, "Mmmmm, oh boy." She then folds the picture in half so that only Gable's face is shown, and holds it up to her own cheek, whispering hoarsely, "Darrrrlink, how I looove you, my darrrlink," in an exaggerated Garbo impersonation. The upbeat musical accompaniment to this scene ends abruptly as Mary realizes that she is late for work, turns off her gramophone, and folds up her Murphy bed. On the way out the door she takes one last look at the photograph of Gable and croons, "Gooodbye, my darrrlink, gooodbye . . ." and makes an exaggerated exit with her head tossed back.

The process by which this character uses each magazine image to construct her own "personal style" is explicitly ironized because of her parodic Garbo imitation. At the same time, Mary clearly enjoys the process of dressing according to the magazine images, and as she gazes at the picture of Gable, she takes possession of his image in "pin-up" fashion, folding Garbo out of the way. The scene also emphasizes what fashion columnists would have called Bennett's "best features," particularly her mouth, calling up a familiar discourse of women's physical self-analysis in fashion culture. The self-objectification enacted here is clearly addressed to female viewers: their familiarity with beauty discourses, their participation in fan culture, and their potential use of fan-related consumerism for their own self-presentation.

The irony expressed in this scene by Mary's Garbo impersonation is maintained throughout much of the film, but it is paired with her seriousness regarding the labor of becoming a movie star. After flubbing her "big break" as a bit player, she doggedly rehearses her single line and her body movements until she has effectively taught herself the protocols of naturalistic acting. She then forces her way back onto the set and performs perfectly, winning a studio contract. Mary's struggle to break into Hollywood by mastering its performative codes is legitimized as labor, and in spite of its parody of Hollywood excess, the film represents Hollywood filmmaking as a populist enterprise (particularly by contrast with Mary's initial failure at breaking into High Society). The status of Bennett's star persona was highly relevant to both the character of Mary Evans and the film's populism. In spring of 1931, Bennett (who was known to come from a socially elite theater family) had received a record-breaking salary of $30,000 per week for the Warner Bros. film *Bought*. News of her salary reached the public at the height of early-depression unemployment. One journalist reportedly wrote a scathing piece estimating, based on the $30,000 per week, how much it would cost Warner Bros. "every time Connie yawned, answered the telephone, changed her dress, or said 'good morning' to the director. She figured that it would take seventy-five dollars worth of time for a lipstick to be used on the famous Bennett lips." According to one fan magazine, this article prompted a flood of letters protesting the amount "being paid a girl in her twenties," and it was suggested that the article "probably hurt the motion picture industry . . . more than any other story written about the films."[69]

Not surprisingly, during the rest of the decade numerous

films were produced in which Hollywood's highly paid female stars played hard-working proletarian women. A letter to *Photoplay* indicated that *What Price Hollywood?* had rehabilitated Bennett to some extent, commenting that "Connie . . . forgot her cultured accent, even forgot her poise, in order to play the role of that cheap but goodhearted little picture star."[70] Such characters humanized Hollywood performers while creating narrative opportunities for the depiction of young women's well-earned rise from the working class to a more glamorous existence. This narrative also created opportunities for the popular trope of the makeover, which tied in neatly with fan and fashion magazine advice on how readers could further their own ends by emulating the stars' performative strategies. The article "Finding Your Type in the Stars" suggests that a favorite movie star could function for the reader like "a sort of finishing school," claiming that "we can all learn much, not only for the benefit of our appearance, but much in the way of the little niceties of life, the fine points that always pave the way for any girl."[71]

The celebration of female stars as archetypes of successful self-fashioning was sometimes characterized as a mere professionalization of traditional femininity. For example, the article "Stop Making Excuses! You Can Learn to Dress!" lectured the reader:

> What to wear and how to wear it! . . . There you have every woman's life work. For irrespective of any other job we do in a home, an office or a studio it most decidedly is our job to be the most attractive individual it is possible for us to be.[72]

Similarly, the article "Glamor Is Not a Gift" stated flatly, "There are some who are born with it. And that's their good fortune. There are others who never do have it. And that's their fault, their lack of gumption. . . . You can learn to be glamorous."[73] But such imperatives do not reflect the range and contradictions among the styles of femininity typified by many new stars who were held up as models for emulation in fan magazines. For example, one article commented that

> Hollywood has created a new woman, a different type of heroine. . . . the leaders of the new school are Garbo, Marlene Dietrich, Tallulah Bankhead [and] Joan Crawford. . . . The new cinema heroine can take care of herself, thank you, since she combines, with her mysterious allure, many of the hard-headed attributes and even some of the physical characteristics—the tall, narrow-hipped, broad shouldered figure—of men.[74]

In this article, changes taking place in what it meant to be "the most attractive individual . . . possible" are pointed out, such as the sudden challenge posed to the girlish rosebud mouth by Crawford's scandalously large lips. Garbo's "deep, throaty" voice, lean body, and "efficient" stride are said to "combine subtly both masculine and feminine characteristics" in ways that were clearly alluring to female fans.

The stars' styles of femininity and glamour are also represented as egalitarian because unlike mythical aristocratic qualities, they are not inherited or "natural." This means that on a lesser scale the power attained by the star is available to those who can teach themselves to feel and act entitled to it. As one letter to *Photoplay* suggested:

> It seems to me that Joan Crawford has accomplished the one difficult thing so many girls dream of doing. Rising from a lower status to her present heights is in truth a modern fairy tale that holds the working girl of today entranced. . . . Is it any wonder she is fascinating to us?[75]

Crawford is perhaps the ultimate "self-made" woman of Hollywood, an image that she also characterized in many films.[76] Her own rags-to-riches life was well known, as well as the story she told of how she went from being a chorus girl to a Hollywood player:

Joan is quoted as saying that . . . she, too, had her first "chance" when a friend gave her money to buy "something decent to wear." . . . Recalling that dress, she said, "I defy Hattie Carnegie to sell me a gown that will make me feel more chic than the little four-ninety-eight model I bought that day."[77]

The importance of clothing as a catalyst for new kinds of social behavior is featured in a range of films that focus on women's ability to act with authority and ability in new or intimidating situations, such as a male-dominated workplace or an urban environment. Such films sometimes feature the use of clothes to create an impression of bourgeois sophistication, as Crawford's anecdote suggests. But some fashion journalism offered a more ironic complicity with the reader regarding upper-class style and pretension. A *Photoplay* winter fashion spread, for example, coyly asserted that "to expect a girl to go through cold weather with only one fur coat is just sheer cruelty," and one caption described "a practical and attractive coat for . . . polo matches, whippet races . . . or what have you." This tone acknowledged that there were limits—both economic and cultural—to the degree to which fashionability could be identified with upper-class taste in mainstream magazines. In another issue, a photograph caption overtly made fun of assumptions that women's fashion emulation was based on psychological identification: "It wouldn't baffle Freud a bit if this gown haunted your dreams. Any good psycho-analyst would tell you your suppressed desire was to look like Dorothy Mackaill."[78]

The concept of star emulation is thus represented in terms of both calculation and fantasy, but rather than being discussed as a matter of psychological identification with particular stars, it is often presented as a conscious move to adopt a particular set of fashion and behavioral codes. In the opening sequence from *What Price Hollywood?* however, this process is also linked to a more playful and pleasure-oriented mode of self-conscious role-playing modeled on the stylized personae of Hollywood stars like Garbo. In either case, it is not a process that can be reduced to a naive or passive adoption of fashion marketing directives but must be seen as one that was inevitably connected to both the imaginative activities of women's fan culture and women's conscious use of fashion's social semiotics.

Deconstructing Class Difference

—I'm afraid he's the kind of man who would only be interested in someone of his own social stratum.

—Stratum? What's that? Something I ain't got? I'll make him forget he ever saw a stratum.

Mae West in *Goin' to Town* (1935)

Debates about consumer emulation and star endorsements are significant in light of the two main types of celebrity endorsers targeting female consumers in this period: Hollywood stars and "society women." It has been suggested that this split represented an attempt by advertisers to divide their advertising between a "class" and a "mass" target market, but I would argue that the two strategies were not necessarily aimed at different markets. They may have been effective because of a broad, popular interest in the representational codes of class.[79] For example, the J. Walter Thompson agency ran the longest-running Hollywood and "society" endorsement campaigns of the decade, for Lux Toilet Soap and Pond's facial creams, respectively. These ads regularly appeared only pages apart in the same magazines, suggesting that they were not addressing different consumer categories but representing different modes of femininity. The attributes associated with Pond's (refinement) and Lux (glamour) were linked to particular categories of female celebrity; each type of femininity emphasized a different kind of cultural capital rather than representing a contrast between class-as-authentic status and Hollywood-as-popular status. Testimonial campaigns by society women in

30

BETTE DAVIS tells you
how to protect
daintiness

"The easiest, most delightful way I know to protect daintiness is to bathe with Lux Toilet Soap. The ACTIVE lather leaves skin really _sweet_—fragrant with a delicate perfume you'll love.

"All you girls who want to be popular—here's something you ought to remember: The man was never born who could resist the charm of perfect daintiness. The least fault against it just ruins illusions—and spoils romance.

"A Lux Toilet Soap bath relaxes and refreshes me. It's a real beauty treatment. Try it next time you're tired and have a date. You'll find it peps you up in no time—makes you feel sure of yourself—ready for conquests!"

WARNER BROTHERS STAR

H AVE you ever thought before of what this lovely screen star says? The charm that's most appealing of all—perfect daintiness from head to toe—is a charm within the reach of any girl.

A regular Lux Toilet Soap beauty bath will leave you refreshed—skin _sweet_—pores freed of hidden traces of stale perspiration by ACTIVE lather. Your skin will have a delicate fragrance that makes people want to be _near_ you. Try this simple, inexpensive way to make sure of daintiness. Famous screen stars use it. You're sure to find it works for _you._

9 out of 10 lovely screen stars use this gentle soap with ACTIVE lather. You can keep your skin soft and smooth the easy Hollywood way.

LUX
TOILET SOAP

Advertisement for Lux soap with Bette Davis, circa 1935.

the 1930s are less a sign of outdated respect for nobility than of its appropriation (as a set of codes) into the commercial and popular fashion vocabulary.

Movie stars were decidedly not in "society," however. Stars were still excluded from elite social gatherings, in spite of the efforts of countless stars from the silent- and sound-film eras to access this realm through liaisons with European aristocrats. Instead, Hollywood was represented as a meritocracy, of sorts: "It must be understood that there is no society in Hollywood as there is in Mayfair, Park Ave., Newport and Palm Beach. . . . You must have a great name, great success, or be extremely amusing if you would belong."[80]

High Society and stardom were still discrete and unequal social realms, and as a result, the wealth of Hollywood stars was often represented as part of a populist struggle against traditional social hierarchies. The resulting characterization of film stars was thus somewhat contradictory. Constance Bennett, for example, was attacked for her excessive salary, while Joan Crawford was both highly paid and a notorious "clothes horse," yet her film roles often maintained her working- and middle-class affiliation. This ambiguity in stars' class affiliation (they are rich but really just like "us") is also evident in films in which a female character's self-transformation and escape from poverty are valorized, but social climbing per se is questioned. This split is particularly visible in "gold digger" films in which the heroine's social climb is unsuccessfully comic or tragic (such as Jean Harlow's *Red Headed Woman* [1932], *Personal Property* [1937], and *Dinner at Eight* [1933]; and Barbara Stanwyck's *Baby Face* [1933]). The gold digger's temporary rise in status often has the effect, however, of underscoring the unfairness of her initial social inferiority, deflating the pretensions of the upper class and commenting cynically on the antidemocratic basis of wealth and social status (this critique is particularly clear in *Baby Face*, in which the impoverished heroine's near-rape in the opening scene gives the audience a clear understanding of her desire for autonomy and revenge).

In musicals, gold-digging showgirls are aligned with popular entertainment and pleasure, while society snobs are often lampooned or shown to be hypocritical (as in *Gold Diggers of 1933* [1933] and *Dames* [1934]). In such films, the showgirl symbolizes Hollywood's embattled status in relation to high culture and traditional morality, since she just wants to live well and have a good time. *Photoplay* invoked this metaphor in 1933, when the effects of the depression finally hit the studios and pay cuts were demanded: "Hollywood has hit bottom. . . . She has been the chorus girl on the world stage . . . and now she is reduced to a diet of beans. How's she taking it?"[81] Depression-era musicals answered by showing that beneath her glitzy veneer the Hollywood showgirl had a work ethic and a proletarian soul. In *Dancing Lady* (1933), for example, Crawford pushes herself relentlessly to make it in show business but rejects the proposal of a society swell (Franchot Tone) in favor of her hard-working boss (Clark Gable).

When female characters do move from the working class into the upper echelons of society, it can be through a career, through posing as a socialite, or through the intervention of a fairy-godmother-like figure. In almost all cases, the resolution of her class transgression comes in the form of marriage—either as a return to her original status (sacrificing money for love) or as a legitimization of her class rise because of her honest love for a man who just happens to be rich. In either case, such Cinderella stories usually focus on the process by which the heroine manages to "pass" in an elite social milieu and perform entitlement to social status. In Crawford films such as *Possessed* (1931), *Mannequin* (1938), *The Bride Wore Red* (1937), and *The Last of Mrs. Cheyney* (1937), the heroine's desire for upward mobility is also explicitly linked to her initial poverty in working-class jobs (at a factory, as a garment worker, as a café singer, and as a shop girl, respectively). Her working-class values and integrity are consistently upheld, however, and in the latter three films, Crawford's character breaks into high society only to reject its values and make an impassioned critique of the rich.

The Bride Wore Red illustrates the detail and fascination with which class difference is explored in these films and links class performativity explicitly to clothing-as-masquerade. *Bride* was the fifteenth film directed by Dorothy Arzner and was not very successful at the box office; some of its limitations have been ascribed to the influence of Louis B. Mayer at MGM, who was determined to soften the story's class critique (the film is based on a play by Ferenc Molnár).[82] Like George Bernard Shaw's play *Pygmalion*, *The Bride Wore Red* begins with a disagreement between two men over the basis of class difference, with one of the men setting out to prove that upper-class status is a matter of money and appearances, not "breeding." Ultimately, however, the narrative works to romanticize seemingly organic class differences and the notion that happiness comes from finding one's proper place in the natural social hierarchy. What makes the film interesting is that this recuperation of class difference is so unsuccessful because of Crawford's star image, her performance, and the ways they conflict with the film's attempted resolution.

The film opens with a callow young aristocrat, Rudi Pal (Robert Young), and the world-weary Count Armalia (George Zucco) playing roulette in a Trieste casino. The Count challenges Rudi with the comment, "Do you suppose that there's anything to distinguish you from that waiter, except your clothes and the fact that you sit while he stands?" Rudi replies that "breeding" makes all the difference, and that breeding is more than clothes and manners. Determined to prove him wrong, the Count secretly invites a poor café singer named Anni (Crawford) to masquerade as a society woman named Anne Vivaldi at the same mountain resort where Rudi and his fiancée are staying. Judith Mayne has pointed out that

> performance is central to *The Bride Wore Red*. . . . [It] emphasizes from beginning to end the extent to which

women's identities—sexual as well as class—depend upon performance. . . . The central performance that [Anni] undertakes in the film, of course, is her attempt to act like a "lady." Two particular elements are significant here: her assumption of arrogant speech with servants, and her entrances in different types of clothing down the staircase of the hotel.[83]

It is significant that both Anni's ability to act like a snob and her fashion sense are indirectly attributed to her observation of upper-class behavior in movies. When queried by the Count about how she learned her manners, she replies, "I go to the movies. I watch the ladies of your world—they're all so simple and stupid and artificial." In addition, the way that Anni later stages her dramatic entrance down the central stairway to the hotel clearly references (cinematic) fashion shows and Ziegfeld Follies–style costume parades.[84] She thus borrows from popular representations of class and glamour in order to successfully pass herself off as a lady. Unlike Eliza Doolittle, Anni is not marked by her accent, which plays no role in the film. Her biggest hurdle appears to be that of unlocking the secrets of restaurant dining. A perceptive waiter, however, tells Anni what to order and how to eat it, in a gesture of working-class solidarity.

The real dialectic of Anni's two identities is played out in relationship to clothes. Anni's initial transformation from wearing a plain, cotton dress with a peasant-yoked neck is marked by a transgression—she enters an exclusive dress shop. Freed from her job at the dark, dingy café, she invades the bourgeois sphere of the dress shop, and then the exclusive mountain resort, literally miles "above" her original social position. The symbolism of clothing is clear in the dress-shop scene, in which Anni declares that she wants a red evening gown with beads on it. Later we are told that at moments of despair, Anni used to fantasize about finding a box containing a beautiful red dress. More significant than money, the red

Joan Crawford goes shopping for a makeover dress in MGM's *The Bride Wore Red* (1937). Courtesy of the Academy of Motion Picture Arts and Sciences.

dress represents Anni's desire for autonomy and passion, both of which eventually conflict with her masquerade. On the night she arrives at the hotel, she is warned against wearing the dress by a chambermaid, who turns out to be her old friend Maria. Seeing the dress she exclaims, "Not this red dress, not here. You may as well wear a sign." Although it is too loud to be worn by a lady, the dress comes to signify Anni's rebellion against both gentility and poverty.

One of Anni's most strategic costumes, however, is a frilly, traditional peasant dress to be worn to the local Tyrolean festival. The dress echoes the square-yoked one that Anni wears on her initial visit to the dress shop, suggesting that this pastoral look reflects Anni's "authentic" self when she is not singing at the café or pretending to be a lady. But the costume's exaggeratedly traditional femininity clashes notably with Anni's modern cynicism and tendency to lounge around her hotel room in negligees, smoking cigarettes. The dress has white puffed sleeves, an embroidered square yoke (lowered by Anni to be more seductive), and a full skirt. For the festival, Anni's hair is crowned with flowers, and she is shown on the night of the festival in a highly picturesque pose: in a medium close-up at her window, Anni's face is framed by the white flowers in her hair and puffy white sleeves of the dress, while the window is bordered by dark green pine branches. The image contrasts pointedly with the image of Anni shortly before in her bedroom, shot from above while reclining, wrapped in a feather boa with her arms stretched languorously overhead. This modern Crawford persona reappears, however, when Anni decides to celebrate her successful masquerade (Rudi Pal has proposed to her) by wearing her outrageous red dress down to dinner.

Anni's red dress is the most contemporary-looking gown in the film: it is cut on the bias from Crawford's broad shoulders to the floor, is made of solid, glittering red bugle beads, and has a small cape of the same fabric held by a band across the collarbone. The gown contrasts dramatically with the more Victorian-inspired, full-skirted evening gowns worn by aristocratic women in the film. Anni's decision to wear it can be seen as a sign that she is still a café chanteuse at heart. But it also suggests Anni's desire to flaunt her contempt for the pretensions and codes of the upper class. Like the red dress that Bette Davis wears to a white cotillion ball in the following

Joan Crawford makes her entrance in the red dress (publicity photograph *The Bride Wore Red*). Courtesy of the Academy of Motion Picture Arts and Sciences.

year's *Jezebel* (1938), Anni's dress is a protest and gesture of reclaiming her original desire for autonomy and pleasure (the fantasy of finding a transformative red dress) rather than accepting the roles offered to her.

Following her exposure, Anni must give up her clothes in order to pay the hotel bill, but she descends the stairs defiantly, wearing a full, floor-length black cape. The cape is the film's coyest use of costume, since it delays the display of Anni's final choice of identity. The film's romantic close reveals that under her black cape Anni is again wearing her frilly peasant dress and that she has chosen to marry the local postman (Franchot Tone). Judith Mayne has noted, however, the irony of the final scene, pointing out that Anni "adopts a costume from the most elaborate performance of the film to claim her authentic self." While this ending suggests that Anni has found her "proper place" in the social hierarchy, her abandonment of her desire for autonomy (the red dress) is far from convincing, particularly since the more modern version of Anni's character is so stylistically linked to Crawford's own glamorous star persona. Anni's final choice thus appears less "authentic" than pragmatic. The film is constructed as an interrogation of class difference, but its unconvincing resolution demonstrates the character's lack of social options in terms of both class and gender; it problematizes the roles available to her rather than successfully naturalizing them.

Class Parody and Imposture

By the mid-1930s, the Cinderella story and its use of fashion to signify class had become so familiar that it was frequently a comedy theme.[85] In *Easy Living* (1937), when a fur coat is thrown from a penthouse and lands on the head of a working-class woman (Jean Arthur), her life changes dramatically as the coat opens doors and gives her an entirely new social status. In such comedies of class imposture, the European aristocracy is often infiltrated by an American, adding to the genre's populism. The wave of exiled Eastern European and Russian aristocrats that arrived in the United States after World War I had by the mid-1930s produced a popular mythology of class reversal. Baronesses and counts were discovered working as servants and taxi drivers, and impostors successfully gate-crashed society. Films with this theme were popular throughout the interwar period.[86] In 1931, Fox star Elissa Landi was

Carole Lombard does Garbo in a publicity photograph for *The Princess Comes Across* (1936). Courtesy of the Academy of Motion Picture Arts and Sciences.

"discovered" to be the granddaughter of the Empress Elizabeth of Austria, and a series of other regal-looking European actresses were brought to the studios in an attempt to capitalize on the popularity of Garboesque European glamour.[87]

As the opening scene of *What Price Hollywood?* shows, Garbo's accent and mannerisms were often caricatured and

Greta Garbo in an MGM publicity photograph, circa 1935.

quickly became a code for foreign, aristocratic femininity. The 1936 film *The Princess Comes Across* features Carole Lombard performing what amounts to an extended Garbo impersonation. Lombard plays Wanda Nash of Brooklyn, an aspiring actress who poses as the Princess Olga of Sweden in order to get a Hollywood film contract (based, according to one review, on actual events). As the princess, she wears her hair in the famous Garbo bob (smooth over the crown and fastened by a comb at the nape of the neck), paints her lips in Garbo's distinctive downward arc, tilts her chin up, wears a cloak with a high "Garbo collar," and utters exaggeratedly pseudo-Swedish mispronunciations. Fred MacMurray plays the American "King" Mantell, a popular musician who is initially snubbed by the faux-princess because he is not a real king, as his title leads her to believe. The film contrasts Wanda and Mantell's status as popular entertainers with old-world authority, as a group of European detectives threaten Wanda's ruse. Although Wanda assumes that her movie career has been sacrificed when she exposes herself as a con artist, Mantell tells her not to underestimate the American public and their appreciation of a good masquerade. This ending implies that Wanda may still get her studio contract because she can act like a princess without being one, which is far preferable to being a real aristocrat.

Like *Easy Living,* in which a fur coat changes a woman's life, the film *Midnight* (1939) is a comic Cinderella story that makes fun of class distinctions and presents status as a matter of appearances. When Claudette Colbert goes from being Eve Peabody of the Bronx to being the Baroness Czerny of Hungary, all she changes is her clothes. Other aspects of her behavior, speech, and etiquette apparently bear no trace of the working class by the time the film opens with Eve in Paris, owning nothing but the gold lamé dress on her back. She first appears in a luminous pool of gold lamé on the wooden bench of a third-class train coach, having pawned the rest of her clothes in Monte Carlo. She has kept only this delicate, draped evening gown to travel in. The dress has a gold lamé hood that clasps at the neck and drapes over her shoulders, which Eve vainly uses to protect herself from the downpour that greets her in Paris. In spite of its apparent impracticality, however, the dress does protect her: first by getting the attention of a generous cab driver (Don Ameche) and then by getting her into society, when she is mistakenly ushered into a formal gathering. Suddenly her dress is no longer comically out of place, and Eve happily plays bridge with the unsuspecting guests. When it is discovered that someone has given the doorman a pawn ticket instead of an invitation, a search begins for an intruder. The "Eve Peabody" who is thrown out, however, is a "terrible old woman" claiming to be the Duchess of Mendola. The fact that Eve fits right in while a genuine duchess is found utterly un-duchess-like and ejected from the party demonstrates both Eve's self-confidence and poise (thanks to the dress), and the arbitrariness of class signifiers.

Georges Flammarion (John Barrymore) finances Eve's continued masquerade in exchange for her agreement to seduce his wife's lover and get him out of the way. Having accepted the deal, Eve finds that she suddenly has a suite at the Ritz, a chauffeured car, and carte blanche in the fashion salons of Paris. Although her clothes are clearly an important aspect of her masquerade, haute couture and its wealthy "fashion victims" are also made fun of—elite women are shown to blindly follow fashion dictates, just as they adhere to codes of social distinction that are no less arbitrary than fashion. In one scene, Eve buys a hat at "Simone Chapeaux" and witnesses the following dialogue between another customer and the designer Simone (who wears a huge, surrealist centipede brooch on one shoulder):

> **Simone.** Bring me that one with the stuff on it that looks like spinach. You know, that hideous thing I made this morning. [turning to customer] Well where in the world did you get that hat, it looks positively moldy.
> **Customer.** I bought it from you three days ago.
> **Simone.** I don't care where you bought it, it's out of style. I decided this morning that all hats should be off the face.

Other films of the late-1930s such as *Vogues of 1938* (1937) and *The Women* (1939) make fun of wealthy socialites who claim to have taste but are simply pawns of pretentious designers. By parodying couture, a highly elite segment of the fashion market, these films suggest that popular fashion is, by contrast, not dictated in such an autocratic manner. ("Simone" is probably a reference to Elsa Schiaparelli, who collaborated with surrealist artists in the 1930s, producing "such memorable eccentricities as the lamb-cutlet hat, the brain hat, [and] the shoe hat.")[88]

In *Midnight,* the parody of haute couture is combined with indications that Eve's taste in fashion is far superior to that of aristocratic women. This confirms that in spite of Eve's ability to pass in society, she is not fooled by the pseudo-sophistication of the wealthy fashion elite. Similarly, Eve's behavior does not change dramatically when she is pretending to be the baroness; unlike Wanda in *The Princess Comes Across,* Eve's aristocratic role is not a caricature. The ease of her imposture reinforces the film's utopian rendering of status-as-appearance, as was often the case in such comedies. Eve's working-class social values are reasserted, however, when she gives up her wealthy suitor in favor of her Paris taxi driver, telling Flammarion, "every Cinderella has her midnight." Again, love wins out over social climbing, but only following a representation of the heroine as essentially indistinguishable from her aristocratic cohort. As in *The Bride Wore Red,* Colbert's star persona makes the film's romantic closure more formulaic than convincing in its presentation of marriage as the resolution of the heroine's desire for freedom. In other Cinderella films, however, marriage sometimes functions to legitimize the status that the heroine has appropriated through work, imposture, or social climbing (cf. *Possessed* [1931], *Sadie Mckee* [1934], *Goin' to Town* [1935], *The Last of Mrs. Cheyney, Easy Living, Mannequin,* and *Fifth Avenue Girl* [1939]).

Just as *What Price Hollywood?* is about Constance Bennett as much as Mary Evans, Lombard's Wanda Nash in *The Princess Comes Across* is never "really" in danger of becoming just another would-be actress from Brooklyn. She is, quite visibly, Carole Lombard, whose dominant impression is that of a glamorous and popular star. The recourse to a "real" identity that is used to resolve class disruption by restoring

Wanda to her proper "place" as a Brooklyn girl is thus, as in *The Bride Wore Red,* a narrative convention that does not override the glamour of star performance. The discourse of stardom makes normalcy an appealing representation because, as Richard Dyer has suggested, the star's charisma erases the negative aspects of normalcy while foregrounding the positive ones.[89] Roles in which stars play characters who choose a normal life over wealth and pretense not only expose such distinctions as economic and performative rather than essential, they also represent the "choosing self" of consumer culture in ways not limited to class envy. Dyer's theory that stars function to embody social contradictions can be seen in the context of 1930s America specifically in relation to tensions between material aspiration and populist or pro-social values. Stars were depicted as "in" the world of wealth and fame but not "of" it because they were a "studio-made" elite whose status was far more ephemeral than that of a true aristocracy.

Both Hollywood films and consumer discourses of the 1930s emphasized the potentially miraculous effects of self-transformation, even when, as for Wanda Nash and Eve Peabody, the change was transitory. The point was not that such changes represented self-discovery, but was rather the power of "image management" and the performativity of social status. This aspect of modern social identity has often been seen as alienating, producing what Georg Simmel described as the monetarized and calculated personality, Herbert Marcuse termed "one dimensionality," and David Riesman called the "other-directed" personality. Less clear is the extent to which it has also had disruptive and egalitarian implications because of the anti-essentialist rhetoric on which consumerism is based. To look at these implications is not to valorize the marketplace as a democratic social sphere or make claims of consumer sovereignty in relation to popular culture. It is, rather, to consider the way that consumer culture opened up an imaginative space between the power of traditional elites and the ways in which their status was enacted in daily life.

Fashion has long been a crucial medium for communicating status, and in the 1930s this process was demystified by the figure of the Hollywood star. The significance of fashion as a populist discourse is central to an understanding of the cultural meanings of female Hollywood stars in this era. It was a decade in which the codes of social status were identified and parodied, undermining commonly held notions that the rich were simply "different" due to lineage and inimitable forms of cultivation. These issues were raised throughout the 1930s, as popular fashion and Hollywood fan culture became a context for examining the basis of social classes and categories.

STYLE AS SPECTACLE

New York and Paris disdainfully looked down their august noses at the dresses we designed in Hollywood. Well, maybe they were vulgar, but they did have imagination. . . . Into this carnivalesque atmosphere I was plummeted. There I wallowed in rhinestone and feathers and furs and loved every minute of it.

Designer Howard Greer

Hollywood's use of fashion as spectacle has its roots in entertainment forms like the theatrical tableau, night club revue, beauty contest, and fashion show. These traditions were directly related to film genres that used costume at its most spectacular, such as the musical, the fashion film, and the costume drama. Female stars like Mae West and Marlene Dietrich drew on such vaudeville and cabaret traditions to form their playfully exaggerated performance styles and images. Others, like Norma Shearer and Greta Garbo, had their careers built around high-budget "prestige" dramas that featured elaborate historical costumes. There is an apparent contradiction between the popularity of these genres in the 1930s and Hollywood's increasing emphasis on "wearable" styles that could be promoted through tie-ins and fashion publicity. These two aspects of costume (the spectacular and the commercial) were surprisingly compatible, however, since fashion and costume films often demystified "high" fashion, in the Hollywood tradition of contrasting high and low culture in favor of the popular appropriation of elite forms.

In films about fashion and couture, populism emerges through an emphasis on making high-fashion's glamour accessible rather than on exclusive design or elite fashion culture itself. This accessibility is provided, in spite of opulent and "impractical" displays of clothing, through the evocation of traditions of popular spectacle, melodrama, and masquerade. For example, fashion shows would seem to be perfect examples of Veblenesque "conspicuous consumption," with their expensive designer clothes, haughty models, and audiences of wealthy women. On the Hollywood screen, however, the fashion show often has an entirely different inflection, in large part because of its association with the musical. Throughout the 1930s, musicals presented sets and costumes that were distinctly utopian—they were outrageously luxurious and yet created an aura of democratic abundance.[1] As Fred Astaire sings in *Top Hat* (1935), 1930s musicals create "an atmosphere that simply reeks with class" but are also a playful critique of snobbery and class difference.

Sets and costumes in Hollywood musicals epitomize artifice. Take, for example, the 1930s "big white set" popularized by Paramount and RKO:

> While, as a visual device, large quantities of lighting added to the beauty of films' sets, they also suggested the abundance and the luxurious sheen of the high life. Light heightened virtually every element of decor in movie night clubs, making objects highly reflective, and stressing smooth surface over texture and mass.[2]

48

Contrasts between brilliant white and jet black were also frequently used in costume design, along with reflective fabrics, which emphasized the surface and tactility of clothing; the MGM designer Adrian often contrasted stark black-and-white fabrics, as well as beaded and metallic ones, to express opulence and luxury.[3] The white evening gown, often worn with a white fur wrap, was an omnipresent signifier of feminine luxury throughout the 1930s, particularly following Jean Harlow's appearance in an Adrian-designed satin version in *Dinner at Eight* (1933).[4] Hollywood musicals also used stylization as a pretext for arbitrary and playful metamorphoses. In *Broadway Melody of 1936* (1935), for example, an invisible cut transforms the female dancers' costumes from black to white at the center of the screen as they move in unison from one side to the other.

Fashion films (movies about fashion or those that present fashion shows and costume revues) thus celebrate sartorial spectacle while maintaining a populist attitude toward fashion diffusion. *Fashions of 1934* (1934), for example, presents an elaborate, Ziegfeld-like fashion show but also features William Powell as a fashion merchandiser who "knocks off" boutique designs that sell for $375 and makes identical dresses available at "Rosenblatz Basement" for $16.95. Such films often parody couture fashion as elitist and eccentric, as in *Midnight*'s scene at Simone Chapeaux, and utilize fashion shows to emphasize the abundance and variety of *consumer* fashion rather than to promote high-fashion exclusivity. The fashion film also frequently features performances by female stars who play fashion models, literalizing the commercial role of the star as an exemplar of fashionable self-presentation.

The act of modeling itself, like the role of the musical performer or chorus girl, is overtly stylized in a way that conflicts with realist film acting. As Charlotte Herzog has described, cinematic fashion shows use a series of poses akin to dance or the Delsarte gestures used in early-twentieth-century performance, interrupting narrative flow with alternating long and

Bette Davis in a Warner Bros. publicity photograph for *Fashions of 1934*.

medium shots. They often begin with static group poses similar to the tableaux used in the silent-film era (collective poses around different themes are used in the fashion show sequence of *The Women* [1939], for example).[5] When playing a fashion model, the star presents herself in a semifrontal stance, usually to an on-screen audience aligned with the camera's point of view. She is thus looking almost directly at and playing to the viewer—a vaudeville tradition that was strongly discouraged with the rise of realist film acting. Although narratively motivated, this direct address, like the musical show-within-a-show, foregrounds the star-as-performer over her characterization. In *Mannequin*, for instance, a sequence in which the character Jessie (Joan Crawford) is seen modeling signals the success of Jessie's struggle to escape poverty and a bad marriage. In this sequence, the cool, self-possessed Joan Crawford persona overshadows and transforms the character of Jessie because of Crawford's familiarity as a Hollywood "clothes-horse" and her association with Adrian, whose designs she models in the film.

The Hollywood star, as Richard Dyer, Barry King, and James Naremore have described, is often in conflict with the self-effacing conventions of realist acting.[6] In the case of 1930s costume drama, the significance of the star was even more pronounced because these films used the glamour of their female movie stars to indicate the power of the historical figures they played. Costume dramas were frequently used as star vehicles, with historical and "prestige" pictures functioning as showcases for the top tier of female stars who could easily carry high-budget films on their own, particularly if costumes were emphasized. The dynamic combination of star, costume, and historical figure was exploited early on by Adolph Zukor, who bought the U.S. rights to the French independent film *Queen Elizabeth* in 1912.[7] The film starred Sarah Bernhardt and was costumed by the most famous designer of the era, Paul Poiret. It was a huge hit, inspiring the

U.S. production of other "prestige" features, which eventually included a cycle of "queen" biopics in the 1930s.

The genre of historical costume drama also has an ambiguous relationship to codes of realism, in part because of its frequent function as a star vehicle, as well as its use of heavily embellished sets and costume. The genre's fetishization of historical "authenticity" has been described as an "imitation of archeology."[8] This form of mimesis, however, often becomes artificial in its very quest for historical accuracy, ultimately drawing attention to itself rather than contributing to narrative realism (the MGM film *Marie Antoinette* [1938] is notorious for this kind of excess). In many instances, the costume drama slips unmistakably into the mode of melodrama, in which realism is secondary to the expressivity of gesture, costume, and mise-en-scène. Codes of dramatic realism use costume primarily to reinforce narrative, social, and characterological meaning, subsuming each element of the mise-en-scène into a unified dramatic effect. But the costume drama clearly overemphasizes details of design, preventing these elements from blending into a formally self-effacing narrative. Pam Cook has called this the historical drama's "design extravagance," which, like the "textual extravagance" of film melodrama, "demands an aesthetic appreciation" that may potentially overwhelm both narrative and emotional affect, becoming pure spectacle. Interestingly, this emphasis on costume as a dramatic and visual element in its own right supported discourses of consumer fashion and display, even as it went against claims that good costuming should only enhance a performance rather than draw attention to itself.[9]

Such costumes can also function as central reference points in the development of the narrative—as a form of visual and dramatic punctuation. This is particularly evident in major star vehicles where costume changes crystallize a significant narrative moment: Bette Davis's entrance at a white cotillion ball in a red satin gown in *Jezebel* (1938), Greta Garbo's change from masculine clothing into her weighty coronation dress in

Queen Christina (1933), and Vivien Leigh's gradual transformation from the girl in a green-flecked barbecue dress to the survivor wearing velvet drapes in *Gone with the Wind* (1939). Historical costume is often less naturalistic and more metaphorical than that of films with a contemporary setting; Adrian's period costumes often use details that symbolize character traits, and period settings allowed costume designers to raid the past for new motifs, often starting stylistic revivals. The centrality of costume in historical films led many designers to abandon historical accuracy for expressive value, and fashion trends in the 1930s were, surprisingly, more directly influenced by historical dramas than by films with modern settings. The costumes and production values of these films were thus heavily promoted, as well as their star value, and they usually had big budgets for both.[10]

Les Girls: The Fashion Show, Beauty Pageant, and Chorus Line

The fashion show originated in the intimate couture salons of Paris (Paul Poiret has been credited with its innovation), but by the early 1900s it had arrived in the United States on a more theatrical scale. Department stores used "dress parades" to attract the growing market of middle-class women, who were shown reproductions of the French designs seen in fashion magazines "at exactly one-third the cost." By 1915, fashion shows were popular attractions in all major cities, and their basic form had become established: "Living models paraded down ramps in store theaters or departments, spotlighted by light engineers to a musical accompaniment, sometimes with 'dramatic effect,' as in the theater."[11]

The models' promenade was also accompanied by a running commentary on the clothing; at a Wanamaker's show in 1908, each model posed in a *tableau vivant* inside a large gold picture frame, stepping out in turn and walking down a ramp as the mistress of ceremonies described each gown. Exotic decor was popular, as in Gimbel's 1911 show, which featured casinos, roulette tables, and a tearoom "converted to look like the 'Monte Carlo de Paris.'" Some stores had an exclusive first-showing that was attended by invitation only, while others, like Gimbel's, lined the promenade with "thousands of seats to accommodate the thousands of women from New York and surrounding suburbs." In New York, fashion shows became so popular that merchants were required to get licenses for them because of the disruption to competitors' business and the "ordinary conduct of city life" they created.[12]

The Americanization of the fashion show coincided with the rise of a large female audience for popular theater. As Gaylyn Studlar has described, "matinee girls" were commonly disparaged by drama critics for their support of "lightweight theatrical fare" and fanaticism for both male matinee idols and "glamorous actresses in gorgeous clothes and stylish coiffures." One critic complained, for example, that he "heard a matinee audience of women applaud the actress' gowns as she lifted them up to pack her trunk," while another described a play in which the action was stopped while the audience applauded the entrance of an actress in a particularly beautiful costume.[13] Musical revues like the *Ziegfeld Follies* allocated huge production expenses to costuming in order to capitalize on this interest, and in 1915 Florenz Ziegfeld hired the English couturiere Lady Duff Gordon (a.k.a. Lucile) to design gowns for his famous chorines, resulting in the number "An Episode in Chiffon," featuring Duff Gordon's famous model Dolores as the "Empress of Fashion."[14] From that point on, both "Lucile" gowns and models became a central attraction of the *Follies*. Ziegfeld's consciousness of the popularity of fashion and its theatrical display is clear from a 1923 *Ladies' Home Journal* article in which he commented on the importance of keeping the *Follies'* costumes up-to-date, "since these musical shows are dependent upon and spread the fashions."[15]

A *Moving Picture World* article of 1910 suggested that theatrical uses of fashion and costume for publicity be emulated by the film industry in order to attract the "refined" women who attended stage productions to see the gowns.[16] Such advice was evidently taken by film producers, who in the teens and twenties released an increasing number of films with fashion themes. Early newsreels regularly covered the Paris openings, and Pathé-Frères even utilized an early Kinemacolor process to enhance the spectacle of haute couture. *The Bioscope,* for example, described Pathé's extension of its fashion coverage in 1911:

Parisian Modes
To meet [the] desire and demand for fashion films, Messrs. Pathé are commencing a series showing the coming models from Paris. The present one gives coloured pictures of hats, dinner gowns, tailor-made costumes, walking dresses, negligees and teagowns.[17]

The biannual New York Fashion Show was filmed for newsreels in 1913, according to *Moving Picture World,* which also suggested that actresses be used for the event instead of models.[18] Other cinematic vehicles for fashion included *Florence Rose Fashions,* a series of thirty-one short films produced between 1916 and 1917, which were tied in to leading newspapers and stores with articles describing the clothes printed twelve days before the films appeared.[19] In 1930, this directly commercial use of the cinematic fashion show was repeated in both *Fashion Features* and a series of short films sponsored by *Vogue* magazine that were released every two weeks; these were screened for one week in selected cities, with a major department store tie-in. According to the magazine, each costume was described by the "voice of *Vogue*" while being modeled, with one announcement suggesting that "you, too, may become a living fashion-plate, for the costumes worn by *Vogue*'s mannequins are on sale at moderate prices in smart shops of the cities where the films are released."[20]

The popularity of large fashion shows in the teens and twenties suggests that many in the audience were spectators rather than serious shoppers, given the expense of department store labels at the time. By the 1930s, however, the wholesale and price-lined production of such designs made fashion shows and fashion-related films increasingly popular and useful as promotional texts. But the fashion show became more than an advertisement for clothing, and its frequent appearance in Hollywood film cannot be attributed exclusively to its use in promoting costume tie-ins. Like Ziegfeld's use of Lucile gowns, the fashion show's glamour, music, mise-en-scène, and descriptive commentary were elements in a performance of fashion-as-spectacle. Such spectacles, along with scenes of informal or showroom modeling, appear frequently in films centering around women who work as models or fashion designers, or in department stores.

A partial list of such films from the 1930s includes *On Your Back* (1930), *Our Blushing Brides* (1930), *Street of Women* (1932), *Employees' Entrance* (1933) *Fashions of 1934* (1934), *Roberta* (1935), *The Bride Walks Out* (1936), *Colleen* (1936), *The Golden Arrow* (1936), *Stolen Holiday* (1937), *Artists and Models* (1937), *Vogues of 1938* (1937), *Artists and Models Abroad* (1938), and *Mannequin* (1938). Although Hollywood's representation of women in fashion retailing was paralleled by increasing numbers of women employed as models, buyers, and stylists, the kind of female labor most common in the garment industry (that of production) is ignored by these films.[21] Female designers and head seamstresses are featured, but they work in salons rather than sweatshops or factories. Their work is more reminiscent of small-scale design or home sewing (sketching, fitting dresses on a model, choosing fabrics, etc.) than commercial production. Thus, although these films acknowledge women's centrality to the fashion industry, their status is idealized.

Fashion shows also appear frequently in Hollywood musicals, indicating the degree to which the popularization of this motif was structured by conventions of the musical revue. The "Artists and Models" films, for example, were adaptations of an actual Broadway revue, while other films, like *Fashions of 1934, Roberta, Vogues of 1938, The Great Ziegfeld*

(1936), and *The Goldwyn Follies* (1938), are revue films that have fashion themes or "fashion parades." *Vogues of 1938* depicts the use of leftover musical revue sets and numbers to enhance a fashion show, creating a subgenre that could be called the "backstage fashion musical." The combination of fashion with musical performance has a history in the association of theater costume with couture, as in the Ziegfeld-style musical revue, but in Hollywood this combination was also aimed at maximizing the audience for fashion spectacles by adding other features, as indicated by the press book for *Fashions of 1934*:

> We know as you do that your fashion tie-ups on this picture are unlimited. However . . . [i]n your ads . . . the atmosphere should definitely convey something big and unusual in Warner Bros. extravaganzas. Style mentions will bring business from the women, but be sure you tell the world you're not just playing a pageant of styles.[22]

It was recommended that advertising emphasizing fashion be "segregated to women's pages," while musical and comedy numbers could be publicized on the "amusement page" in order to attract younger or male viewers.

Gold Diggers of 1935 (1935) marks the beginnings of the "integrated" musical, in which musical performances are seamlessly interwoven into the narrative flow so that songs and dance numbers represent a story progression. Dick Powell sings "I'm Going Shopping with You" throughout a fashion makeover sequence, but this takes place in a shopping arcade rather than on stage, and the song is never repeated in the concluding show. The integration of music and fashion is also present in *Roberta* (released the same year), in which Fred Astaire plays a bandleader who helps out at a fashion show by introducing the clothes in verse with musical accompaniment. This integration is only partial, however, because as the models promenade to the accompaniment of music, they are shot in a stylized manner specific to the cinematic fashion show,

Bette Davis and William Powell in a Warner Bros. publicity photograph for *Fashions of 1934.*

with the camera following the profile of each model down a staircase, cutting from a wide to medium shot as the model poses directly for the camera, pivots, and reveals the details of her gown.[23] This fashion show is followed, however, by a musical number in which Ginger Rogers dances in a stunning evening gown, providing a display similar to that of the fashion show but without its overt, "direct address" presentation of clothing for the audience. The success of the subsequent

Roland Young and Kay Francis in a Warner Bros. publicity photograph for *Street of Women* (1932). Courtesy of the Academy of Motion Picture Arts and Sciences.

Astaire-Rogers RKO musicals at integrating plot, music, and a degree of fashion display foreshadowed the eventual demise of the musical fashion show: like the revue, fashion display was gradually integrated into narrative flow rather than foregrounded within the highly stylized format of the fashion show.

The revue format is distinctly non-narrative, as suggested by its frequent description as "a show-stopper."[24] One of the main features of such spectacles is the female chorus line, which provided the primary formal link between the Hollywood musical and the fashion show. The presentation of collective feminine pulchritude was a major feature of the pioneer Broadway musical revue the *Ziegfeld Follies,* which ran between 1907 and 1931, establishing many of the conventions visible in film musicals from the "Broadway Melody" cycle to Busby Berkeley's choreography for Warner Bros. and its later adaptation in his work at MGM.[25] As Ziegfeld described the *Follies* in 1925, "the glorified girls, the galaxy of stars, and marvelous scenic effects and costumes . . . hold up to the world all the elaborateness and the beauty that are to be associated with a shop-window of life."[26]

Theatrical genres using a female chorus, such as the "extravaganza" and the burlesque, appeared in the United States by the mid-nineteenth century; they often included scandalous European features like a female "corps de ballet" in tights, or a group of "British Blondes" in trousers who satirized male roles.[27] Ziegfeld's first use of a female chorus, in *The Follies of 1907,* was suggested by his wife, Anna Held, who admired French musical revues like the *Folies Bergère.* To the French-style musical revue, Ziegfeld added elements of vaudeville-like comedy and costume theme pieces, held together at a quick pace by a unifying mise-en-scène and precise choreography. Ziegfeld considered himself a connoisseur of female beauty and described his chorus as a collection of women who were each uniquely attractive but "glorified" by their presentation en masse in lavish settings and costumes that made them a harmonized entity. He argued that "costumes should not be standardized. They should blend together like the various sounds issuing from the many sections of a symphony orchestra, yet every girl must stand out as an individual."[28]

To create this sense of multiplicity rather than uniformity, women in the chorus often appeared as variations on a particular motif, such as articles of female clothing, salad vegetables, items in a trousseau, taxi cabs, battleships, and flowers.

Other variations on a theme included the most famous beauties of world history, the months of the year, different kinds of animals, soft drinks, and songs (the latter is lavishly reenacted in the number "A Pretty Girl Is Like a Melody" from *The Great Ziegfeld* [1936]).

After 1915, the designer Lucile increased the shows' use of high fashion as both a theme and a production value, popularizing much of the performative style associated with haute couture and salon modeling. Lucile was reportedly the first English designer to use fashion shows in her couture shop, instructing her models to use Delsarte gestures to give an air of drama and sophistication to the clothes.[29] In 1917 the "Ziegfeld walk" was introduced to the show; this was a slow promenade down a stairway that usually began high in center stage and ran in a V-shape down to the left and right. The chorus women walked with hips and outer arms toward the wings, and shoulders and faces turned toward the audience, so that the twist in their bodies gave them a contraposto look.[30] This stylization was heightened in the *Follies* by the weight and complexity of the women's costumes. Headdresses were weighted by beads, braid, feathers, and rhinestones, and required balanced movement, accentuating the women's measured steps. Ziegfeld was obsessed with the quality of costuming materials and argued that the finest fabrics, silk linings, and expensive lingerie made the chorus girls "act and feel more feminine and enhanced their grace and movement on the stage."[31]

The appearance of the *Ziegfeld Follies* and subsequent revues, like *Earl Carroll's Vanities* and *George White's Scandals*, coincided with another presentational format for collective femininity: the beauty pageant. Like the revue chorus, beauty contests presented women as units of a whole; in the Miss America Pageant, for example, winners of regional contests represented each state, forming the collective entity "American beauty." The first beauty contest is said to have been held by P. T. Barnum in 1854, as one of a number of contests evaluating "dogs, flowers, babies, and birds" for the amusement of an audience. The Miss America Pageant began, as did other "bathing beauty" contests, as a publicity event to boost beach tourism. The contest took place in Atlantic City amid a festive series of events, beginning with the parade of King Neptune, mermaids, and "sea nymphs" on the boardwalk, a Night Carnival with a masked ball, and a costume competition featuring a female impersonator. The following day festivities concluded with a Bathers' Revue, which could be entered by anyone as long as they wore a swimming costume. Participants, said to number in the hundreds, included the mayor of Atlantic City, firemen in red bathing suits, and policemen in blue bathing suits. The Miss America Pageant lapsed twice, continuing again after 1935. In the 1930s the pageant was cleansed of most of its carnivalesque qualities, but other beauty contests sprang up across the country, often as a form of publicity for products or businesses.[32]

The Ziegfeld-style female chorus clearly has much in common with the early, carnivalesque beauty pageant in its emphasis on social inversion (women in military uniforms, police in blue swimming costumes) and libidinal release.[33] The post-Ziegfeld chorus line, however, tended to move away from the organic metaphors and cross-dressing themes of the stage revue toward more modernist, abstract forms. In the musical revues choreographed by Busby Berkeley, for example, the stylization of the female chorus via costuming, abstract sets, and synchronized movements often creates a uniformity among the women, who become indistinguishable units of the whole. This effect is occasionally paired with organic metaphors, as in *Dames* (1934), in which an overhead shot of the chorus stylizes their fluffy skirts into a circular bouquet of white flowers. A single chorine is then catapulted toward the overhead camera, like a flower being pulled from the bouquet.

Such organic metaphors soften the uniformity of the chorus, while nevertheless subordinating individual differences to an overall effect. But Berkeley often used more geometric motifs and stark tonal contrasts in *mise-en-abîme*, surrealist sets. This style required much greater uniformity among chorus women than did the Ziegfeld or beauty pageant paradigm, replacing it with formations of meticulously matched chorines. Berkeley claimed once to have spent an entire day selecting three women from 723 chorus auditioners: "after I picked the three girls I put them next to my special sixteen and they matched, just like pearls."[34]

The style of Berkeley's musical sequences has inspired comparisons with machinery, mass production, and military formations (Berkeley served briefly in the army, where he choreographed military drills).[35] Ziegfeld had put chorus girls in military uniform since about 1910, using cross-dressing as burlesque "trouser roles" had—to expose women's legs.[36] Berkeley's musical choruses, by contrast, emphasize military rationalization: complex group formations and precise, uniform physical movements. Berkeley's choreography, his cog-like interlacing of bodies in circular movements, and his foregrounding of technology in the form of complex set and camera movements produced a vision of abundant but seemingly "mass-produced" and -organized female bodies.

In the backstage musicals of the early 1930s that Berkeley choreographed at Warner Bros., however, assembly-line femininity is combined with surreal or ironically excessive musical numbers. *Gold Diggers of 1933*, for example, contrasts a tracking shot of glossy chorus women with one of men on a depression breadline in the socially critical "My Forgotten Man" sequence. In *Gold Diggers of 1935*, the film's setting in a modern luxury hotel is combined with a theme of financial graft and worker exploitation by the hotel management. The "mass ornament" presented by Berkeley's films is thus tinged with social critique and reflexivity, particularly in the backstage musicals, which offer a Goffmanesque commentary on the vulnerability of performance (last-minute substitutions, near disasters, etc.). These films also foreground artifice, as spatial realism is abandoned in favor of moving sets and multiple dissolves between vast, seemingly connected spaces.[37]

While Berkeley unified the chorus line only to highlight its artifice, tension between conformity and individuality is resolved somewhat differently in fashion films. Each model wears a different outfit, but they all conform to the prevailing silhouette and fashion types. The effect is one of variety within conformity. Lucy Fischer has suggested that there is little difference between the visual uniformity of the chorus line and the use of "types" to represent women: "the very concept of stereotype . . . denotes having no individuality, as though cast from a mold . . . indeed, the entire history of cinema can be seen as constituting an on-going fashion show of popular female 'styles.'"[38]

Individuality and conformity in style are a theme in a number of fashion films, but primarily in terms of the split be-

Ginger Rogers and chorines flaunt parodic uniformity in RKO's *Shall We Dance?* (1937).

tween elite, couture exclusivity, and ready-to-wear fashion. This cinematic contrast usually supports ready-to-wear rather than the individualized whims of high-fashion culture. In *Vogues of 1938*, for example, models are seen prior to a fashion show wearing identical robes backstage, huddled together in friendly conversation. Although the film's star, Joan Bennett, is in the center of the group, she is almost indistinguishable from the others until a close-up is inserted; the film continually contrasts Bennett's classical features and gowns with other women's exaggeratedly eccentric couture. The fashion show context thus presents each model as just different enough— with her moment on center stage—while remaining within a style paradigm defined by popular, commercial fashion.

Vogues of 1938 also visually reinforces the relationship between women's ready-to-wear fashion and mechanical production, but in a positive light rather than the dehumanizing one often attributed to Berkeley's use of mechanical motifs in female chorus numbers. Both of the film's fashion shows feature moving, conveyor-belt-like catwalks, smoothly propelling the models forward toward the camera or rotating them on a pedestal. This automation of the models' movement creates an effect of mass-produced abundance, in which the stage becomes a mechanical cornucopia, pouring endless well-dressed models out of the House of Curson and into the audience. It thus illustrates the rhetoric of MGM's promotional film *Hollywood—Style Center of the World,* discussed in the introduction. That film's narrator emphasizes not only the new influence of film costume on fashion design but also its role in creating demand for the mass production of new styles: "Commercial designers pattern gowns reflecting the latest mode, and dress factories hum with activity. Materials are piled high, and as many as twenty-five coats or dresses are cut from the same pattern at the same time by keen circular blades, power-driven."[39] This description is accompanied by a montage of power tools and clothing, with dissolves and superimposed images to emphasize the film's synthesis of fashion, mass production, and modernity. Hollywood fashion spectacles often foreground these positive associations with consumer fashion, or contrast popular forms of spectacle (masquerade, music, and dance) with the pretensions of high fashion.

The Fashionable Meets the Popular in
Roberta and *Vogues of 1938*

The film *Roberta* takes place in Paris and features a series of contrasts between American and European fashion culture and a number of characters who use fashion to alter their identities. These include Irene Dunne as Stephanie, a fashion designer for the House of Roberta who is really an exiled Russian princess; "Roberta" herself, who is really "Aunt Minnie" from Indiana; and the Russian Countess Scharwenka, an American dancer (Ginger Rogers). When Minnie dies, the House of Roberta is inherited by her nephew John Kent (Randolph Scott), an ex-football player and band manager. As Jeanne Allen has described, the film offers "[a] veritable rule book in a poker game of social positioning," with "the struggle for social position . . . enacted on the field of clothing."[40] This struggle, however, is also about the nature of fashion, as articulated in a contrast between American practicality and European aesthetics; this contrast is ultimately mediated by the popular stylishness of American music and dance, represented by Fred Astaire and Ginger Rogers.

On inheriting the salon, the ex-football player Kent tells a fashion reporter that he is going to "design women's dresses the way men think they should be," and the film aligns American practicality with masculinity and European design with femininity. After Kent quarrels with his designer Stephanie, his former bandleader "Huck" (Fred Astaire) attempts to prepare a new line for the season openings. When shown his designs, Stephanie comments that "the men may like them but the women won't." In the end she averts a crisis by redesigning the entire show at the last minute, but the proper balance between American and European taste is found when Huck suggests, "we'll give them some entertainment, too," and Stephanie exclaims, "a musical fashion show!" The result is a spectacle in which the fashions are authentically European, but their presentation is irreverently American. Huck's lyrical introduction of the gowns begins,

> 'Tis the hour for dry Martinis.
> . . . The Ritz Bar is serving caviar and weenies; Madame
>   is there.
> And from Roberta she has something "too divine" on,
> The sort of thing your jealous friends would love to spill
>   their wine on.
> For your inspection, our cocktail collection.

The film's musical sequences with Fred Astaire and Ginger Rogers contrast with Stephanie's aristocratic style, providing the synthesis of high and low culture that characterizes many Hollywood musicals. Rogers's masquerade as Scharwenka both lampoons the implied superiority of European aristocrats and makes Rogers's character a mixture of "real" American earthiness and "put-on" glamour. Astaire's Huck combines American popular culture with simple, well-suited elegance. In their final dance, which concludes the film's fashion show sequence, Rogers's performance also underscores the film's integration of fashion-show and musical elements. She appears just as the last model has traipsed down a stairway and exited. Adopting the same slow, gliding walk of the other models, she pivots midstage to show her gown. Astaire removes her fur-trimmed satin wrap, and Rogers strikes another modeling pose while he sings; finally they dance together, abandoning the fashion-show format.

Roberta was a triumph for tie-in merchandiser Bernard Waldman, whose Modern Merchandising Bureau reproduced fifteen of the film's Bernard Newman designs under the Cinema Fashions label. Waldman also staged his first large publicity stunt with the opening of *Roberta*. According to *Fortune* magazine, Waldman sent an armored car to the theater where the

Ginger Rogers and Fred Astaire model clothing with style in a publicity photograph for RKO's *Roberta* (1935).

film would premiere with a sign proclaiming that the car contained "$40,000 worth of gorgeous gowns worn by Irene Dunne and Ginger Rogers and other stars in RKO's Roberta," which would be modeled at the theater following the premiere. The dresses were apparently Waldman's own copies, not Newman's original designs, and were worth "a couple of hundred dollars."[41]

Another of Waldman's major costume tie-in successes was with Walter Wanger's *Vogues of 1938,* which generated fifty-two dresses, twenty-four hats, and a variety of accessories for

Cinema Fashions. An early Technicolor musical, *Vogues of 1938* does not achieve the synthesis between fashion and popular culture seen in *Roberta*; its mediation is, instead, between the aesthetic pretensions of European couture and the accessibility of American ready-to-wear. Although the musical revue format is utilized, along with a hackneyed plot requiring the characters to "put on a show" in order to save the fortunes of an American designer, the musical elements are minimal and serve primarily as window dressing for the fashion presentations. The film does, however, make a pointed critique of fashion elitism; it revolves around the American House of Curson, which is shown to operate, like most U.S. designers at the time, by buying sketches from the Parisian openings each season and producing them for department stores. The designer Mr. Curson and his head seamstress Sophie are compared favorably with the eccentricity and pretension of a Russian would-be couturier, Count Muratov (Mischa Auer). This contrast underscores the film's promotion of American ready-to-wear design (and, of course, the film's own mass-produced costume reproductions).

Vogues of 1938 also illustrates a number of the connections I have suggested between the fashion show and other forms of spectacle like the beauty pageant and the musical chorus. The film begins with a runaway bride story in which Wendy van Klettering (Joan Bennett) escapes her arranged marriage by becoming a fashion model at the House of Curson. She falls in love with Curson, whose wife has convinced him to invest all of his money in a stage show for her to star in. When the show flops, Curson is on the brink of bankruptcy. Meanwhile, Muratov has stolen the Paris designs Curson was planning to use, and begins luring away Curson's clientele. The film concludes when Muratov is exposed, and Curson uses the leftover props and performers from his failed stage revue to put on a musical fashion show, rescuing his collection.

The film contains informal modeling scenes, one non-musical fashion show, a musical-revue finale, and a sequence that combines masquerade and beauty pageantry called the "Fete de Rayon Fantastique." This is a charity fancy-dress competition in which society women parade before judges in a Technicolor extravaganza of glittering Orientalist, historical, and fantasy costumes. The Fete is also, like the beauty pageant, a form of promotion—in this case for rayon, which was being used increasingly in ready-to-wear clothing as an inexpensive substitute for silk. Cinematically, the "Fete de Rayon" scene illustrates the film's overall emphasis on fashion as sensuous visual abundance: it begins with a backstage shot of numerous women running playfully across the frame in glittering, multicolored costumes, filling the screen as the camera tracks to accentuate their rush of movement. This is followed by a reverse angle of the costumed women as they pour out into a ballroom, and two more shots framed with movement across and off the screen, making the flow of dazzling colors and textures appear limitless. After a number of costumes are shown in detail, as women parade before the judges in medium-low angles to accentuate the designs, the women are shown from overhead, once again filling the screen in an image of overflowing gaiety. This scene is also used to highlight the ridiculousness of wealthy Mrs. Lemke, who wears a gold beaded gown with gold plumes sticking out of shoulder epaulets and from the top of her gold turban. Her garish outfit illustrates the eccentricity and incompetence of its designer, Muratov, who has charged his fashion victim a "mere ten thousand dollars." The pretentious gown dissolves into a cascade of gold beads when a single thread is pulled. Curson's entry, by contrast, is a white Grecian gown draped from the shoulders, epitomizing stylish classicism.

Muratov passes himself off as a Romantic artist who creates entirely unique dresses for each client, while in fact he has simply raided Curson's Paris design sources. When a client consults him, he "composes" a gown for her while playing the piano and pretending to consult his muse. His wealthy clients are told that their gowns are absolutely unique, inspired only by their beauty and the music of Chopin, Beethoven, or Mendelssohn. Curson exposes Muratov by duplicating three gowns for van Klettering to wear at society events. When a woman exclaims in horror that someone else is wearing "her" gown, her husband replies, "What of it? There are thousands of men here wearing exactly what I'm wearing." The woman snaps, "Well, I didn't pay that Russian to make me a uniform."

Hollywood's debunking of fashion exclusivity is directly linked to its promotion of consumer fashion, both in general and in direct merchandising tie-ins. Fashion individuality, other than alterations made by home sewers, was not a significant aspect of popular style.[42] As Angela Partington has suggested, popular fashion is less focused on cutting-edge designs and their "center-periphery" diffusion than on the reception and circulation of styles within particular fashion cultures.[43] Most popular fashion journalism from the 1930s suggests that fashion individuality was less important than being "in fashion" and that minor differences in fabric or detail, for example, would be an adequate form of differentiation. For this reason I would question some aspects of Charlotte Herzog's reading of *Fashions of 1934*:

> William Powell plays a fashion pirate who makes it possible for a working-class woman to buy for $16.95 at Rosenblatz Basement, what appears to be the very same dress that an upper middle-class woman would pay $375 for at an exclusive dress shop after she is told the dress is straight from Paris and that there is not another like it in the world. The message is that even for $16.95 one can be part of the fashionable elite. The film (which presents each gown individually to each woman) covers up the fact of mass production: in order for one woman to buy the fantasy dress for $16.95, thousands of similar dresses had to be manufactured for thousands of other women.[44]

But this mass production only devalues the dress if one assumes that the shoppers at Rosenblatz Basement were concerned about design exclusivity, which fashion journalism from the 1930 indicates would have been unlikely.

Instead, marketing discourses valorized fashion types over individual or unique design, with female stars representing idealized but appropriable and *reproducible* styles. A description of the "Studio Styles" costume label from the *Fashions of 1934* press book illustrates the decade's emphasis on accurate duplication and generic value rather than exclusivity: "Costumes worn by Warner Bros. screen stars originally designed by Orry-Kelly, Hollywood's fashion creator; faithfully reproduced from the most exact seam to the most elusive elan."[45]

The dress's "elusive elan" results from its association with a screen star and a Hollywood designer, but this elan, if "faithfully reproduced," apparently loses none of its value or Hollywood aura. Similarly, the cinematic fashion show presents fashion as spectacular and glamorous but not unique, since it also epitomizes an ideal of variety within conformity. The Hollywood fashion show thus mediates between the rarefied glamour of couture, figured in terms of the fashion designer-as-artist, and the democratic abundance of mass-produced consumer fashion. The Hollywood fashion show is a spectacular, but demystified, appropriation of couture glamour because of its cinematic association with more familiar modes of theatricality and self-adornment (the carnival masquerade, musical revue, and beauty pageant). It borrows the glamour of elite fashion but recodes it in terms of theatrical spectacle and thereby downplays its elitism and instead celebrates the abundance, accessibility, and transformative potential of consumer fashion.

The Costume Drama as Fashion Spectacle

A curious state of affairs now seems to exist in Hollywood. Every one has gone into perpetual fancy-dress. There apparently isn't a female star out there who doesn't want to

72

put on pantalettes, do her hair up in curls and a frizz, and
go bouncing her hoops in front of the camera.
Helen Brown Norden, Vogue, March 1937

The genre of historical costume drama has an ambiguous relationship to codes of realism because of its excessive use of costume and mise-en-scène, which draw attention to themselves
rather than contributing to a realism effect. Within codes of
realist drama, costume is meant to reflect a character's interiority and social background. This mimetic relationship between costume and character is in the costume and period
drama destabilized by the genre's overt "theatricality." Often
promoted as star vehicles, such films make it difficult for the
leading actress to "recede" behind her performance; the costume drama thus brings together a contradictory set of representational codes: it carries on the trappings and historical
subject matter of nineteenth-century realism but regularly sac-
rifices authenticity in favor of expressivity. Its "authentically"
embellished star, though often enacting a historical person's
biography rather than a fictional character, actually presents
one of the least self-effacing modes of performance in the
Hollywood oeuvre. This emphasis on expressive over realist
effects parallels the discourses of consumer fashion and its
separation of interiority from self-presentation.

The realist mode of performance and costume, according
to Richard Sennett, was related to the waning of eighteenth-
century notions of "natural character," which was unchang-
ing and fixed at birth. The nineteenth century, by contrast,
was an era in which the self was thought to be individual and
expressed in every gesture and item of clothing worn. The
anxiety produced by this sense of visibility (particularly in relation to class and sexuality) led to a fashion culture of arcane
and "miniaturized" dress codes that shielded the wearer from
exposure or misinterpretation—the purpose of fashion was
to express as little as possible about the individuality of the
wearer.

Sennett argues that anxieties around how one's always visible self would be construed, and the corresponding encoding and veiling of the body, inspired new codes of realism in theatrical performance:

> What these people tried to find in the theater was a world where you could indeed be absolutely sure that the people you saw were genuine. The actors really represented what they played. . . . In the theater, unlike the street, life was unshielded; it appeared as it was.[46]

Significantly, according to Sennett, "[t]his desire for believable and true appearances on the stage first surfaced as a demand for accuracy in historical costuming." Beginning in the 1830s, this quest for authenticity also inflected performance styles, as stage gestures were modified to represent naturalistic movements: "even in melodrama, melodramatic motion on the part of an actor was in bad taste in the 1850s."[47] By the end of the century, early cinema had also begun the transition from gestural codes of acting, via the transitional Delsarte system of "idealized" naturalism, toward the use of close-ups and codes of facial expression.[48]

Part of the controversy over Hollywood's silent-era "vulgarity" in costuming was that it represented the continuation of melodramatic and pantomimic forms of expressivity rather than self-effacing realist codes. Jane Gaines argues that Hollywood costume never adhered to a strict naturalism, but that "the legacy of the silent era was . . . a tendency toward metaphorical literalization in costume design," which provided not only a visual reinforcement of character but also a nonrealist symbolism that added drama and insight.[49] The distance between star and character that is presumably bridged by naturalistic acting in contemporary films is in the costume drama bridged instead by metaphorical connections between the star's preexisting persona and the character portrayed. As Gaines points out, female stars' personae were crucially structured by both their previous film roles and their offscreen style of dress, which added an intertextual element to each new performance.

In 1936, the *Motion Picture Herald* defined the "prestige picture" as having four possible sources: the nineteenth-century novel, Shakespeare, award-winning novels and Broadway plays, and biographical/historical subjects. These source materials had the distinction of being "acclaimed by the classes and bought by the masses." But Tino Balio also describes the prestige picture as one with "plenty of star power, glamorous and elegant trappings, and elaborate special effects."[50] This broader description is more useful in conceptualizing the relationship between fashion and costume drama. My discussion of the costume drama will thus refer to films outside the studio-defined "prestige" category, but it will be limited to films set in a historical period. Historical settings eliminate the need to adhere to strictly contemporary fashion codes (although these are always visible), and often allow for a more baroque use of costume.

American costume features date back to D. W. Griffith's epics and Paramount's "Famous Players" productions, but in the 1920s an emphasis on modernity and luxury briefly overshadowed the status of the historical epic. By the mid-1930s, however, the prestige picture had become "the most popular production trend of the decade."[51] Throughout the 1930s, the audience for historical costume film was presumed to be largely female: "costume dramas, with heavy emphasis on glamour, became known in the trade as 'women's pictures.'"[52] Studios often used such films to capitalize on the popularity of charismatic actresses such as Greta Garbo, Norma Shearer, Marlene Dietrich, Claudette Colbert, Bette Davis, and Katharine Hepburn.

Like the musical and the fashion film, the costume drama draws an "excessive" amount of attention to its own stylization and performativity. Both Pam Cook and Sue Harper have described the way that historical drama uses costume to present a conjunction of "femininity, foreignness and masquerade." Cook sees the English Gainsborough costume dramas of the 1940s as transgressive in their "lavish dress and decor and their conjuring up of an erotically charged feminine world."[53] Likewise, Harper sees the Gainsborough "bodice rippers" as films that rewrite the past in order to appeal to working-class women, a social group usually left out of academic history. The costume and mise-en-scène of such films, more than their stories, are seen to transgress the conventional representations of class and gender relations by accentuating women's sexuality and social power: "Gainsborough languages of costume and art direction displayed the past as a series of intense, illuminated moments, resonant with sensual meaning. The scripts were more rigorous in ascribing a class basis to social experience."[54] Vivien Leigh's performance as Scarlett O'Hara exemplifies this rewriting of history in terms of (white) feminine power and emotion. Such roles were consistently popular in the 1930s, and costume was a central vehicle for fans' engagement with such roles (Scarlett's famous "barbecue dress" was knocked off by countless department stores and wholesalers). Publicity for these films often focused on costuming, in keeping with the studios' targeting of a female audience. Unparalleled in the amount of publicity generated around a film's costumes is MGM's *Marie Antoinette* (1938), for which the studio wrote endless press releases and stories in *MGM Studio News*. Other films from the 1930s that generated large numbers of costume-related articles were *She Done Him Wrong* (1933), *Romance* (1933), *Cleopatra* (1934), *The Scarlet Empress* (1934), *Anna Karenina* (1935), *Mary of Scotland* (1936), *Romeo and Juliet* (1936), *Camille* (1937), and *Gone with the Wind* (1939). The only non-historical films to receive a comparable amount of costume publicity, according to Susan Prichard's exhaustive bibliography, were *As You Desire Me* (1931), *Letty Lynton* (1932), *Roberta* (1935), and *Vogues of 1938*.[55] In an essay on the Hollywood historical epic, a category that overlaps with the costume drama, Vivian Sobchack argues that the publicity surrounding such films often generates a rhetorical parallel between the spectacular production values of the film and the epic significance of the historical events and characters: "The genre formally repeats the surge, splendor, and extravagance . . . [of] its narrative's historical content in both its production process and its modes of representation . . . in a manner and at a magnitude that is *intelligible as excess*."[56]

In the case of *Marie Antoinette,* this parallel between production values and historical importance can be seen in the way that the film's publicity implies a similarity between the aristocratic excess of the court of Louis XIV and the movie's excessively opulent costuming. Articles repeatedly describe the film's unparalleled twelve hundred costumes—including thirty-four different gowns worn by its star, Norma Shearer—and the quantities of expensive materials that went into them. The hyperbole of the film's costume publicity itself repeats this excess, with headlines like "Facts That Make 'Antoinette' Most Fabulous Picture Screen Ever Attempted," "Heavy Costumes" (giving the total weight of Shearer's costumes as 1,768 pounds), "Royal Robe Uses 2500 Ermine Pelts," and "Shearer Gowns Set New Record." A souvenir program, "The Making of 'Marie Antoinette' in Pictures," was also produced, with photographs of wardrobe women constructing the costumes. This detailing of the labor involved in producing such costumes is typical of the period film more generally, as seen in the press release for *Queen Christina* that noted, "one gown alone required a hundred yards of material, and ten women worked for eight weeks completing the seed pearl embroidery on it."[57]

This publicizing of the intense labor and craftwork that such costumes required again raises the question of the relationship of mass production to popular fashion culture. While, as I argued earlier, design exclusivity had been the goal of an elite fashion market rather than a popular one, craftwork and quality were more populist values. In contrast to the invisibility of garment production in most fashion-related films, the detailed description of construction processes on costumes for period films recognizes the painstaking labor involved in such work. But this emphasis on craft would not have implied that mass-produced ready-to-wear was, conversely, seen as lacking

Norma Shearer is upstaged by her gown in a MGM publicity photograph
for *Marie Antoinette* (1938).

in quality. Mass production, contrary to what is often assumed, represented an overall improvement in clothing quality for the majority of consumers. As Ben Fine and Ellen Leopold point out, mechanization both improved the quality of clothing construction and continued to "increase expectations" of fashionable detail, leading to "the production of ever more elaborate clothing."[58] The value of simplified, retail versions of film costumes (like the Cinema Fashions tied in with *Queen Christina*) may thus have been enhanced by association with publicity about the labor-intensive originals and their design details.

The emphasis on costume, craftwork, and historical authenticity in many of these films appears to function, like the stardom of their lead performers, as an enhancement of the "splendor" and significance of the narrative events. Sobchack suggests, for example, that stardom is particularly central to historical costume drama because the star gives significance to the historical character portrayed: "stars literally lend magnitude to the representation."[59] Although the primacy of stardom over characterization is particularly apparent in costume drama, I would argue that historical roles were also a way of articulating and enhancing an existing star persona. The films *Queen Christina* and *Mary of Scotland*, for example, were discussed in fan magazines in terms of the fascinating similarities between their protagonists and their stars (Greta Garbo and Katharine Hepburn, respectively). A *Photoplay* article on *Queen Christina* called "Two Queens Were Born in Sweden" notes that "the parallel between the lives of Greta and the Christina she interprets is truly remarkable." Their common characteristics are said to be androgyny and the desire for independence rather than marriage:

> Christina . . . wore as near to man's attire as was possible in those days . . . [her] hands were beautiful and white, but strong and virile; her eyes might have belonged to either sex . . . her voice was clear, deep and emotional. It would be difficult to find a more exact description of Garbo. . . . "I

Katharine Hepburn in an RKO publicity photograph for *Mary of Scotland* (1936).

would rather die than be married," [Christina] once said . . .
"My ambition and my pride are incapable of submitting to
anyone." Could not those very well be Garbo's sentiments?[60]

Similarly "uncanny" resemblances are drawn between
Mary Stuart and Katharine Hepburn in the article "How
Hepburn Is 'Queening' It." Referring to Hepburn's role in
Mary of Scotland, the article claims that "before she ever ap-
plies her screen make-up as Mary, Katharine has an advantage . . . she *looks like the* woman she is to portray. Moreover,
she *thinks* like her." To illustrate this, a scene from the film is

Greta Garbo in an MGM publicity photograph for *Queen Christina* (1933).

described: "when the Lords propose that she should marry one of them, Mary asks, 'Suppose I don't choose to marry at all?' (A question that you could imagine Katharine, herself, flinging at an annoying questioner.)"[61]

A more general interpretation of these parallels is made in the article "They're All Queening It," which features the subtitle, "And Each Will Thrill to the Power That Was Once a Monarch's." The writer notes that "four of Hollywood's greatest picture stars are about to become Queens" (along with the Garbo and Hepburn films, Dietrich and Shearer had been cast in *The Scarlet Empress* and *Marie Antoinette*), and suggests

> it's much, much more than a mere costume picture these women are making. Isn't it really a gratifying—unconsciously perhaps—of the suppressed desire that burns within the breast of nearly every woman in these modern times? To the housewife of only yesterday who believed that "woman's place is in the home" those famous and powerful women monarchs were strange people in history books. . . . Then something happened . . . they battled their way into the professions, business and politics. They swept aside the old stigmas against actresses, and they set up screen and stage stars as women of ideals and purpose.[62]

This homage to female stardom goes on to note that what is particularly empowering about modern screen-queens, by contrast with historical ones, is that any "obscure youngster, cleverly managed [can] become a great star," and that "any great movie star [can] attain queenly beauty." These films, then, display the power of their stars, but the stars themselves are not unique—rather, they are creations of the clever manager and the Hollywood glamour machine. The representation of femininity in the queen cycle is thus both empowering and accessibly populist; it also echoes marketing emphases on fashion as a vehicle of social mobility and self-invention. In the costume drama, however, the emphasis is not on transformation but on display.

The fashion influence of Hollywood costume drama was reinforced by the fact that historical revivals were popular with Paris designers throughout the 1930s, in a symbiotic relationship to Hollywood's cycle of costume films. The French designers acknowledged Hollywood's influence on their stylistic nostalgia; when an American reporter covered the French openings in 1935, she asked whether Hollywood films influenced current designs. Lucien Lelong replied succinctly: "We all take inspiration from the same sources. . . . We, the couturiers, can no longer live without the cinema any more than the cinema can live without us. We corroborate each other's instinct." Edward Molyneux mentioned *The Barretts of Wimpole Street* (1934), and Marcel Rochas admired Walter Plunkett's costumes for *Little Women* (1933), noting that "at a time when everyone was feeling the need for something 'new' . . . these types of clothes offered the solution." In 1940, a fashion reporter for the *New York Times* concluded, "It cannot be denied that clothes in period pictures do affect the modes of the moment. . . . costume pictures add notes, bars, and passages to the symphony of dress."[63]

This process was dependent on the relationship of films to the design cycle, however, a dynamic that was described by Adrian when asked whether he thought the costumes for *Camille* would have a fashion influence:

> "It is difficult to say," he answered. "The picture will probably not be released until around Christmas and it will depend upon what the newest silhouette is at the time. In other words, if the crinoline influence, with its accompanying details, is in the fashion picture at the time, then further novel details may be added by this film. It is possible, however, that these styles may be too early or too late to influence fashion, with the exception of hats. The hat picture is always flexible."[64]

Adrian gives the example of *Romeo and Juliet,* which was released just after there had been a major Renaissance influence on Paris design, minimizing the film's fashion impact (it did, however, popularize Norma Shearer's "Juliet cap" and hairstyle). The most famous example of Hollywood's influence on French fashion is Mae West's 1933 film *She Done Him Wrong,* which is credited with having revived the hourglass shape of the Gay Nineties. According to *Photoplay,* "Mae West parties" became the rage in Paris following the film's release, and Elsa Schiaparelli based an entire collection on the "Mae West Look." As a result, Paramount commissioned Schiaparelli to costume West for the 1937 film *Every Day's a Holiday,* and the couture designer's work was unusually successful on-screen, perhaps due to her stylistic playfulness and frequent use of exaggerated, surrealist details and colors.[65] Previous attempts to use couture designers for costumes had highlighted the differences between screen costumes, which required formal exaggeration, and the subtlety of much French design. Coco Chanel's well-publicized visit to Hollywood, sponsored by Samuel Goldwyn in 1931, typified this incompatibility, in spite of one reporter's approving comment that "Chanel does not pull any artistic stuff about 'inspiration.'"[66]

Hollywood's period costumes usually subordinated historical accuracy for the sake of fashion and visual effect, with details exaggerated and proportions modified to fit the current silhouette (in a particularly bold move, Sam Goldwyn moved *Wuthering Heights* [1939] from a Regency to a Victorian setting because he found the styles more flattering).[67] Along with the liberties taken with period design motifs, an emphasis on the symbolic significance of clothing is frequent in costume films. As W. Robert LaVine has described, *Gone with the Wind* uses costume not only to show the effects of the Civil War on its heroine, Scarlett O'Hara, but also to show the way that Scarlett herself uses clothing in a highly strategic manner. While the first half of the film presents her in the flowery, crinoline-filled dresses of a girl preoccupied with flirtation, the

Norma Shearer displays an unlikely Renaissance neckline in an MGM publicity photograph for *Romeo and Juliet* (1936).

second shows her making a gown out of old velvet drapes in order to feign an economic status that she no longer has.[68]

In *Jezebel*, the heroine's willfulness is made irreversibly public when she wears a red gown to the cotillion, a gesture of disregard for codes of dress and femininity that dooms her to a tragic end. This role also referred tacitly to Bette Davis's well-developed star persona as a strong, "difficult" woman, seen in previous films like *Dangerous* (1935) and *Marked Woman* (1937). In *Queen Christina,* Garbo's well-known preference for men's clothing is echoed by Christina, whose appearance indicates both her ability to do a "man's job" as a monarch and her desire for freedom and independence. The film dwells on her changes of costume as a barometer of her conflicts between duty and desire, and her unhappy sense of confinement as queen is figured in the heavy, motionless gown she wears for her coronation. This symbolic use of costuming is not limited to period films (there is, for example, Cynthia Darrington's sudden appearance in a silver lamé moth costume in *Christopher Strong* (1933) a metaphor for her tragic compulsion toward a love that results in her death-in-flight). But the inevitable "fancy dress" aspect of historical costuming makes it more open to metaphoric uses.

In the costume drama, the distance between contemporary star and historical character makes naturalism impossible; it is replaced, instead, by such characterological metaphors. For example, in *Romance,* set in the "gilded age" of New York, the Italian diva Nina Cavallini (Greta Garbo) bids farewell to her adoring fans wearing a cap adorned with two entire bird wings; they summarize what we already know about her— that she is a restless songbird who must fly from place to place, finding solace only in her music. She is also frequently seen in gowns with wide, off-the-shoulder shawl collars that form a deep, V-shaped neckline, sometimes with pointed, wing-like lapels. Her dramatically exposed throat and shoulders are contrasted with the high-necked, Victorian collars of other female characters, who appear both trussed up and weighted down by their dark clothing. (This film also introduced the feather-plumed "Empress Eugenie" hat, which became wildly popular.)

Adrian has written that in designing the costumes for *Camille,* he had difficulty finding images of the demimondaines of the period, since they were rarely painted. He decided to express Camille's "theatrical legendry" by dressing her in every conventional style of the era, "snoods, fringed parasols, bustles, and pyramided skirts," but with added "taste and flair," set off by "hats a shade more unconventional than her life." This exaggeration and theatricality were, according to Adrian, set off by Garbo's own persona: "She brought to the sets, with her quality of aloofness, that mystery which is a part of her and a part of the theatre's integral glamour."[69] The theatricality of period costume thus enhances the way star performances turn history into melodramatic spectacle.

Both period drama and the fashion spectacle thus present an intensification of the role of costume (and, by association, fashion) through their use of star performativity, masquerade, and melodrama. Far from contradicting consumer fashion marketing and its emphasis on "wearable" costumes and star emulation, these stylistically excessive modes of costuming can be seen to represent the apotheosis of both costume and fashion as agents of self-invention and the malleability of social identity.

Clothed in Emotion: Costume Melodrama

A number of contemporary-setting melodramas of the 1930s utilized costume as a featured expressive element, just as costume dramas did. Such films were closely linked to their stars' shifting fashion styles, which changed periodically in order to keep them from becoming too predictable. After Norma Shearer became the reigning queen of sophisticated, flirtatious elegance in films like *The Divorcée* (1930), *A Free Soul* (1931), and *Private Lives* (1931), publicity for her next film, *Smilin' Through* (1932), read: "Leave it to Norma Shearer to change her type when she felt there was danger of its becoming a rubber stamp. When you see her in *Smilin' Through* she will be as quaintly demure as an old valentine."[70] Contemporary melodramas often functioned to indicate new trends or changes in stars' appearance, and letters to fan magazines indicate that viewers may have evaluated such films as much for their presentation of particular stars as anything else.

The melodrama was thus a privileged genre in its use of the formal expressivity and the star-related semiotics of costume. The basic principles of costume design (to convey information about characters and situations without "upstaging" them) are still relevant in such films, but the heightened visual and emotional vocabulary of the "woman's film" allowed for the intensification of the costumes' expressivity. While Edith Head has argued that highly dramatic scenes require unobtrusive designs (and, conversely, that elaborate costumes can make incidental scenes more exciting), high-budget melodramas in the 1930s (particularly those produced by MGM) tended to feature eye-catching costumes for the star in each of her scenes.

One of the most notorious costume melodramas of the decade was *Letty Lynton* (1932), which solidified the transformation of Joan Crawford's image from that of a youthful party girl to an elegant "clotheshorse." One gown in the film, of white starched chiffon with huge ruffled shoulders, became famous as the Letty Lynton dress and was reproduced in numerous forms, including a version for Waldman's Cinema Fashions. Though it is unclear how many copies of this dress were actually retailed, *Fortune* magazine printed Waldman's claim that Macy's had sold five hundred thousand of his design, and that number became legendary.[71] As it appears in *Letty Lynton*, the dress defies Head's dictum about using subtle designs for particularly emotional performances.[72]

Letty wears the dress in a scene that is pivotal in establishing her as a sympathetic character rather than a jaded socialite. Having broken off a cynical "foreign affair" with a domineering man named Emile (Nils Asther), Letty takes up with a more sympathetic bachelor on board the ship carrying her back to New York (Robert Montgomery). The ship provides a space for Letty to fall properly in love and become more vulnerable, but it is also a conducive space for her depiction in several highly cinematic outfits. On the evening she wears her famous dress, Letty breaks down in tears over her mother's ongoing rejection of her and takes refuge on the deck of the ship. Like publicity stills of Crawford in the dress, the scene is designed around the fabric's ability to catch the light, and takes full advantage of the white clouds of starched ruffles that extend up from the shoulders. Letty stands in the dark, but the waves of fabric that frame her face glow in a soft pool of moonlight and echo the ocean waves on which she gazes unhappily. The dress is a crucial component of the scene's lighting, since its softness and diffusion of light give Crawford a look of innocence and vulnerability. At the same time, the architecture of the dress broadens Crawford's shoulders dramatically and lengthens her torso, while the smooth, flaring skirt extends the line of her long back and erect shoulders in a posture of youthful stoicism.

The popularity of this dress and its widespread adaptation illustrate the way that Hollywood designs could both take up and inflect broader fashion trends. After the lowering of hemlines in the Paris collections of fall 1929, dresses became particularly formfitting, often cut on the bias to accentuate the line of the body. This look was widely hailed as a rejection of the "mannish" look of the late-1920s chemise dress, but the long hemline also required a sylphlike body and narrow hips in order to avoid looking pear-shaped. As a result, this silhouette was increasingly combined with retro details like puffy sleeves and feather boas for eveningwear, and slightly padded shoulders for suits. These made the waist and hips look narrower and allowed the long, narrow silhouette to become flattering to more women. Schiaparelli is credited with having started the trend by emphasizing broad shoulders in her 1930 and 1931 collections, but Adrian's Letty Lynton dress combined the look, which particularly suited Crawford's figure, with a neo-Victorian femininity that remained popular in U.S. eveningwear for the rest of the decade.[73]

The dress was quickly disseminated in a variety of forms,

Joan Crawford wears the popular *Letty Lynton* dress in an MGM publicity photograph (1932).

and Crawford wore similar ones in subsequent films, which became generically known as "'Letty Lynton' type" gowns. One columnist described Crawford's own fashion "tip," which was to wear a plain, sliplike gown with a "puffed sleeve blouse tying high about her waist." Such sleeves were referred to as "mutton" sleeves "à la gay '90s," indicating their association with retro-feminine charm and a more hourglass-shaped body (nevertheless, 1930s evocations of this silhouette were—Mae West notwithstanding—uniformly narrow-hipped).[74] The femininity of the puffed sleeve cannot, however, be separated from the simultaneous appearance of the padded shoulder in suits. This aspect of Adrian's new broad-shouldered silhouette for Crawford was equally influential, but one that had distinctly masculine connotations. The exaggerated shoulders of the Letty Lynton dress can thus be seen as simultaneously feminine and powerful, a combination that resonated with fan-magazine descriptions of Crawford's modern, strong but alluring sensibility.

The scene in which Letty kills her possessive former lover again uses the formal aspects of Crawford's costume to heighten the emotional rendering of her character's situation. Forced to visit her former lover, Letty wears a two-piece dress made of a brittle-looking silver lamé, and the metallic, armorlike outfit suggests her desire to protect herself from him. Since he expects Letty to spend the night, the metallic dress indicates her need for a barrier between their bodies and also works to heighten the scene's dramatic lighting. The hotel room is dimly lit by a fire and one small table lamp, and the refraction of light on the dress is riveting in almost every shot, as Letty's body glimmers in the ominously dark room.

After Emile strikes Letty twice, she crumples onto the floor, a figure of abject pathos whose wealth (the silver lamé) suddenly looks no more protective than aluminum foil. Thrust into a chair beneath the table lamp, Letty reaches out to drink the champagne she has poisoned. Huddled in the chair, the pool of lamplight accentuates her huge eyes, which widen as

Emile unknowingly takes the poison from her and drinks it. As he raises the glass, the camera pulls back dramatically from a close-up of Crawford to a high angle shot from over his shoulder as she stares up, accentuating Emile's physical power as he looks down at her contemptuously. Letty's costume is thus integral to the success of a difficult scene, the purpose of which is to make her responsibility for his death not only justifiable but a form of self-defense. The scene's costume and other formal elements emphasize her repulsion from Emile, her vulnerability in his hotel room, and her inability to protect herself physically.[75]

The extent to which what Gaines calls melodrama's "empathic costuming" inflected the meaning of those designs as they circulated in retail versions is impossible to gauge. Like the fashion influence of the costume drama, much of the impact of particular costumes depended on whether their appearance coincided with broader fashion trends. When that was the case, particular costumes could epitomize that trend and amplify its significance because of its association with a particular star or character, as with the Letty Lynton dress or Scarlett O'Hara's barbecue dress from *Gone with the Wind*. More generally, costume melodramas indicate the popularity of costume as a foregrounded feature of Hollywood filmmaking, since fan magazine reviews of such films frequently evaluate the quality of the clothes on display in them.

Not least of all, these films formed the framework of female stars' images and marked the cyclical changes that kept their "looks" from getting stale. This process both mirrored the emphasis on constant change in consumer fashion marketing and demonstrated the transient nature of each star's current "type." These changes were almost always represented as adaptations to changing public taste or viewers' boredom with a particular image, and were consequently discussed in fan magazines as calculated career moves. Consequently, the deployment of fashion as both spectacle and for melodramatic affect was always couched in a framework of star popularity in which the ability to adapt one's style was a necessary strategy for stars as workers in the studio system. The studios' struggle to maintain their stars' glamour value and popular appeal was often described as an "object lesson" to women struggling to maximize the value of their own self-presentation. Thirties Hollywood fan discourse was thus one in which the pleasures of fashion as artifice and self-transformation were overtly linked to a particular industrial economy. This economy was one that depended on and celebrated artifice and affect, but in doing so de-essentialized rules of dress and appearance in ways that may have been far more provocative in their social reception than studio publicists might have imagined.

HOLLYWOOD 3 EXOTICISM

Thirty years ago, no lady ever made up. . . . And now, from
the greenish or umber sheen of her eyelids to the flame or
saffron of her lips and nails, the lady of to-day is a subtle
and marvelous creation based on the entity that is—Herself.
Vogue, June 1934

Since the early days of the star system, Hollywood femininity
has been closely tied in with the marketing of cosmetics, and
one of the most important stylistic vehicles for this relationship was the glamour of exoticism. The stereotypes of exotic
ethnicity deployed in Hollywood films were both repeated
and modified within cosmetics advertising of the 1930s, and
numerous female stars endorsed makeup brands. It has been
argued that the use of exoticism in cosmetics advertising has
historically "displaced" discourses of race and gender via a
"language of 'color' and 'type.'"[1] This can be seen as a sup-
pression of racial difference, but commercial discourses have
also worked to normalize difference by treating it euphemisti-
cally. For example, in the early 1930s Max Factor began de-

signing cosmetics to correspond with a range of complexion, hair, and eye colors, and this "personalized" color-matching system (which was widely adopted by other brands) avoided issues of race by describing differences in skin tone as aesthetic categories or "complexion types." Cosmetics advertising of the 1930s certainly utilized stereotypes (popular makeup products used "Tropical," "Chinese," and "Gypsy" colors), but the advertising was, nevertheless, significant because it described beauty in terms of multiple points on a spectrum, rather than a single, monochromatic ideal.

The paleness that many women, both "white" and of color, had struggled for years to create with bleach creams, arsenic and lead powder, veils, and parasols was, I would argue, significantly modified by Hollywood's familiarization of the sensual, painted face. This relativization of beauty norms also resulted from the expansion of a commercial beauty culture that relied economically on the promotion of new looks, new faces, and new colors. The 1930s' exotic makeup lines can thus be seen as an early form of commodified multiculturalism aimed at maximizing cosmetics sales. By mid-decade, most cosmetics manufacturers had stopped advertising traditional, lily-white facial powder altogether.

By the end of the decade, the cinematic projection of sexuality onto nonwhite women, typically characterized as dangerous "vampires" or tragic native-girls, had also been modified. Sensuous and dusky dark-haired sirens like Dolores Del Rio, Dorothy Lamour, Hedy Lamarr, and Rita Hayworth had replaced pale platinum blondes as icons of glamour. It is difficult to interpret such changes in fashion iconography, but what is clear is that in the 1930s a relative increase occurred in the range of beauty types on the American screen and in advertising, suggesting that the dominance of white, monoracial beauty was significantly challenged by previously marginalized female identities.

From their first appearance at the turn of the century, Hollywood's ethnic stereotypes were predicated on the notion

Cover of *Screenland* featuring Greta Garbo's cosmetic exoticism, circa 1933.

that there exists a category of nonethnic whiteness. Even in the late 1930s, when Mendelian genetic theory had disproved the concept of "pure" races with that of the human gene pool differentiated only by temporary geographical isolation, Hollywood perpetuated myths of racial purity and the dangers of "mixed blood." Films and publicity materials continued to

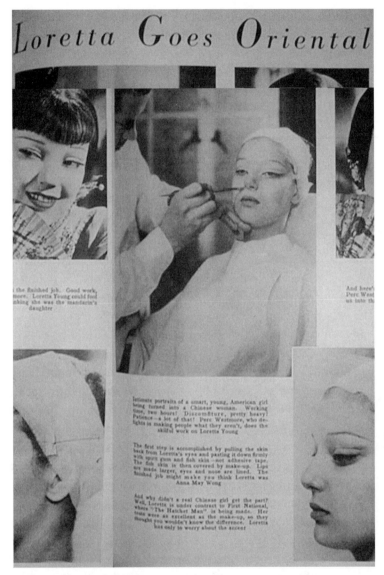

Article "Loretta Goes Oriental," *Photoplay,* March 1932, p. 71.

refer to racial purity even as genetic theory was becoming popularized in the form of pro-assimilation arguments, which gradually displaced hereditarian and eugenicist racism in mainstream ideology.[2] At the same time, however, Hollywood's constructions of race were visualized in the form of clearly artificial "ethnic simulacra," the cosmetic basis of which was often described by publicity in terms of the wonders of Hollywood makeup illusionism.

These "simulacra" are the material of what Ella Shohat calls Hollywood's "spectacle of difference"—its creation of ethnicity as a consumable pleasure.[3] One of the primary products of this spectacle, the image of exotic beauty, was indispensable to the recuperation of cosmetics. The frequent use of exotic female stars as endorsers of women's beauty products was thus at odds with nativist norms of beauty, just as women's obsession with Rudolph Valentino, Ramon Novarro, and Charles Boyer's passionate sexuality was seen as a rejection of culturally approved but boring WASP masculinity.[4] One way to explore the controversial popularity of "ethnic" beauty is to look closely at the discourses around it, such as the way that racial difference was used in marketing, and the range of readings that such strategies made available.

The artificiality of Hollywood's ethnic categories was visible not only in discourses about cosmetics but also in publicity about nonwhite stars and films that represented hybrid racial identities. Notes from the Production Code Administration's censorship of *Imitation of Life* (1934), for example, are symptomatic in their unease about Peola, the film's mulatta character (played by Fredi Washington). Washington's image on screen clearly undermined the myth of racial "purity," but the Hays office, which coordinated the industry's self-censorship, responded by referring to the character of Peola as "the negro girl appearing as white." The film disturbed the Production Code Administration because it undermined the visual inscription of race as color, as well as implicitly reflecting to the history of miscegenation. The Hays office insisted that the invisibility of Peola's race was "extremely dangerous" to "the industry as a whole" and stipulated that the film script attribute her lightness to an albino-like aberration within "a line of definitely negro strain."[5] The difficulty of inscribing racist essentialism in terms of skin color also emerges in *Photoplay*'s description of Nina Mae McKinney, star of *Hallelujah!* (1929), which begins, "Nina isn't black, she's coppery," and concludes with the comment, "She may be black, but she's got a blonde soul."[6] The visual culture of Hollywood consumerism made it increasingly difficult to assign fixed identities to glamourized racial stereotypes.

Ella Shohat and Robert Stam have pointed out how the "racial politics of casting" in Hollywood effectively "submerged" the multiculturalism that is at the center of American national identity, replacing it with a visually coded racial hierarchy.[7] But the constant publicizing of Hollywood's cosmetic illusionism, along with marketing discourses obsessed with the "makeover," undermined the racial essentialism that required stereotypes to be taken as signs with real-world referents. Hollywood's exoticism of the 1930s was a product of centuries of Eurocentric representations and decades of racist production practices. But these films also popularized a form of exoticism as masquerade within an increasingly diverse market for both Hollywood films and associated goods like cosmetics, subjecting their images to an idiosyncratic process of consumer appropriation.

Western Beauty and Split Femininity

Modern cosmetics have been promoted in terms of a fairly recent concept of "democratic" beauty, based on the proposition that with good grooming and makeup, every woman can be beautiful in her own, unique way. In the early 1930s, beauty columns began to suggest that facial beauty was simply a matter of effort and technique. This concept of beauty as universally attainable was predicated on a sense of the body's malleability and constructedness, and like the notion that one's personality could be endlessly modified through fashion, it supported the requirements of a consumer economy. Within the Judeo-Christian tradition, however, concepts of physical beauty have been even more controversial than debates over the legitimacy of fashion. Beauty as a social value continues to be highly problematic from a range of perspectives, including contemporary feminist ones. But the condemnation of physical beauty has a long history in relation to the moral condemnation of women's sexuality, and a discussion of the rise of commercial beauty culture needs to take account of this.

Christian warnings against "vanity" and the cultivation of physical attractiveness have often clearly articulated anxieties about the expression of female sexuality. Historian Arthur Marwick has traced the discourse of English, European, and American beauty manuals from the sixteenth century onward, arguing that their emphasis on the cultivation of feminine virtue was linked to fears of female physical beauty as a form of power. Until the nineteenth century, many books on beauty were, in fact, written by church officials or professional moralists, and reflect a long-standing European model of split femininity iconically represented by "the Madonna and the whore." Real feminine beauty is said to reflect moral goodness (the beauty of the Madonna), but it can also exist physically in the absence of goodness (the seductiveness of the whore). In Gabriel de Minut's 1587 book *Of Beauty*, for example, the author explains that an attractive woman who is not virtuous is only *seemingly* beautiful, while in fact stimulating "the pollution and contamination of vice and ordure."[8] Beauty is thus a sign whose meaning can only be determined by the feelings it invokes in men: if it stimulates lustful desire, it is not "real" beauty but a sign of the *woman's* immorality. The usefulness of this ideology for inhibiting women's expression of their own sense of attractiveness is clear, given the risk of inspiring the "wrong" kind of appreciation.

In spite of this moralizing split between physical and spiritual beauty, by the late eighteenth century there was a large market for practical advice on techniques of cosmetic self-improvement. As the nineteenth century progressed, the value of beauty for both men and women within a growing capitalist and service economy became obvious, and the recognition of beauty as social capital is evident in its absorption into a feminine work ethic. Women's cosmetic self-maintenance came to be seen as a process that might not *produce* beauty but could help retain positive attributes and was, therefore, dutiful rather than unethical. This view led to a plethora of beauty guides that originated and circulated in England, France, and the United States. Their authors included "society beauties," professional writers on fashion and etiquette, and purveyors of scientific beauty treatments.

In the nineteenth century a fairly limited range of cosmetic aids were used, however, particularly by comparison with the earlier popularity of cosmetics among social elites in the seventeenth and eighteenth centuries. Bourgeois women limited their use of beauty products to items like refined soap, lotions and astringents for softening the skin, hair oils and tints, and facial powder. In 1866, poisonous white facial powders made from lead or arsenic salts were finally replaced by an oxide of zinc, which was cheap and became available to working-class women.[9] Christian anxieties about physical beauty and cosmetic self-adornment remained powerful, however, until the popularity of cheaper cosmetics after World War I began to mitigate the social stigma of makeup.[10] In the transitional, prewar period, bourgeois women's interest in cosmetics was made morally acceptable by the quasi-spiritual philosophies of "beauty culturists." These were primarily female entrepreneurs who, like Elizabeth Arden and Helena Rubenstein, had some knowledge of dermatology and a lot of marketing skill. They made cosmetics morally acceptable by promoting a philosophy of "Natural Beauty" to be achieved through good health, expensive massage, and "scientific" skin treatments. Their approach combined moralizing about the need for inner perfection with the pleasures of salon pampering: as one advertisement asked, "Is your complexion clear? Does it express the clearness of your life? Are there discolorations or blemishes in the skin—which symbolize imperfections within?"[11]

But this mind-body philosophy, which was carried over from the nineteenth century, also implied that individuals who were less than beautiful could be judged as to their moral interiority, a theory popularized by the pseudoscience of phrenology. In addition, it presumed to set the standards of "Natural Beauty" according to northern European ideals, implying that racial "difference" could be read as both an aesthetic and a moral imperfection. Such theories represented a nativist bias in the United States that became increasingly virulent in response to new patterns of immigration and resulted in the eugenics movement. Eugenics brought together Christian notions that the body was a mirror of the soul, a Darwinist emphasis on heredity, and a pseudoscientific notion of racial purity. It aimed to purify the "white" race by restricting immigration and miscegenation, and by preventing "deviant" bodies from reproducing.[12]

Following World War I, however, nativist claims to physical and aesthetic superiority became increasingly incompatible with the demands of the new consumer economy. Given the requirements for "Natural Beauty"—a WASP pedigree, lots of fresh air, and virtuous thoughts—most American women would have been doomed to an inferior visage. But consumer-marketing professionals needed women to look in the mirror and see potential beauty so that new products could be positioned as a means of self-improvement. The cosmetics industry had also begun to shift from a "class" to a mass market in the nineteenth century, when white-collar women were confronted with the value placed on their personal appearance in the commercial service sector. This market of working- and middle-class women gradually became far more significant to the cosmetics industry than its traditional market of elite female consumers.[13]

The Makeover and the Max Factor

The growing presence of women in service-sector work and the entertainment industry throughout the nineteenth century meant that female beauty became increasingly visible as a form of social capital. New women's magazines and self-help literature facilitated the rise of a commercial beauty culture that increasingly looked to actresses to legitimize new modes of self-adornment.[14] Throughout the nineteenth century, cosmetics manufacturers had solicited letters of endorsement from reigning theatrical divas to be printed in publications aimed at bourgeois women.[15] In the early twentieth century, however, endorsements by cinema stars began to outnumber those from "legitimate" stage actresses, as popular appeals to a mass market for beauty products displaced reliance on elite consumers.

Helena Rubenstein opened a salon in London in 1908 and by 1916 had begun a chain that included salons in several major U.S. cities. Mainstream American women were still reluctant to adopt her eye shadow, however, and Rubenstein turned to Hollywood for promotional help by designing the Orientalist eye makeup for Theda Bara in *A Fool There Was* (1915).[16] With their heavy, seductive eyes and "vampire lips," Hollywood silent-film stars like Bara, Nita Naldi, Pola Negri, and Alla Nazimova successfully challenged American norms of childlike beauty epitomized by Dorothy and Lillian Gish and Mary Pickford. Their success can be seen in the popularity of Clara Bow's huge eyes and "bee-stung lips," which were incorporated into the innocent but assertive sexuality of late-1920s flappers like Colleen Moore and Joan Crawford.[17] By 1934, the style pedagogy of Hollywood was metaphorized in a film featuring Thelma Todd as a model who demonstrates the miracle of cosmetics in the window of a beauty emporium, while a simultaneous huge "close-up" image of her face is projected alongside her in the shop window, attracting a crowd of onlookers (in *Hips, Hips, Hooray*).

Makeup played a significant technical role in the production of the Hollywood screen image. The use of heavy makeup on film actors was initially necessary to conceal the skin's red corpuscles, which were visible on orthochromatic film; it also hid imperfections exaggerated by the camera and provided a more consistent image for continuity purposes. By the early 1930s, panchromatic film stock allowed the use of a thinner greasepaint, and studio makeup artists began producing a carefully shaded and contoured face for the Hollywood screen—a look that was further stylized by studio lighting and photographic retouching.[18] To maintain the image he had created of Marlene Dietrich, Josef von Sternberg supervised all her studio portraiture: to make Dietrich's nose more aquiline, he once painted a thin silver line from the bridge to the tip of the nose and focused a small spotlight on it, with effective results.[19]

The stars' faces were individualized with a range of signature features: the shape of the mouth and eyebrows, the color and form of the hair, and the amount and style of eye makeup worn. Stars usually maintained a consistent makeup style from film to film, except when playing a "character" role, although they adapted to and modified broader fashions in makeup. Joan Crawford's mouth, for example, was painted inside her natural lip line throughout the 1920s to make her mouth smaller and rounder. In 1932, however, the films *Letty Lynton* and *Rain* display a fuller, somewhat overpainted mouth. As one article noted, "The lipstick extended beyond the corner and the mouth was greatly exaggerated in both thickness and length." In spite of the controversy this caused, Crawford's trend setting established what came to be seen as the "natural"-shaped mouth.[20]

The logic of an expanding consumer market for cosmetics helps to account for steady increases in the variety of products available from the early twentieth century onward. In 1931, an article in *Harper's Magazine* commented:

> A quarter of a century ago perfume, rice powder, and "anti-chap" for the hands constituted the entire paraphernalia of a woman's boudoir table. Now that table looks like a miniature chemist shop. No detail of appearance which can

safely be entrusted to artifice is ever left to nature. . . . As a result feminine beauty, once the Creator's business, is now Big Business's.[21]

The article reported that more than two billion dollars were spent each year on beauty products, and that forty thousand beauty shops were scattered across the United States. The marketing strategies that fueled this growth were based on a few key concepts, most of which had also been applied to fashion marketing, as discussed in chapter 1. These included the cultivation of a personal style chosen from a range of "types," the idea that this style could be changed at will, that an openness to change was necessary for finding or perfecting one's style, and that Hollywood stars represented idealized types for emulation and also demonstrated the effectiveness of cosmetic self-transformation.

Profiles of female stars in Hollywood fan magazines inevitably include a photograph of the star when she had just arrived in Hollywood. Much is made of the quaintness of her appearance in contrast to the astounding beauty she has cultivated since, which is credited to both her drive for self-improvement and the skill of studio makeup artists and designers.[22] In the 1933 article "These Stars Changed Their Faces—And So Can You!" this process is described in terms of facial features that have been "remodeled" by particular stars:

> Though styles may change in dresses and hats, most of us cart about the same old face . . . year in and year out. And sometimes we'd be glad to exchange the old looks for some new ones. But how can it be done? The movie stars are showing you! . . . In the new films, there are many "new faces," which have been remodeled over familiar frames. And something tells us that these new eyebrows, lips and hairlines are going to be as avidly copied by Miss America as the Hollywood clothes styles have been.[23]

Beauty advice columns of the early 1930s focused increasingly on the use of cosmetics, as indicated by the article, "What Any Girl Can Do with Make-Up." The columnist describes a young woman who went from "demure" to sophisticated, thanks to "a new coiffure, a different line in clothes, and most important of all, a new make-up scheme." The column concludes by suggesting, "why don't you try a few changes . . . we girls of 1930 have waked up to make-up!"[24] A Max Factor advertisement in the same issue repeats this narrative in the form of a testimonial by Bessie Love (an MGM star) titled "I Saw a Miracle of Beauty Happen in Hollywood": "She was just like a dozen other girls, but Max Factor, Hollywood's Make-Up Wizard, by the flattering touch of make-up, transformed her into a ravishing beauty . . . Revealing the secret of how every girl may obtain New Beauty and New Personality."[25]

The degree of artifice employed by Hollywood makeup artists was actually played up in beauty articles, and the very artificiality of the made-over face was celebrated as evidence of the democratization of beauty:

> There is a corrective formula for everything that is wrong with the feminine face. . . . The miracle men know what that is. They put it to work. And they transform those who are average . . . into individuals whose attraction and charm circle the globe.[26]

The concept of the "makeover" is regularly promoted in Hollywood fan magazines, although the first use I found of the term itself was in January 1939: in a beauty column, several female stars describe their New Year's fashion and beauty resolutions, which articulate concisely the cosmetics marketing strategies noted earlier. Anne Shirley, for example, "feels that only by experimenting can a person discover what's most becoming to her," and Joan Blondell states categorically, "the whole secret of beauty is change. . . . A girl who neglects changing her personality gets stale mentally as well as physically. So I'm going to vary my hair style, my type of make-up, nail-polish, perfume." In this article, constant self-transformation is also described as a source of pleasure rather than just a means to an end. The makeover epitomizes consumer marketing because it is a process that is simultaneously goal-oriented *and* its own reward—it offers the pleasure of potentiality: "If you get bored with yourself at times, let your resolution be to do something about it. Experiment with new make-ups, change your hairstyle and make yourself over into a new person."[27] Advertising for beauty products, however, still emphasized the positive results of their use—like romance or a job—and cinematic makeover sequences often had even more dramatic consequences.

Along with self-transformation and change, the promotion of color was a successful cosmetics-marketing concept. Just as product stylists in the 1920s stimulated the market for household products by designing them in vibrant colors, cosmetics began to be produced in an ever wider range of tones by the end of the 1920s. For cosmetics, the fashion "type" became linked to hair and eye color rather than personality, encouraging women to try a variety of makeup hues to see which ones matched their own coloring. In 1928, Max Factor changed the name of his cosmetics line from "Society Make-Up" to "Color Harmony Make-Up," on the advice of his marketing agency, Sales Builders, Inc. Their research showed that women usually bought cosmetics items in different brands; if the need to buy "harmonized" products was stressed, however, women would buy every article in the same brand. The result was the Max Factor "Color Harmony Prescription Make-Up Chart," which indicated the complementary shades of powder, rouge, and lipstick to be used according to complexion, hair, and eye color. This "harmonizing" concept was part of a widespread technique of marketing women's fashion separates and accessories as complementary "ensembles." Richard Hudnut cosmetics used it successfully in an "eye-matched makeup" line, which offered a variety of cosmetics chosen according to eye color, while advertising for "Lady

Esther" cosmetics cautioned that "the wrong shade of powder can turn the right man away! . . . so I urge you to try all my shades."[28]

One of the most significant aspects of the use of color to promote the growth of cosmetics was the introduction of new facial powders and rouges that were meant to accommodate a wider range of skin tones. In previous centuries, women had bleached, enameled, and powdered their faces with an array of frequently toxic substances. A gradual change took place, however, as outdoor activities like bicycling and tennis became popular among upper-class women, and working-class women moved from farm to factory labor. Suntanned skin became associated with bourgeois leisure, while pallor represented long hours worked in sunless factories. In addition, beach resorts like the Riviera became meccas for social elites in the 1920s, resulting in a vogue for suntan as a visible sign of upper-class travel; as a writer for *Advertising and Selling* mused,

> What inherent urge causes people to paint upon their faces the visible marks of their political or social levels? . . . The outdoor complexion has now met with consumer recognition . . . prompted by the desire to imitate leisure—that leisure which may go to Florida, Bermuda or California and bask in the sun.[29]

Cosmetics manufacturers took notice of the new acceptability of nonwhite skin and began to produce darker powders, as well as artificial bronzing lotions. By 1929, Jean Patou and Coco Chanel had introduced suntan products, and Helena Rubenstein was selling "Valaze Gypsy Tan Foundation." Other cosmetics manufacturers were blending powders to be "creamy," rather than white, and producing "ochre," "dark rachel," and "suntan" shades. Joan Crawford was credited for spreading the trend among Hollywood flappers—in addition to tanning her face, Crawford browned her body and went stockingless, a style that was popular "for sleeveless,

Joan Crawford tans with Douglas Fairbanks Jr. in a publicity photograph
for MGM, circa 1931.

backless frocks." Predictably, hosiery soon became available
in darker colors as well.[30]

The end of the suntan fad was predicted periodically in
early-1930s magazines, and Crawford was reportedly told by
MGM to stop tanning because she looked "like a lineal de-
scendent of Sheba," and "contrast[ed] strangely with the pale
Nordics in her films."[31] Instead, it became the norm for
women to tan in the summer, or even year-round if they lived

109

in a warm climate. Golden Peacock Bleach Cream and other facial bleaches, which were advertised regularly in women's magazines until the late 1920s, appeared only rarely after the early 1930s, although skin lighteners were still marketed to the African American community.[32] But as the racist quips about Crawford's suntan attest, the end of idealized pallor did not mean the end of the color line in American culture. What it accompanied, however, was a period of intensified commercial and cinematic representation of non-Anglo ethnicity, in the form of an appropriable exoticism. But the implication of such marketing was that nonwhite beauty cultures had an increasing influence on the mainstream. The cosmetics industry's maximization of its market through exoticism, in other words, resulted in a diversification of aesthetic ideals rather than the promotion of exclusively nativist, "white" beauty.

Hollywood Exoticism and Beauty Culture

An expanded range of color tones had been introduced into mainstream cosmetics by the late 1930s, but the discourses surrounding this change had a complex history both in Hollywood and in the marketing of cosmetics. Silent-screen "vamps" and the love goddesses who succeeded them were products of Hollywood's participation in a long tradition of projecting sexual licentiousness and exoticism onto colonized subjects. In the United States, European obsessions with the East were augmented by political and economic designs on Latin America and the South Pacific, giving rise to additional ethnic stereotypes and erotic "others" associated with those cultures. From its beginning, cinema had played a significant role in the popularization of imperialist fantasies and ethnic stereotypes, and the Hollywood studios found that the sexual exoticism associated with these themes was consistently popular.

Hollywood offered a range of nonwhite characterizations throughout the 1930s, from the "Latin Lover" roles of Ramon Novarro and Charles Boyer to the Latin, Asian, and South Seas beauties played by stars like Dolores Del Rio, Lupe

Velez, Dorothy Lamour, and Hedy Lamarr. The European stars Greta Garbo, Marlene Dietrich, and Lil Dagover were also "Orientalized" in many films and described as embodying a "pale exoticism." The casting of Euramerican actors in "ethnic" roles was commonplace in Hollywood, and the process of transforming them via elaborate character-makeup techniques was often discussed and illustrated in magazines.[33] Most non-Anglo Hollywood performers had their names anglicized, however, to eliminate any reference to their cultural background. Others were chosen to represent foreignness and rarely allowed to do anything else. On occasions when a star constructed as "ethnic" played a "white" role, it was noteworthy: when the Mexican actress Dolores Del Rio was cast as a French-Canadian lead in *Evangeline* (1929), *Photoplay* noted that "after winning a place on the screen because of her sparkling Spanish beauty and the fire of her performances, [she] now steps into a role that might have been reserved for Lillian Gish. It's a tribute to her versatility."[34]

More frequently, non-Anglo actors played a wide range of exotic roles; Lupe Velez was cast as a Chinese woman in *East Is West* (1930), a Native American in *The Squaw Man* (1931), and a Russian in *Resurrection* (1931). There was an interchangeability between all "ethnic" roles, but movement from "ethnic" typecasting to "white" roles was rare. One of the most notorious cases of casting discrimination in the 1930s took place when MGM asked Anna May Wong to audition for the role of the maid, Lotus, in their 1937 production of *The Good Earth*. The Los Angeles-born Wong had performed successfully on the stage in London and Europe and was the most popular Chinese American performer in Hollywood. In spite of Wong's status, the leading role in *The Good Earth* was given to Austrian actress Luise Ranier. Disgusted, Wong refused to play Lotus, questioning why MGM was asking her to play "the only unsympathetic role" in the film, while non–Chinese Americans played the main characters.[35]

In the United States, these characterizations were screened

in the context of a nativist backlash against immigration aimed at both Asians and the "new immigrants"—Jewish, Italian, and Eastern Europeans who arrived in the late nineteenth century. Unlike their Anglo, German, and Nordic predecessors, the "new immigrants" were perceived as being unfit to assimilate into a nativist-defined American identity, which was in danger of being "mongrelized" by their presence. In 1907, Congress established an "Immigration Commission" to look into the impact of the new immigrants on the country; two years later, the report granted Congress broad powers to exclude and deport specific categories of immigrants. According to David Palumbo-Liu, "from 1921 to 1925, nearly thirty thousand people were deported," and over the next five years that number doubled; the Tydings-McDuffie Act of 1934 effectively restricted all Asian immigration.[36] Hollywood's exotic ethnicity of the 1930s thus arose in the context of social anxiety about race but also represented an ongoing attraction and fascination with idealized forms of ethnicity.

Hollywood ethnicity in the 1930s also had hierarchical distinctions, with Castillian Spanish "blood" as the most idealized and assimilable form of nonwhiteness possible. Like the Mediterranean-influenced French and Italians, the Spanish were seen as both exotic and European. Dolores Del Rio was repeatedly described as having an "aristocratic" family in order to distinguish her from mixed-race Mexicans, and the studios' disregard for Spanish-speaking countries' linguistic differences led them to dub films into Castillian Spanish, even when they were set in Mexico, Cuba, or Argentina. Actresses described as Spanish appear to have outnumbered any other "ethnic" category in the late 1920s and early 1930s; in addition to Del Rio and Velez, the performers Raquel Torres, Conchita Montenegro, Arminda, Rosita Moreno, Movita Castaneda, Maria Casajuana, and Margo all appeared, for a while at least, on-screen and in the pages of fan magazines. The sex appeal of the "Latin type" is clear from an article noting that Casajuana was discovered when Fox, "on the look-

Anna May Wong in a publicity photograph for Paramount (no date).

out for sultry types, staged a beauty contest in Spain."[37] Like the "Spanish blood" that redeems Valentino's character in *The Sheik* (1921), Spanishness is often Hollywood's ethnically acceptable alibi for hot-blooded sexuality. It was also used as a racial default-setting for performers who played a range of

Lupe Velez in a publicity photograph (no date).

ethnic roles; a magazine profile of Margo, whose biggest Hollywood role was as a Russian in the Orientalist fantasy *Lost Horizon* (1937), notes, "Margo's exoticism is not an affectation. It is an inheritance bequeathed by her Castillian ancestors."[38]

Nativist ideology had often stressed women's role in maintaining "racial purity": in 1922, feminist Charlotte Perkins Gilman supported the eugenics movement by calling on women

Dolores Del Rio in an advertisement for Richard Hudnut eye-matched cosmetics, 1937.

to utilize "their racial authority" in order to "cleanse the human race of its worst inheritance by a discriminating refusal of unfit fathers." The same year, the Cable Act declared that any female citizen who married an immigrant who was unable to naturalize would automatically lose her own citizenship. As Palumbo-Liu notes, the only other act for which one's citizenship could be revoked was treason; a woman's conception of a child with an "alien" man was thus seen as the equivalent of treason.[39] Miscegenation was identified as "race suicide," and was included in the Motion Picture Producers and Distributors of America (MPPDA) list of representational prohibitions when Will Hays became president in 1922, removing the possibility that any Hollywood film narrative could include a non-tragic cross-racial romance.[40] Nevertheless, by promoting stars who represented a sophisticated ethnicity designed to be mass marketed internationally, Hollywood utilized "the spectacle of difference" in ways that allowed for anti-essentialist readings.

Hollywood's émigré performers were a crucial part of the film studios' attempts to maximize international distribution, and numerous production decisions about casting, dialogue, and representational issues were also made in relation to the requirements of nondomestic markets.[41] The consideration of different national codes of censorship was a particularly relevant factor, as was the popularity of specific stars overseas. In 1933, *Variety* took stock of the value of Hollywood stars in foreign markets, noting that

> there are some picture stars in the U.S., very popular here, who are even more popular abroad. . . . The foreign stars in the U.S., of course, like Marlene Dietrich, Maurice Chevalier, and Lillian Harvey can be figured on to garner at least as large a harvest outside the American boundaries as within them. Not true of Greta Garbo or Ronald Colman, however, because of the amazing strength both have at home.[42]

The importance of stars as global commodities was highlighted when the studios, attempting to maintain their foreign markets following the transition to sound, tried making multiple foreign-language versions of selected films; in most cases, a completely different cast was used—without the English-speaking star. But when the original star happened to be bilingual (as were Dietrich, Garbo, and Novarro), a foreign-language film could be produced with equal star value, doubling profits.[43] This desire for international appeal accounts for much of Hollywood's consistent poaching of foreign talent. Arguing in support of Hollywood's use of non-American labor in 1937, an attorney for the MPPDA told a congressional committee on Immigration and Naturalization that "[s]ome of the world-wide character and appeal of American motion pictures must be credited to the employment of foreign actors."[44]

Hollywood's use of stars representing "foreignness" can therefore be seen as an attempt to target three distinct audiences: (1) Anglo-American viewers who liked exoticism, even if only in terms of racist stereotypes; (2) an immigrant-American audience interested in multicultural characters; and (3) nondomestic viewers with various linguistic and cultural preferences. The desire to create a global product thus put the studios somewhat at odds with the racist xenophobia of 1930s America. Such a conflict between audiences was also evident in the studios' battles with the Christian Right over what mainstream moral standards were, resulting in stricter Production Code enforcement after 1934. Hollywood's glamorization of racial difference and simultaneous pandering to racist stereotypes can thus be attributed, in part, to marketing conflicts and the desire to create non-Anglo characters that were acceptable both at home and abroad.

The Technicolor Face: "Jungle Madness for Cultured Lips"

Twentieth-century cosmetics advertising vividly documents the importance of Hollywood exoticism to the construction of a new kind of beauty achievable through a more colorful use of makeup—a discourse linked to Hollywood's gradually increasing use of Technicolor from the mid-1930s onward. Early Technicolor sequences had been used in black-and-white films of the 1920s to highlight spectacular scenes such as fashion shows or elaborately decorated sets, while color simultaneously appeared in consumer product design and advertising graphics. In 1932, however, the Technicolor company developed a three-strip process that, although expensive, was used for big-budget costume and adventure films. Big-budget productions became increasingly popular by mid-decade on the theory that, as David Selznick argued, money could be made during the depression only by producing either a lot of cheap films or a few expensive ones.[45]

The new Technicolor process was first tested in the Disney cartoon *Flowers and Trees* (1932), then in a two-reel short called *La Cucaracha* (1934), and finally in the feature *Becky Sharp* (1935). Three-strip films initially tended, like earlier two-strip sequences, to be in spectacular rather than realist genres because of anxieties that viewers would find the color jarringly stylized when paired with a realist mise-en-scène. Color was thus used in musicals or backstage entertainment/ fashion films like *The Dancing Pirate* (1935), *A Star is Born* (1937), *Vogues of 1938* (1937), and *The Goldwyn Follies* (1938); in Westerns such as *Dodge City* (1939), *Drums along the Mohawk* (1939), and *Jesse James* (1939); and in fantasy/ costume dramas like *The Garden of Allah* (1936), *Ramona* (1936), *Adventures of Robin Hood* (1938), *Gone with the Wind* (1939), and *The Wizard of Oz* (1939). Selznick International Pictures also produced a successful Technicolor comedy, *Nothing Sacred,* in 1937. The question of whether Technicolor would be accepted by viewers as compatible with Hollywood's realist conventions focused, in particular, on the importance of the face as a privileged signifier. In 1920, a producer warned that Technicolor threatened to overwhelm the screen with visual information, which conflicted with established goals of focusing attention on performers' faces and eyes through lighting and cinematography: "The human being is the center of the drama, not flowers, gardens, and dresses. The face is the center of the human being. And the eyes are the center of the face."[46] Another critic complained of early Technicolor that "when the figures retreat to any distance, it is difficult to distinguish their expression."[47] Anxiety that facial features could not be photographed in color with the same attention-riveting results that had been achieved in black and white became central to the Technicolor firm's research. As David Bordwell has noted, "The firm was at pains to compromise between developing a 'lifelike' rendition of the visible spectrum and developing a treatment of the human face that would accord with classical requisites of beauty and narrative centrality."[48]

One way that the chaos of the Technicolor palette was adapted to Hollywood norms of facial representation and beauty was to use performers whose style could be "naturally" associated with bright colors. Female stars who were "the Technicolor type" had "vivid" features and personalities, which often meant that they were exotically ethnic. When *Motion Picture* ran a profile of the actress Steffi Duna called "Steffi Is a Perfect Type for Color," Natalie Kalmus, Technicolor's production advisor, was asked why Duna had been chosen for the first three-strip films (*La Cucaracha* and *The Dancing Pirate*). She listed Duna's qualifications: "A colorful complexion; a contrasting shade of hair; natural rhythm (color accents a woman's gracefulness you know); a personality vivid enough to counter-balance the most brilliant kind of setting; and she's the type that can wear picturesque clothes." Along with having "natural rhythm," Duna was described as exotic: "Steffi of Hungary . . . and all the bright romance of it sings in her blood. In Budapest, you see, children are weaned on the gypsy music. . . . Steffi could dance to it before she could talk."[49] The description of ethnicity in terms like "vivid," "colorful," and "picturesque" was also commonplace in the promotion of stars like Dolores Del Rio (the

"Sparkling Spanish beauty"), Tala Birell ("she's as exotic as a red camellia"), and Anna May Wong ("she brings to the screen . . . the mysterious colors of her ivory-skinned race").[50] But the advent of Technicolor produced even more emphasis on the relationship between color and exotic beauty, with Hollywood stars playing a central role in the promotion and naturalization of "colorful" femininity.

Along with Duna, a new style of tropical exoticism appeared in the mid-1930s that contrasted sharply with Garbo's "pale exoticism."[51] It had been visible in the 1920s' deluge of South Seas island films, which usually featured romance between a white hero and a native woman, since the Production Code Administration considered such couples relatively nonthreatening and ruled in 1937 that romance between "white" characters and the "Polynesians and allied races" did not constitute miscegenation.[52] The island girl made a dramatic reappearance in the early 1930s just in time for a major fashion vogue in tropicalism. Balinese batik appeared in beachwear, along with the "Goona-Goona bathing suit" and a general "Javanese Influence." In 1935, an advertisement for brassieres declared that "Women of the Isle of Bali have always had the most beautiful breasts in the world," and a Tahitian-style bathing suit advertisement noted that "it all started in the Riviera. Smart women . . . adopted the daring costumes and colors of primitive islanders." *Vogue* concluded that "it's smart, this year, to look like a Balinese maiden when you have the figure for it," and also advised:

> If you are wearing a swathed Oriental evening frock . . .
> your make-up should be as glamorous as possible—deep,
> mysterious eye shadows, with perhaps a touch of gold or
> silver. This is the moment to use mascara on your lashes,
> and even indulge in kohl, and to make yourself, in general,
> as exotic as you possibly can.[53]

The following year, Dorothy Lamour made her sarong debut in *Jungle Princess* (1936) and became synonymous with the tropical look in subsequent films, like *The Hurricane* (1937), *Her Jungle Love* (1938), *Tropic Holiday* (1938), and others. By 1938, Lamour's long dark hair, sultry brown eyes, and prominent red mouth were being emulated widely, as an advertisement for lipstick in "a wicked new shade" indicates: "Jungle madness for cultured lips . . . the sublime madness of a moon-kissed jungle night . . . the most exotic color ever put into a lipstick."[54] Also available was "tropic beauty for your fingertips," with nail polish in shades like "Congo," "Cabaña," and "Spice."[55]

The Lamour "type" was a boon to the cosmetics industry, as well as to Technicolor, because her dark hair and skin tone could accommodate a wide range of cosmetics. The perfect expression of this type appeared in 1938 when Hedy Lamarr caused a sensation with her appearance in *Algiers*. While Lamour was called "untamed and torrid," Lamarr was a "red-lipped, tawny-eyed, black-haired girl" whose "lush, exciting beauty" combined sensuousness with an aloof glamour.[56] The Max Factor company was central to the promotion of sultry new stars like Lamarr, Ann Sheridan, and Rita Cansino (soon to be Hayworth), using them to endorse the new, multicolored approach to cosmetics. One Max Factor advertisement, featuring a photograph of Lamarr, stated: "Beauty's secret attraction is color . . . for it is color that has an exciting emotional appeal." Soon older stars followed the new "brunette trend"; Joan Bennett switched from blonde to raven hair and even duplicated Lamarr's long bob with a center part, her distinctive, downward-curving eyebrows, and wide, red lips. Bennett noted that with her new coloring, she could tan her face and wear stronger shades of makeup and heavier, "more Oriental" perfumes.[57]

Max Factor had been commissioned to devise an improved makeup foundation for use with Technicolor, one that could be layered in different shades without being too thick or reflective. The result was "Pan-Cake" makeup, which made its official debut in Walter Wanger's *Vogues of 1938*. Accord-

Hedy Lamarr sets the style in a publicity photograph for MGM (no date).

Rita Hayworth in a publicity photograph for Columbia Pictures (no date).

Joan Bennett looks demure, circa 1932.

Joan Bennett after her Lamarr makeover, circa 1938.

Dorothy Lamour gives the sarong new style in a publicity photograph for
Paramount, circa 1936.

ing to reviews of the film, the goal of Technicolor realism had been reached with a "natural" rendering of facial tones and features. One critic devoted most of his review to a discussion of the new makeup, while another wrote that the actresses "were so lifelike . . . it seemed like they would step down from the screen into the audience at any minute."[58] Once Technicolor and cosmetics manufacturers had established both the beauty advantages of color and the naturalism of the new representational palette, it remained for Pan-Cake makeup techniques to be promoted to consumers. Referred to as "shaded" or "corrective" makeup, it was said to give Dietrich "that lovely exotic high-cheekboned look" and to disguise numerous structural imperfections in other stars' faces. Contoured makeup could, in effect, give anyone high cheekbones, a "new nose," or "larger eyes." Most important of all, the process required the use of more than one foundation color—potentially doubling sales of facial powder. To make cheekbones stand out, they could be powdered with a light shade, while a darker "shadow" was applied underneath. If, like Dietrich, one applied the shadow in a triangle shape, the results would be "positively Oriental."[59]

Technicolor makeup techniques were thus said to increase the transformative qualities of makeup and the range of complexions and colors located within the new norms of natural-looking beauty. A *Photoplay* beauty column of 1938 was devoted to a discussion of the "Technicolor . . . school of beauty"; in addition to exoticism, the Technicolor face is said to represent the full range of different complexion and coloring types among women. Using *The Goldwyn Follies* as an example, the writer suggests that there are at least thirteen different "variations of coloring" represented by women in the film, offering female viewers the opportunity to find their own "color harmony" among the many facial shades available. In addition, she points out that film stars now wear "different make-ups for different color gowns, so that the whole ensemble is a perfect blending of color." The column is essentially an advertorial for the Max Factor company's "personalized color palette," system, even incorporating the company's slogan of "color harmony" into the text. But it also demonstrates the way that the growth of the cosmetics industry was predicated on women's use of an ever greater range of products and colors on their faces.[60]

Hollywood exoticism was thus central to discourses that fueled the renaissance in cosmetics, as were Technicolor and the desire for export-market appeal. The high point of Hollywood's vivid exoticism was reached in the 1940s with the Technicolor figure of Carmen Miranda. "Good Neighbor" films like *The Gang's All Here* (1943) presented not only the archetype of the Hollywood Latina (with huge eyelashes, red lips, and a multicolored "tutti-fruity hat") but also a pro–Latin American sensibility designed to foster Pan-American solidarity against the Axis powers. Miranda's first Hollywood film, *Down Argentine Way* (1940), features a musical number in which the blond-haired Betty Grable emulates Miranda's look, wearing vivid makeup, an ornamented turban, costume jewelry, and a ruffled, off-the-shoulder gown. Gable represents the consumerist assimilation being promoted by such films, in which Latin American style is domesticated via music and comedy. Soon numerous American women would also emulate Miranda by wrapping their hair in colorful floral scarves for factory work and using bright red lipstick and costume jewelry to make their rationed outfits more exotic.

Going Native: From Primitivism to Tourism

> The whites went, not to . . . hear Shakespeare, who had bored most of them in school, but to get something different— that something at once innocent and richly seasoned, child-like and jungle-spiced, which is the gift of the Negro to a more tired, complicated, and self-conscious race.
>
> *Vogue* review of the Federal Theatre Negro unit's
> *Macbeth,* November 1936

Encounters with exotic beauty in Hollywood film are motivated by a range of scenarios, particularly that of interracial romance, which allowed Euramerican characters to (temporarily) appropriate aspects of an exotic identity. Although racial
difference is often reinscribed in such films, its attractions are
also foregrounded. Primitivist constructions of femininity emphasize an Edenic sexuality that is libidinal but innocent, providing a mediation of Western split femininity. This mediation
was crucial to cosmetics marketing, which was dependent on
the decorative aspects of exotic beauty but had to negotiate
associations of immorality that still clung to the image of the
nonwhite and "painted" woman. Edenic female primitivism
thus represented an idealization of racial difference that mini-
mized the potential transgressiveness of such encounters.

The arrival of Josephine Baker in Paris in 1925 signaled a
shift from the influence of the Orient on European designers
to that of Africa and the tropics. Primitivism in European art
and fashion had an impact on American trends, as did the rise
of the phonograph and its dissemination of jazz and African
American dance styles, followed by the mainstream appropriation of these forms in musical theater. In contrast to the
image of decadent, pre-crash "jazz babies," depression-era
Africanism often stressed the cultural virtues of the supposed-
ly less civilized African American community. As in the blues-
based opera *Porgy and Bess* (1935) and the film *Hallelujah!*
(1929), this community was seen as emotionally elemental
and less "complicated" than dominant white culture, which
was fraught with the "self-consciousness" and worry of having to reestablish its economic hegemony. From a less conde-
scending perspective, the ongoing effects of the depression
caused many to wonder whether modernity was worth the
costs being paid, and even whether the entire course of modern civilization might have gone astray. This critique took
place across the political spectrum, from libertarian populism
to a progressive socialism that often relied on American nostalgia for preindustrial, communitarian values. According to

these arguments, the depression was the result of a flawed system that not only failed to provide a secure labor base but had made Americans lose sight of their real values: community, nature, and meaningful labor.

Hollywood responded to the popularity of primitivism in a range of films, some emphasizing a critique of civilization, others offering a romantic, if temporary, return to Edenic innocence. The latter include South Seas films like *Tabu* (1931), *Bird of Paradise* (1932), and *The Hurricane*, as well as those that emphasize a more muscular exoticism like the *Tarzan* cycle.[61] Critiques of civilization were made in back-to-the-land narratives like *The Good Earth* (1931), *The Purchase Price* (1932), *The Stranger's Return* (1933), and *Our Daily Bread* (1934), which are structured around a city/country dichotomy emphasizing the personal and moral regeneration possible through a return to agrarian values. Such films may reject urbanism in favor of a return to the simple life, but only when that life is found outside North America do these films' connections to discourses of exoticism become apparent. In Pearl S. Buck's 1931 novel *The Good Earth,* the hero, Wang Lung, and his wife, O-Lan, survive the opium-induced collapse of ruling elites by proclaiming, "We must get back to the land"; the book was a best-selling novel and successful film (1937), suggesting that the image of peasant dignity could be held up as a model of noble primitivism. But some back-to-the-land films combined the nobility of peasant labor with a slightly more hedonistic exoticism in order to depict the pleasures of premodernity as well as its virtues. *Lost Horizon* replaces Western agrarianism with the myth of Shangri-la, offering the lure of innocent sexual exoticism combined with Christian communalism. Because of its setting in the inaccessible and pristine mountains of the Orient, Shangri-la is represented as a place of mystical wisdom as well as uncorrupted, natural sensuality.

Lost Horizon opens in war-torn China with the hijacking of a small plane carrying the diplomat Robert Conway

(Ronald Coleman), his brother George, and three Americans, who are taken to the mountain utopia of Shangri-la. Sondra (Jane Wyatt) provides the film's love interest. Although she appears Eurasian, Sondra has been brought up in Shangri-la following the death of her European explorer-parents. Dressed in Chinese-style robes, her cultural Orientalism and racial "whiteness" give Sondra a hybrid femininity that is at once exotic and innocent. Her Edenic sexuality is demonstrated when she flirts with Conway by riding past him on horseback and diving nude into a mountain pool while he looks on. She has a rapport with nature represented by the sound of the small pipes she has tied to numerous pigeons, whose music creates a faintly mystical aura around her whenever she goes outside. The costumes and mise-en-scène of *Lost Horizon* reflect the mid-decade vogue for Chinese-inspired design, combining Chinese furnishings with an international-style modernism to evoke Asian metaphysics rather than the excessive opulence of much Hollywood Orientalism. Like Sondra, Shangri-la combines Western and Eastern virtues: Christianity, the ancient wisdom of the Orient, and the virtuous labor of a happy peasantry.

Unashamed sexuality was one of the qualities frequently projected onto African American women during this period. The characterization of Chick (Nina Mae McKinney) in *Hallelujah!* (1929) illustrates a somewhat infantilized mode of female sexuality, while Josephine Baker performed a more sophisticated version in her French film roles. In *Vogue*'s article on the Federal Theatre's *Macbeth*, the popularity of Harlem nightspots is attributed to Anglo-American emotional repression, which is described in some detail:

> Civilization—call it that while it lasts—is for most of us poor white trash a barrier between ourselves and life. . . . But the Negro seems to carry that flame right inside of him. You can tell he does by the way he laughs. White laughter is by comparison so often uneasy, hysterical, insincere, thin. . . .

We find it hard, except vicariously in some Harlem, to be wholeheartedly sad or glad. The Negro, at least as he appears to us, is either high or low, either tasting the full joy of being alive or bottomlessly blue.[62]

Most films that celebrate ethnic primitivism do not make a particularly convincing critique of whiteness or civilization but instead offer a more escapist paradigm of cultural tourism that, like the night out in Harlem, offers a safe and reinvigorating form of contact with "primitive" vitality.[63]

The film *Bird of Paradise* displays many qualities popular in jungle and island films: a natural paradise, lots of exuberant, native female sexuality, a "beefcake" display of the hero's body, and a safe return to civilization for the Americans. The heroine, Luana, is played by Dolores Del Rio, whose aristocratic background and marriage to MGM art director Cedric Gibbons made her a career-long icon of sophisticated ethnicity in fan and fashion magazines, as well as cosmetics advertising. As Ana López describes, "Hers was a vague upper-class exoticism articulated within a general category of 'foreign/other' tragic sensuality."[64] The character of Luana combines a childlike but assertive sexuality with loyalty and self-sacrifice (her inevitable suicide saves the hero's mother, as one character comments, from the heartbreak of having her son come home with a native bride). Luana's unabashed sexuality is represented positively throughout the film, however, and is not used to justify her death; instead, her self-sacrifice is attributed to her irrational refusal to become "civilized." Unimpressed by both Christianity and modernity, she is doomed to die. Luana's appearance is elegant and yet untamed—she wears makeup accentuating her dark eyes, lips, and sculpted features but has a loose, curly mop of dark hair. In ceremonial sequences she wears a long, geometrically patterned cape from her shoulders and a large feathered headdress, while only a double lei and thin grass skirt cover her breasts and legs, making her look both regal and sexual. Luana is frequently associated with food and nourishment, making her an ideal hybrid of untamed sensuality (displayed in exotic tribal adornment) and pastoral, nurturing femininity.

By the end of the 1930s, tourism had become a popular cinematic context for the representation of exoticism. A mode of temporary adventure, it contributed to the marketing of cultural exoticism as a "spectacle of difference" available via the travel package or the luxury cruise. The musical *Flying Down to Rio* (1933) celebrates Pan-American Airways' new route to Brazil, and *Honolulu* (1938) centers around a shipboard romance en route to Hawaii. Tourism thus made exoticism safe for mass consumption: in 1936, *Vogue* noted that in Hawaii "the medley of natives, American military officers, and sundry Orientals makes the location scene colorful without being alien."[65] In *Honolulu*, Eleanor Powell has the opportunity to wear a gold-lamé-and-grass skirt and do a hula dance number, suggesting tourism as another way for consumers to try out new self-images.

Significantly, no native Hawaiians have speaking roles in this film; instead, service-sector workers, entertainers, and a Chinese houseboy represent local culture. Romance between fellow travelers replaces jungle love, and the innocent aggressiveness of Luana's desire is transposed into the female tourist's opportunity to perform exciting native dances. In *Flying Down to Rio,* cultural appropriation is highlighted in the form of the Carioca, the sensual new Latin dance, which is learned by Fred Astaire and Ginger Rogers during their visit so that it may be imported to North America. The tourism film thus tends to offer an assimilated or picturesque form of exotic femininity rather than a dangerously alluring one. The tourist is a cultural shopper rather than the liminal subject seen in Orientalist adventure films like *Morocco* (1930) or *The Bitter Tea of General Yen* (1932), which addressed more transgressive desires to cross the cultural borders of identity.

Orientalist Fashion and Exotic Masquerade

European Orientalist fantasy was integral to the marketing of cosmetics and self-adornment from the eighteenth century onward. As Kathy Peiss has noted: "Advertisers created narratives about beauty culture through the ages, bypassing the Greco-Roman tradition in favor of Egypt and Persia. Cleopatra was virtually a cult figure, displayed in advertising to all segments of the market."[66]

In the early nineteenth century, English and French Orientalist salon painting popularized myths of Islamic beauty, centered around fantasies of the harem. In Ingres's painting *Bain Turq* (The Turkish Bath, 1862) a group of women lie entwined in each other's arms, adding a frisson of lesbianism that was not uncommon to the genre. Reina Lewis has argued that the myth of the harem is typical of Orientalist discourses, with the desire to breach the harem walls symbolizing the drive to colonize and possess Eastern lands. However, Orientalist paintings frequently depicted the most desirable harem women as light-skinned. A common alibi for this was their identification as Circassian women, a Turkish ethnic minority said to be light-skinned and more beautiful than any other women on earth. Lewis concludes:

> The pale harem women oscillate between being like and not like European women, i.e. as both the permitted and the forbidden object. Part of the frisson of the white odalisque comes from the projection of the white wife (the licit object) into what amounts to a brothel situation (an illicit site): she is pitied but desired as the fantasy combination of Europe's splitting of female sexuality.[67]

Orientalist beauty can thus be seen as a fantasy of feminine beauty unfettered by Christian taboos against female sexuality. Notwithstanding Lewis's reading of their potential meaning for male viewers, such images may also have resonated with European and American women's interests in the possibilities beyond Victorian norms of female sexuality and self-presentation. The cult status of Cleopatra within twentieth-century beauty discourses, for example, suggests that the power associated with Eastern sensuality had a strong appeal among women as well as men. Beauty salons were often described as sites of collective female pleasure that emulated the harem's luxurious baths, massages, and all-female exercise rituals. Throughout the late nineteenth and early twentieth centuries, Orientalist beauty was offered to Western women as a means of transgressing the strictures of split femininity: by temporarily adopting signs of exotic sensuality via makeup and clothing, Western women could present themselves as a combination of (white) virtue and (nonwhite) sexuality.[68]

The projection of female desire onto a fantasy of Eastern and Southern eroticism was particularly visible in Orientalist women's fiction, most notoriously in the 1919 novel *The Sheik* (written by Englishwoman E. M. Hull), which was filmed in 1921 with Rudolph Valentino, turning him into an icon of female desire for non-WASP sensuality. Similarly, in Robert Hichens's 1904 novel *The Garden of Allah,* the English heroine, Domini, travels to North Africa, "aching" to experience "elemental forces" and be "free from the pettiness of civilized life."[69] Domini has a passionate love affair with a Russian man, although he leaves her in the end and returns to the monastery from which he has fled. The book was a huge success in the United States; it was filmed in Hollywood three times (1916, 1927, 1936) and staged twice as a theatrical spectacle, in 1907 and 1912, complete with sandstorms and live animals. According to William Leach's history of American consumerism, "The Garden of Allah" became a shorthand term for Orientalist luxury in a range of contexts, from numerous "Allah" fashion shows to the lavish Sunset Boulevard estate of Hollywood star Alla Nazimova, which she named "The Garden of Allah."[70]

The eighteenth century saw the first wave of widespread fashion Orientalism in clothing, with the use of embroidered

Chinese silk and Indian cotton, the styling of gowns *"a la turque,"* and the wearing of Arab burnooses. The mid-nineteenth century saw a huge renaissance of Orientalist fashion with the "opening" of Japan and its influence on the visual arts.[71] Throughout the late nineteenth and early twentieth centuries, the rich threw *Arabian Nights* parties and dressed up like rajas and harem dancers, or decorated their homes with the ornate carpets, cushions, and curtains associated with Islamic luxury.[72] Orientalist style could also express rebellion or bohemianism, as it had for Victorian female dress-reformers when they wore loose "Turkish" or "Syrian" trousers under their tunics. French designer Paul Poiret became the undisputed master of Orientalist fashion in the early twentieth century: his vision combined modernist formal simplicity with decorative pastiches of Islamic and Asian motifs. In 1911, Poiret gave a "Thousand and Second Night" party to celebrate his new "Oriental" look and appeared costumed as a sultan while his wife, Denise Poiret, played the "favorite of the harem" in a gold cage with several women attendants.[73]

Orientalist fashion, in both couture design and ready-to-wear markets, had an upsurge in popularity in the middle to late 1930s. In *Mata Hari* (1931), Greta Garbo appears in gold lamé from head to toe, with tight gold leggings and boots worn under a long jacket and turban. In one scene, Garbo wears a more revealing gold lamé costume while performing a slow, writhing dance around a large deity-sculpture, demonstrating her "pale exoticism," if not her dancing talent. The promotion of cosmetics as a form of self-transformation was also linked in a number of films to Orientalist associations with luxury and female sexuality. Lacquer red was an important Orientalist color, according to a 1936 advertisement for Helena Rubenstein's Chinese Red lipstick and rouge:

> Flaming flowers, lush vivid fruits, the bright plumage of an exotic bird. . . . Chinese Red is high, clear, brilliantly attuned to this season of intense color. It is vivid, young—

with lots of red for flattery and just a hint of gold to give you a touch of the exotic. To pallid skin it lends a lovely glow. To dusky skin it adds a vibrant accent. It lifts every skin to new heights of enchantment.[74]

The phrase "Chinese Red" thus evokes a number of key cosmetic and marketing concepts: natural vividness, exoticism, and youth, as well as adaptability to a range of skin tones. The same year, Elizabeth Arden introduced a summer line of "Chinese and Copper" makeup; the Chinese foundation is in an "amber tone that makes you look like a Manchu princess," and is to be worn with "Dark Nasturtium" lipstick and rouge, black eye pencil, and blue green "Eye Sha-do."[75]

Greta Garbo in an MGM publicity photograph for *Mata Hari* (1932).

Greta Garbo in an MGM publicity photograph for *The Painted Veil* (1934).

Along with the opulence of the Manchu princess, the Orientalism of the middle to late 1930s also signified stylistic modernity. As in the art direction of *Lost Horizon,* which combined Chinese and modernist design, Chinese-inspired fashion appears, in several films, to indicate a character's aesthetic sophistication.[76] *The Painted Veil* (1934) stars Greta Garbo as Katrin, a German woman who moves to China, where her elegant Chinese-style outfits contrast dramatically with the old-fashioned, ruffled dresses and wide-brimmed hats of other expatriate European women. Katrin embraces the Orient, as demonstrated in a scene in which she walks dreamily through a chaotic street festival and enters a temple containing gigantic statues of Buddha and Confucius. In this scene, she wears a white turban and floor-length white coat; their elegant streamlining and Orientalist details make her look both modern and mystically elegant.

Orientalism had been a defining aspect of the 1930s silhouette since 1931, when the *Exposition Coloniale* in Paris exposed designers to wide-shouldered dancing costumes from Bali and Thailand, which Schiaparelli immediately incorporated into the shoulder-padded silhouette she had used in suits the year before.[77] The peak of Orientalist fashion diffusion, however, was in the mid-1930s, when the ever adventurous Schiaparelli was pictured in the August issue of *Vogue,* having "gone native" in Tunisia to learn "the mysteries of Oriental sewing, draping, and veil twisting," just as her travels to India had inspired the presence of several saris in her line the previous year.[78] Hollywood followed, and occasionally introduced, such Orientalist trends because of the continued popularity of exotic narratives. From the mid-1930s onward, studio designers created numerous costumes with turbans, sari-wrapped bodices, and "Persian draping."

By the late 1930s, these styles had become decisively mainstream. *Photoplay* exclaimed in 1939 that "all smart women are going Oriental for fall," listing required accessories such as a "Maharaja's turban," several "heavy ropes of golden beads," "earrings that jingle like Hindu dancing girls'," and "a wide silver bracelet fit for a Maharanee."[79] The "let's dress up" tone of this description, like *Vogue*'s article on Schiaparelli's adventures in Tunisia, highlights the importance of fashion throughout the 1930s as a vehicle for fantasy. Accessories and cosmetics were the least expensive means of subtle self-dramatization and masquerade; simply by drawing one's eyebrows up slightly at the ends, instead of down, and wearing Chinese colors like red and black, an air of adventure and sophisticated chic could be assumed.[80] Frank Capra's film *The Bitter Tea of General Yen* (1932) incorporated this trend into its Orientalist captivity narrative, with a "makeover" sequence that offers a transgressive appeal second only to the film's interracial romance.

In *The Bitter Tea of General Yen,* the heroine's desire for the exotic is initially cloaked by her intention to pursue missionary work in Shanghai. Megan Davis (Barbara Stanwyck), a plainly dressed member of an old New England family, instead becomes trapped in the midst of civil war fighting, is knocked out, and is rescued by the elegant, French-speaking warlord General Yen (Nils Asther). Megan wakes surrounded by the opulent luxury of Yen's summer palace but also to the sound of prisoners of war being shot outside her window; this contrast between aesthetic refinement and moral barbarism is repeated throughout the film as a characterization of Chinese culture. After three days of refusing to dine with Yen, Megan sits on her balcony watching young lovers on the riverbank outside her room and falls into a dream. In this surreal vignette, an evil-looking caricature of Yen enters her room and reaches out with long, clawlike fingers while she screams. Suddenly another man, wearing a dapper suit, white hat, and mask, bursts in through the window and rescues Megan by destroying the evil Asian. They embrace, and she removes the mask from his face, happily discovering that he, too, is Yen. They gaze into each other's eyes, Megan lies back on the bed, and they kiss.

Megan's conflicted desire for Yen is paralleled by her fascination for his courtesan Mah-li (Toshia Mori), who always appears elaborately made up and dressed. Mah-li convinces Megan to join her at dinner with Yen, offering to help her dress. In a montage sequence with multiple dissolves, Megan is bathed, perfumed, and dressed in silken lingerie by Mah-li and her servants, and a range of ornate Chinese gowns are displayed before her. She chooses the most elaborate one, with huge, glowing silver sequins, loose, embroidered sleeves, and a sequined fringe below the knee. The gown contrasts dramatically with the plainness of Megan's own dress. Mah-li then has her carved vanity table carried in, commenting that Megan is "in need of powder and paint." Megan appears intrigued by Mah-li's display of cosmetics, and picking up a powder puff, she muses, "yes, perhaps I am." Following another dissolve, Megan is seen transformed, wearing the glittering dress with long, ornamental earrings, her hair coiffed, face powdered, eyes shadowed, and lips painted the same dark red as Mah-li's. For the first time in the film, Megan is shown looking like a glamorous movie star, and her satisfaction with this image is immediately followed by a flashback to her fantasy of kissing Yen. As the image disappears, Megan looks unhappily at her beautiful reflection, scoops cream onto her fingers and begins removing the makeup. She is next seen coming to dinner with her face bare, hair primly tied back, wearing the disheveled dress she arrived in.

This makeover sequence clearly associates Megan's pleasure at being groomed and gowned by Mah-li with her illicit desire for Yen, but while her desire for him remains taboo, her makeover offers viewers the satisfaction of seeing Stanwyck's star glamour restored in a particularly opulent style. The makeover is repeated at the end of the film, when Yen declares his love for Megan. She begins to cry and runs to her room; in her confusion she sees the vanity table and begins to transform herself again. Still in tears, Megan is shown in close-up, putting on Mah-li's makeup in a sequence intercut with Yen's preparation of poisoned tea for himself, having lost his political power and failed to gain Megan's love. As he is about to drink the tea, Megan enters his darkened room wearing the sequined gown. The scene is shot with heavy lens diffusion, making the gown's large sequins burst into luminous circles of light as she moves through the shadows. As Yen strokes her hair, Meagan begins to cry again, and he drinks the poison. Megan's desire for Yen is figured as a *Madame Butterfly*-like tragedy that requires the death of Yen so that he can await

Nils Asther and Barbara Stanwyck in a Columbia Pictures publicity photograph for *The Bitter Tea of General Yen* (1932).

Megan in heaven, where, as he suggests, there is no racial difference. Megan's emulation of Mah-li, on the other hand, creates the film's most visually dramatic moments and represents within the film's racist narrative an acceptable resolution of her desire for the exotic via fantasy and self-adornment.

Orientalist fashion and cosmetics tended to aestheticize particular forms of cultural and racial difference so that they could be visually appropriated. These stylized forms of cultural referencing helped to promote the expansion of a commercial beauty industry from one that idealized normative "white" features to one that thrived on exoticism as a form of commodified multiculturalism. Orientalist and primitive femininity had long functioned as a Western fantasy of a non-split female sexuality, and the association of cosmetics with exoticism gradually helped overshadow the stigma of the "vamp" attached to women's use of cosmetics. Clearly, the ethnic stereotypes that circulated on-screen and in cosmetics marketing were mystifications of cultural difference and the politics that structured them; they also perpetuated a sexualization of non-whiteness that could be oppressively deployed. At the same time, the popularization of sultry, darkly hued feminine glamour and the marketing of cosmetics in terms of a spectrum of colored features helped to displace nativist beauty norms that non-Anglo-American women had long been seen as inferior to. This relativization of norms, on which cycles of stylistic change and product development depended, exposed exotic beauty types as signs of imaginary ethnicity. To some extent, Hollywood's exploitation of the "spectacle of difference" worked against the mimetic inscription of ethnicity that linked exterior appearance to essentialist racial categories. The popularity of these styles also suggests that in spite of the exclusionary immigration policies of the 1930s, international markets and domestic product diversification led to the erosion of nineteenth-century nativist beauty norms, changing the face of popular culture to a significant extent.

SUITABLY FEMININE

Vain trifles as they seem, clothes have, as they say, more important offices than merely to keep us warm. They change our view of the world and the world's view of us.
Virginia Woolf, *Orlando*, 1928

As Elizabeth Wilson has argued, "It is possible that the advance of the trouser for women is the most significant fashion change of the twentieth century."[1] This chapter will trace the media representation of menswear for women and the stars who popularized it, linking them to specific films in order to see how Hollywood participated in these changes both visually and thematically. One of the primary sites of struggle over gender roles in the 1930s was the workplace, and working women figured significantly in Hollywood films. These characters enact, as did many female stars, a range of tensions around women's social and economic autonomy. Such tensions can be seen in the decade's contrast between the adoption of menswear by women and a simultaneous revival of neo-Victorian femininity. Costume played a significant role in

Hollywood's negotiation of the contradictory roles that working women played in the 1930s. Like the use of fashion to denote status and mobility, clothing was central to the characterization of white-collar women, while casual menswear also provided a means of articulating a more transgressive femininity. Stars' offscreen dress often reinforced this quality, most notably Marlene Dietrich's frequent appearance in men's suits, Greta Garbo's fondness for army/navy pants, and Katharine Hepburn's overtly feminist wearing of slacks. Conversely, some films about working women used feminine costume to indicate women's inescapable sexuality, which was shown to cause inevitable "gender trouble" in the workplace.

The popularity of films featuring working women, and the representation of many female stars as archetypes of professional achievement, was clearly related to the fact that an ever increasing percentage of female film spectators were likely to be working outside the home. But the growing acceptability of masculine-coded clothing in the 1930s resulted from a complex relationship between such social changes (including the popularization of women's sport and leisure activities), the media (and female stars' use of pants to publicize their own iconoclasm), and marketing (the fashion industry's promotion of menswear as a way to expand the variety of separates purchased by women). This was not, however, a case of "top-down" fashion movement, since women had worn pants or overalls during World War I for factory work and continued to wear them at home throughout the 1920s (they were advertised for gardening and housework). Female stars' adoption of pants was, in large part, a response to the French vogue for *garçonne* lounging suits and beach pants of the late 1920s, but it was also an elevation of American work and play clothes to the status of Hollywood streetwear. In addition to a discussion of these fashion changes, this chapter will explore consumerism's promotion of women's workplace "impression management." Erving Goffman's concept of how performance is used by participants in social interactions as a

form of self-protection is helpful in thinking about the importance of clothing for women who wanted to get ahead at work
but avoid the endemic workplace sexual harassment that was
frequently blamed on women themselves. Proper dress was
discussed in magazines as a way for women to appear professional and avoid unwanted attention, and tips were offered on
choosing clothes that would appear neither offensively "mannish" nor dangerously feminine.

In spite of the struggles against job discrimination that
working women faced throughout the depression, many Hollywood films assume both women's need and right to work (at
least before marriage). But for the Hollywood working woman,
a job is more than survival; it is a way of attaining a more desirable lifestyle and social identity. More than a reiteration of
the "pin money" theory that women's work is usually for dis-
posable income rather than need, this emphasis on consumption represented work as a means to a more important end:
the autonomy, pleasure, and adventure of being able to reinvent
oneself. This consumerist work ethic, unlike Max Weber's
Protestant work ethic, valorized work because it provided the
resources for self-transformation as pleasure. Fashion is a
major source of such pleasure in numerous films, underscoring the more malleable aspects of social identity over fa-
milial *or* occupational ones. While these aspects of consumer
culture have, like fashion itself, often been seen as a corruption of social values, this critique does not account for the
way that consumer culture's more fluid social identities allowed women to contest traditional roles and identities. Consumer fashion could be used by women to signify rebellion,
social mobility, and increased autonomy, especially when they
participated, as in the appropriation of menswear, in a discursive reworking of gender roles and stereotypes.

Ladies with Legs: Reading the Man-Suited Woman

When Marlene Dietrich sailed for the United States in 1930 to
work at Paramount, her legs were already famous.[2] *The Blue*

Angel (1930) had made the cabaret singer Lola-Lola's legs, one knee clasped as she leaned back, a synecdoche for Dietrich's persona that resonated throughout her career.[3] It was a calculated move when Dietrich's first American-made film, *Morocco*, delayed the display of her famous legs until the second act of her cabaret performance as the singer Amy Jolly. In the celebrated first act, Amy appears in a top hat and tuxedo, which initially elicits rude disapproval from her audience. Boos change to applause, however, as Amy's gestural élan and coolly ironic voice persuade the crowd to enjoy the transgression of her mannish appearance. A similar process took place in Hollywood, as Dietrich and others boldly sported menswear in a range of social settings.

Initially, Dietrich's style was taken for a publicity stunt, since she was eager to be photographed by the press in her trousers, sometimes performing high kicks to illustrate the freedom of movement they gave her. She was photographed in menswear with Amelia Earhart, who was said to be "all for the trouser fad," and with Dorothea Wieck (star of *Maedchen in Uniform* [1931]).[4] But as one article described the reaction to *Morocco,* "People gasped, said 'How continental!', and let it pass."[5] Gradually, however, it became clear that Dietrich was not going to stop. While Garbo was known to don menswear for her daily hikes and was spotted buying pants in army/navy stores, she avoided the press and used these clothes for camouflage as well as comfort. As one article described, "She piles her hair beneath a tan beret. Her shoes are low. She wears a mannish walking-suit of brown, with leather jacket. . . . She swings a stick with masculine effect."[6] Dietrich, on the other hand, openly promoted women's adoption of menswear. In the *Motion Picture* article, "Marlene Dietrich Tells Why She Wears Men's Clothes!" she comments,

> Women's clothes take too much time—it is exhausting, shopping for them. . . . Then the styles change—and it must all be done over again, every few months. It is very extravagant

Marlene Dietrich in a Paramount publicity photograph for *Morocco* (1930).

to dress as most women do. Men's clothes do not change; I can wear them as long as I like.

However, she denied that she wore menswear as an anti-fashion statement, asserting, "I am sincere in my preference for men's clothes—I do not wear them to be sensational. . . . I think I am much more alluring in these clothes."[7]

146

But the contrast between the fame of Dietrich's exposed legs on film and the audacity of her means of covering them offscreen also played with fashion's sexual dynamic of concealment. Dietrich commented on this dynamic but in a noncommittal manner: "First, I uncovered my legs, and people were excited over that. Now I cover my legs, and that excites them, too."[8] In spite of Dietrich's denial that she was creating a deliberate gender contrast between her glamorously feminine persona and her coolly sexual, trouser-suited image, this sort of contrast is stylistically central to many of her films, particularly those she made with Josef von Sternberg. Sybil DelGaudio has described this strategy as von Sternberg's method of using gender masquerade to emphasize Dietrich's distant but tantalizing sexual self-possession.[9] It is also clear that Dietrich's publicity deliberately elicited associations with glamorous, European lesbianism, if only, as Andrea Weiss suggests, because it sought "male voyeuristic interest." Nevertheless, as she points out, such innuendo "worked for a range of women spectators as well, enabling them to direct their erotic gaze at the female star without giving it a name."[10] Weiss suggests that the transgressive sexuality of stars like Dietrich may also have appealed to female viewers of color whose sexuality did not rely on identification. Weiss cites a black lesbian viewer who recalled her fascination with Dietrich:

> I was just enthralled with Dietrich. . . . She has a sustaining quality about her that I know has turned on thousands of women in this world. I can't say I identified with her. I wasn't thinking in terms of black and white in those days. . . . [It was just] lust, childhood lust, I'm sure.[11]

The outcry caused by Dietrich's frequent appearances in pants also inspired an ironic response from the comedy team of Bert Wheeler and Robert Woolsey, who went to the Brown Derby in skirts. Wheeler commented, "As long as it's legal for women to wear pants, what's there to stop a man wearing skirts?"[12] This stunt may have resonated with gay fans, particularly in relation to Wheeler and Woolsey's campy performances in films like *Hips, Hips Hooray,* in which they sleep together in a car, "accidentally" kissing in their sleep, and Wheeler frolics in a faux ballet tutu. Hollywood's fascination with gender ambiguity, particularly before the increased enforcement of the Production Code in 1934, may have provoked a range of responses, from "childhood lust" to a desire for the mobility and freedom associated with pants. In a social context in which working women were struggling to maintain their right to jobs and were (inaccurately) blamed for male unemployment, however, Dietrich's assertion of her right to dress in either masculine- or feminine-coded clothing—simply depending on her mood—was a provocation. Her rejection of a circumscribed feminine social identity is illustrated by a publicity photo taken of her with her family: Dietrich stands dutifully beside her husband and daughter but wears a man's jacket and tie.[13] In films such as *Sylvia Scarlett* (1935), with Katharine Hepburn, and *She Loves Me Not* (1934), with Miriam Hopkins, female cross-dressing is a sexually provocative form of gender play that is cast off in the end as a "disguise" of true heterosexuality. Dietrich's film roles, however, rarely resolve the gender ambiguity that arises from her ironic use of both male and female clothing and gestures. This ambiguity can be seen as one way in which consumer fashion allowed women's play with gendered dress to become part of an increased freedom to move between social roles and identities.

Earlier attempts at women's dress reform had been unsuccessful, in part because they were seen as a mode of antifashion rather than a fashion trend. In 1851, Amelia Bloomer began wearing a short dress with loose, matching trousers underneath, scandalizing the general public. Referred to as "bloomers" or Turkish trousers, the full, bifurcated garment was appreciated by many women, but the risk of social ostracism, public attack, and even police arrest prevented popular uptake. Although the overtly feminist dress reform movement had disbanded by 1900, the growing popularity of

Katharine Hepburn in an RKO publicity photograph for *Sylvia Scarlett* (1935).

women's sports produced garments like bicycle bloomers, hiking knickers, and riding jodhpurs. In 1909, the influence of both sportswear and "the Orient" on European fashion resulted in a French outfit surprisingly similar to Bloomer's. Designed by Paul Poiret, this look was a "lamp-shade tunic" worn over full pants that tapered at the ankle. Poiret's outfits were worn by a fashionable vanguard in rich colors and textures, accessorized with turbans, beads, and tassels.[14] A number of explanations for this dramatic shift in early-twentieth-century women's dress (the demise of the corset and crinoline, the shortening and narrowing of skirts, and the gradual adoption of trousers) have been offered, from theories of fashion as a reflection of broad political and social changes to psychosocial readings of the erotics of dress. Many explanations highlight the impact of World War I, but as Poiret's designs indicate, the most significant changes associated with this transformation had already begun to take place around the turn of the century.[15]

The failure of dress reform, followed by the gradual uptake of similar designs during subsequent generations, suggests that reconfiguration of the female form took place through incremental stylistic adaptations to women's changing social activities.[16] But pants did not simply become fashionable as a result of being depoliticized. Women's experience wearing boilersuits and overalls for wartime factory and munitions work maintained much of the dress-reform, feminist significance of wearing pants. One group of railroad shop workers penned a verse to this effect: "We're independent now you see / Your bald head don't appeal to me . . . We're truly glad we got the chance / To work like men and wear men's pants."[17] In addition to women's adoption of male-coded clothing for work, there were many popular-culture representations of women in military uniform throughout World War I, although their emulation of the male soldier was presumably seen as a gesture of patriotic solidarity rather than a feminist statement. Mary Pickford proudly posed in a doughboy uniform, with breeches, boots and jacket, and the famous aviatrix Ruth Law wore similar clothes in her perilous flights over the Western war front.[18]

The first long pants to appear widely in high-fashion culture, however, were associated with the bedroom rather than the workplace. The lounging suit with wide "pajama" pants, popular throughout the second decade of the twentieth century, was elevated to a casual outdoor garment in the early 1920s, and by 1926, lounging pajamas were a favorite casual dress item of female film stars. A continental variety, the "smoking suit," was reminiscent of men's formal wear, worn with narrower trousers, jacket lapels, shirts with collars, and neckties.[19] The Hollywood variety, however, was generally full-legged and more feminine. The real breakthrough in Hollywood's fashion influence came when the lounging pajama moved from the poolside to the street; long pants quickly became casual streetwear, representing fashion legitimation of popular activewear like knickers, overalls, and slacks.

Marjorie Garber has suggested that the erotics of concealment are part of the impact of cross-dressing, which functions not simply to appropriate or displace one gender onto another but as "a sign of the provocative destabilization of gender that is the very signature of the erotic."[20] In this sense, Garber suggests, cross-dressing is "not just a category crisis of male and female, but the crisis of category itself."[21] This would explain the contradictory criticisms of women's adoption of pants, which, it was claimed, would make women less feminine (by exposing their physical likeness to men) but also more sexual (by blurring sexual difference). In 1895, for example, a fashion magazine worried that "the wearing of such garments [bicycle bloomers] will do more to unseat womankind and rob her of that innate modesty which is her greatest charm than aught else."[22] Yet a prominent designer commented in 1899 on the "faccination [sic] which a woman dressed in masculine garments exercises over many of the public."[23] In 1929, an article by psychoanalyst Joan Riviere proposed a theory of the "masquerade of womanliness," which described feminine behavior as a form of protective compensation for women's inevitable possession of traits considered "masculine." She concluded that it was impossible to define the difference between "genuine womanliness" and masquerade: "whether radical or superficial, they are the same thing."[24]

The concept of masquerade has been discussed more recently in relation to Judith Butler's work on the performativity of gender. In both *Gender Trouble* and *Bodies That Matter,* Butler uses J. L. Austin's definition of performative speech acts to describe gender as a product of the reiteration of behavior defined as masculine or feminine rather than a product of these categories' a priori existence.[25] Butler asks:

> [W]hat is meant by understanding gender as an impersonation? Does this mean that one puts on a mask or persona, that there is a "one" who precedes that "putting on," who is something other than its gender from the start? Or does this miming, this impersonating precede and form the "one," operating as its formative precondition rather than its dispensable artifice?[26]

Butler clearly sees gender as a "formative precondition" of social subjectivity, and rather than positing a "utopian beyond" to gendered identity, she is concerned with the inherent instabilities within the "constitutive categories that seek to keep gender in its place by posturing as the foundational illusions of identity."[27]

But even if gender is seen as performative rather than a priori, questions remain as to the social significance of gendered dress and its modification. Valerie Steele has added a contextual dynamic to discussions of twentieth-century women's fashion change, suggesting that the rejection of the corset was part of a general environmental adjustment in women's dress. Although women had done physical labor while wearing corsets for years, nineteenth-century fashionable dress had been designed primarily for occasions of social self-presentation. But as women's labor became more visible in offices and department stores, and bourgeois leisure pursuits like bicycling and tennis became popular, strict divisions between formal and informal dress became more loosely maintained. The result was that women's fashion became both more professional and more casual in the late nineteenth century, producing styles like the shirtwaist and skirt ensemble, which wedded fashion and function. As Steele describes,

> One important factor of new looks is the existence of specific settings for fashion-oriented behavior. What a person does and where affects the style of self-presentation, which encompasses such variables as posture, movement, and expression, as well as dress. . . . Costume links the "natural" body to its cultural surroundings and decor.[28]

Such factors are evident, for example, in the impossibility of sitting at a typewriter while wearing a hoop or crinoline under one's skirt. The large numbers of women required to staff the growing infrastructure of corporate business in the 1890s made dress accommodations to such labor essential.[29]

While the steady movement of women into visible, mixed-gender workplaces helped to align their professional dress and body movements with that of young men doing similar work, the growth of women's sports was also a significant factor. The popularity of bicycle bloomers and gymnastics suits, which became part of college women's everyday dress, helped to modify rigid conceptions of how women should appear in public.[30] Both work and leisure activities were thus important factors in the shift from a Victorian to a streamlined female body. However, this new silhouette and its association with athleticism were accompanied by the idealization of a youthful slenderness that few women could maintain beyond adolescence. Dieting crazes became epidemic on women's college campuses in the 1920s, and a particular favorite was the "Hollywood eighteen-day diet."[31] In the early 1930s, the goal of slenderness was ubiquitously addressed in women's magazines. *Photoplay* magazine registers a dramatic shift between the late 1920s and the early 1930s, from a tendency to warn women against drastic dieting to its promotion. In 1929, *Photoplay* ran the articles "Diet—The Menace of Hollywood," emphasizing "why the average woman risks her health when she attempts to achieve a movie figure," and "Eat and Be Merry," which notes the rise of bulimia among stars.[32] Yet by January 1933, *Photoplay* had begun a regular column by diet-and-exercise guru Madame Sylvia, who told readers struggling unsuccessfully to become thin that they were simply "lazy."[33]

On a more positive side of the trend toward sporty svelteness, Hollywood actresses' love of sportswear helped to integrate physical comfort and freedom of movement into public dress protocols. After film production relocated from the East Coast to Hollywood around 1910, informal California beach- and leisure-wear became steadily more popular in mainstream fashion. Sporting styles whose popularity was attributed to Hollywood in the 1920s included tennis clothes, jumpers, sweaters, brown-and-white shoes, and berets.[34] But the ability of Hollywood stars to turn the most casual of popular play clothes into a sophisticated fashion was made abundantly clear from 1926 on, when female stars began wearing pants in public. By 1930, trendsetters like Greta Garbo, Ina Claire, and the newly arrived Marlene Dietrich and Katharine Hepburn were wearing white duck sailor trousers, fitted riding pants, and wide-legged, flowing "pajamas" in a variety of contexts. By the summer of 1931, Hollywood publicity photographs were regularly depicting actresses in the popular Riviera beach style of white sailor pants and a striped shirt. This outfit, along with a variety of "beach pajamas," appeared throughout summer issues of movie magazines, and stories increasingly circulated about Hollywood women who even wore satin pajamas to formal social events.[35]

In August and September of that year, *Motion Picture* ran articles on the popularity of pants: "Hollywood's Newest Fad" claimed that "Women are wearing the pants in Hollywood today. . . . Despite wild protests from the men." The article lists numerous stars who "refuse to accept any restrictions" on when and where they dress in pajamas. A newspaper ran an article with the headline, "Artists, Showmen and Psychologists—

Unidentified newspaper article, "Strange Spectacle of Women in Trousers," circa 1933.

They All View with Alarm the Strange Spectacle of Women in Trousers," which referred to Hollywood as "Trouser-Land" and cited a "professor of abnormal psychology" who claimed that the fad was the result of women's "blind striving for accomplishment in a man's field."[36] A California newspaper conducted a survey on a corner of Hollywood Boulevard and counted eighteen women in pants and twenty-nine in skirts in the course of five minutes. The article noted that "radicals declare that within another year working women will be wearing the tailored suits to the office and store."[37]

During the summer of 1933, sailor pants and pajamas were omnipresent in the pages of movie magazines, in spite of reports that the designers Adrian and Travis Banton were opposed to the trend. Banton argued that pants were "entirely out of place in the public restaurant or ballroom, no matter how sophisticated the gathering or place," while Adrian noted

155

that he had contributed to the fad by adapting "so many masculine garments to feminine clothes," but added that the trend
had "ceased to be amusing" and predicted that it would be
dropped by most women. Similarly, the chairman of the
International Association of Clothing Designers sniffed that
the fad would be "short lived" because "there isn't a designer in
America who will ever try to cut men's clothes for women."[38]
But numerous actresses continued to be cited as regular wear-
ers of "slacks" on the street and in restaurants. In 1936, a
"man-tailored slack suit of beige angora flannel" was modeled in *Motion Picture,* and the slack suit had become widely
available by 1937.[39] Thus, although most actresses wore
dresses and skirts on-screen, Hollywood's offscreen style culture, as depicted in publicity photographs, newspapers, and
newsreels, was a significant factor in the diffusion of pants
and sportswear.

The specific ways in which these fashions were worn and
photographed are as significant as their design. If, as Valerie
Steele suggests, new environments like the workplace required
changes in women's clothes, new fashions like pants also
changed the kinds of gestures and movements adopted by
women in publicity and fashion photographs. Their poses
were distinctly different from those used by models in traditionally feminine clothes. The majority of them enact masculine modes of assertiveness, such as standing or sitting with
one leg propped up or with legs apart, sitting cross-legged, or
straddling a chair backward. These gestures are expressive of
a relaxed but confident physical presence, since many of the
poses actually take up a larger amount of physical and photographic space than traditional feminine poses (standing with
knees together, sitting with legs crossed at the knee, etc.). Thus,
a whole vocabulary of gestures was associated with Hollywood
stars that were unusual in the context of mainstream women's
streetwear, which was still dominated by narrow dresses and
skirts. Such images resonated with film roles that featured
similarly androgynous elements. As Weiss argues:

Not only did the Hollywood star system create inconsistent images of femininity, but these images were further contradicted by the intervention of the actress herself into the process of star image production. Certain stars such as Katharine Hepburn, Marlene Dietrich and Greta Garbo often asserted gestures and movements in their films that were inconsistent with the narrative and even posed an ideological threat within it.[40]

One can assume that such gestures went through a process of social diffusion just as the clothes did, a process evident in a *Life* magazine article of 1940 called "College Girls in Men's Clothing." The accompanying photographs show young women standing in slacks, suspenders, and suit jackets with skirts, bobby-socks, and loafers. They stand with legs apart and hands in pockets; they sit on railings with their legs propped up, or cross-legged on the ground. Interestingly, the women in skirts also take the wide-legged, "masculine" stance of those in pants, suggesting that the popularity of pants may have influenced the late-1930s flaring of skirts from the hip rather than the knee, allowing for more leg movement.[41] A *New York Times Magazine* article of the same year, "Girls Will Be Boys," wondered

> what deep meaning lies within the fact that so many college girls have outfitted themselves with strictly masculine clothing. . . . there are stylists who predict that within the next ten years women will be wearing trousers—well-cut, comfortable, becoming trousers—to work in just as casually as they now wear them to play in.[42]

The 1930s was a contradictory decade, however, since from the autumn of 1929 onward there was a significant backlash against the short, waistless flapper chemise of the late 1920s, referred to as the "mannish" look that had emanated from Paris. In fact, it was the 1929 Paris fall season that brought hemlines back down and waistlines in; Hollywood

Katharine Hepburn in a characteristic pose for an RKO publicity photograph, circa 1938.

designers responded quickly, however, adapting the new sil-houette into a style referred to by designer Howard Greer as the "Hollywood Line," which popularized the bias-cut designs of French designer Mme Vionnet.[43] These dresses, which were fitted to the torso, hips, and thighs, flaring just below the knee, were hailed as the salvation of femininity in the early 1930s and were often embellished with retro details like puffy sleeves, feather boas, and bow bustles. Hollywood, it was said, had

Carole Lombard in a Paramount publicity photograph, circa 1936.

rejected continental mannishness and redeemed the curvaceous body. The rhetoric of renewed femininity was seen in Paris lines as well, however; as Coco Chanel stated, "The 1933 Winter mode imposes the return to femininity. Severe and masculine lines . . . have disappeared. Velvets, lamés, brocades, lend new luxury to fashion."[44] This elaborate femininity was eagerly taken up by the press as the representation of a hopeful, post-austerity style: "Depression dresses are out-of-date—dresses drably devoid of glamour. . . . For the New Deal modes

Greta Garbo in an MGM publicity photograph for *Queen Christina* (1933).

are modes that express hope of returning gaiety and good fortune and the revival of romance and joy in life."[45]

The 1930s saw periodic celebrations of the refeminized
body, often utilizing Victorian motifs; however, the growing
popularity of women's broad-shouldered, tailored suits and
athletic sportswear continued unabated. Contrary to publicity
claims that the new femininity was a celebration of the Mae
West–style figure, its silhouette actually required an even thinner and more elongated body to conform to its ideal propor-

Cary Grant and Marlene Dietrich in a Paramount publicity photograph for
Blonde Venus (1932).

tions than had the flapper chemise. As a 1931 advertising
campaign for cereal emphasized, "Each dress has become a
subtle revelation of gracefully rounded curves. . . . Those
whose contours are a little too full must diet."[46] Only the addition of padded shoulders, first used by Schiaparelli and increasingly popular throughout the 1930s, kept most women
from looking pear-shaped in dresses that clung to the hips.
Harper's Bazaar reported in 1930 that "at Schiaparelli's, I

Marlene Dietrich in a Paramount publicity photograph, circa 1933.

hear that the padded shoulders in coats and suits are very successful. She handles the shoulder exactly as it used to be handled in a man's coat. This, she says, makes the hips and waist look slimmer, because the shoulders are built up."[47]

An interesting result of the advent of padded shoulders (a practice popularized by Adrian's costumes for Joan Crawford) was that this shape revived a masculine style: men's suits had become soft-shouldered in the 1920s and 1930s, and when they began to have padding again in the late 1930s, the fashion press attributed this to the influence of *women's* suits. Nevertheless, the female padded shoulder was usually described as an emulation of masculine, military style.[48] Thus, in spite of all the talk about refeminizing women's clothing in the 1930s, the popularity of pants as a Hollywood fad grew throughout the decade, and by 1940 the woman's trouser suit had entered the mainstream, along with women's slacks and jeans. At the same time, women's suits became increasingly broad-shouldered, with shorter jackets and flared skirts. As the *Life* magazine article shows, college women were often seen as an important fashion vanguard because they tended to have more economic resources and freedom from mainstream dress codes than other women. The white-collar woman, however, was often depicted in a much more vulnerable relationship to the social semiotics of clothing. A number of films foreground what have been called "scenarios of exposure," in which the contrast between professional clothing and more feminine dress is often used to suggest that working women embody an essential contradiction between female autonomy and feminine sexuality.

These characterizations usually emphasize women's need to work rather than their desire to have careers, and this need is often attributed to the failure of men to be adequate providers due to the depression. In these cases, work is seen simply as a temporary measure until marriage, when traditional roles will be resumed (as in the Crawford film *Dance, Fools, Dance* [1931]). The "gold digger" is a predatory version of this characterization, because when she takes a job, it is primarily to find a successful man (as in, for example, Jean Harlow's *Red Headed Woman* [1932]); the gold digger's career, like that of her doppelganger, the prostitute, is tainted by illicit sex, which she uses to facilitate her rise. Needless to say, this form of work was increasingly punished, in accordance with the Production Code. In the "pre-code" film *Possessed* (1931), for example, Crawford escapes poverty by becoming a rich man's mistress, but the film concludes with their marriage rather than her punishment. In *Kitty Foyle* (1940), however, the heroine's love affair with a wealthy man ends tragically in pregnancy and miscarriage.

Both films, however, emphasize "the difficulties of women living alone in the city," which in 1940 was the topic of a *Life* magazine cover story on the "habits and habitat of an important species of American woman, the White Collar Girl." These "20 million" women were said to appear "neither too grubby nor too glamorous" and "spend their youth—and sometimes more than their youth—in offices or shops before they settle into marriage or a career."[49] In films such as *Employees' Entrance* (1933) and *Skyscraper Souls* (1932), the plight of the white-collar girl includes a critique of male dominance and harassment in the workplace, but on balance they present a fatalistic view of women's position in masculine commercial culture. Working women are presented as vulnerable to corruption and sexual predation, and female ambition is presented as a displacement of more "natural" feminine desires for security and love. The Barbara Stanwyck film *Baby Face* (1933) epitomizes this scenario. Stanwyck's character, Babe, is a working woman whose ambition is shown to be an aberration brought on by her father's abuse. Her contempt for men is explained by the opening scenes of the film, in which her father forces her to service a man to whom he owes money. After escaping and finding work, she determines to sleep her way to the top of the company through a series of calculated seductions. The connection between work and sex that is explicitly drawn in gold-digger films is also seen in a number of films in which women struggle vainly to keep them separate. In such films, the commercial sphere is presented as a corrupting influence because the boss assumes a husband-like proprietary power over his female employees.

Gender Trouble in the Workplace

> She had a marriage contract she couldn't live up to. Because she had to "Love, Honor and Obey" her boss to keep her job. The real lowdown on girls in business!
> Publicity for *Big Business Girl*

An advertisement for *Smart Set* magazine in 1930 featured a drawing of a woman on a psychoanalyst's couch with the caption, "Are you self-conscious? . . . You can cure yourself!" The magazine offers tips from a prominent psychoanalyst on gaining "freedom from the torture of self-consciousness," along with articles on "The Problems of the Working Wife" and "The Business of Sex in Business."[50] This juxtaposition of topics is revealing in light of the conflicting demands being made on working women at the time, and the difficulties of moving from domestic labor into the male-dominated workplace. In 1916, *The Efficient Secretary* noted that some white-collar women made the mistake of wearing "fluffy, frilly, chiffon-like garments" on the job, while others went to the "opposite extreme" of "tweeds and cheviots, cut in masculine lines." The former was considered unprofessional, while "[t]he latter is permissible, to be sure, but unbecoming, except when worn by a woman who is dainty, girlish, and very feminine."[51] This advice reflects the fraught position of working women, who were supposed to avoid resembling either an "imitation man" or a distractingly sexual woman, and instead project a demure but professional femininity. In spite of their efforts, however, male employers could easily take advantage of women's need to work.

Working women could face resentment at home as well as

harassment at work; according to one depression-era sociological study, when young women living with their parents
earned an income, they were conventionally given no more
autonomy in the family than other children, whom they were
supporting.[52] In addition, women who left home often provided for their parents rather than pursuing an education or marriage, or starting their own family. One study conducted in
Chicago between 1934 and 1935 noted that

> this attitude is not a result of the depression but seems to
> rest upon the middle-class family solidarity which makes
> it difficult for the parents to regard the daughter as an in-
> dividual and which often causes the girl to identify herself
> completely with the family, or in some cases, with the
> mother. The same situation was found among Chicago girls
> in 1927–28.[53]

This denial of the rights of working daughters was also seen in
relation to working wives; married women (who made up
28.8 percent of the female workforce in 1930) could be legal-
ly fired from numerous jobs in order to hire a man, in spite of
figures showing that nearly one-third of these women were the
sole support of their husbands and children.[54]

A number of films address these tensions, with various de-
grees of support for or reservations about working women
and the impact of their wage labor on the stability of traditional gender roles. Constance Balides has described several
nickelodeon-era films in which women working in the public
or commercial sphere are sexually "exposed" to the viewer, either through the use of an on-screen voyeur, or an "accident"
in which a woman's skirt is raised, for instance. Balides suggests that the films represent an attempt to contain these
women within patriarchal norms of female sexuality and do-
mesticity in spite of their new work roles. She contextualizes
this reading with a series of articles published from 1910 onward that address problems faced by growing numbers of
working women in American cities. Sexual harassment was

commonplace, as was the employment of women on the condition that they sexually "accommodate" their employers. The urban presence of prostitutes in increasingly respectable attire was said to cause "confusion" among men, who could not distinguish between the new working woman and the "better-known" female sex worker.[55] Maureen Greenwald has documented how women's dress was used against them to shift the blame for sexual harassment. Reports indicate that female workers in the early twentieth century were regularly pinched and handled, and given wage increases—or not—depending on their response to office molestation. Complaints filed indicate that most women tolerated such treatment because those who complained were accused of "flirting with their bosses or wearing provocative clothing on the job." As one harassment file describes, "It was another case of Adam pointing to Eve as the cause of trouble."[56]

The film *Employees' Entrance* emphasizes this masculine dominance of the workplace, and, significantly, the issue of sexual harassment was used to publicize the film. Its press book asks, "has the depression brought BARGAINS IN LOVE?" and clearly announces its targeted audience, claiming, "Department store girls—this is your picture—about your lives and your problems."[57] The story concerns a young woman named Madeline (Loretta Young) who needs work because she is destitute, and is therefore easily exploited by her boss until she is rescued by another man. What is interesting about the film is the way that this positioning of her character and gender is presented via costume and mise-en-scène. Madeline is first seen in the "model home" section of a large department store, which is run by a tyrannical figure named Mr. Anderson (Warren William). At closing time, Anderson walks past the white picket fence and cottage facade of the "model home" and hears someone playing the piano inside. He enters the cottage and finds Madeline, who has made herself quite literally at home, playing a slightly melancholy tune on the display piano. When Anderson questions her presence there, she replies playfully:

Madeline. Don't you know better than to break into a
   lady's house without knocking?

Anderson. Oh, so you're the lady of the house, are you?

Madeline. Yes—and besides how did you know, I might
   have been taking a bath or something. Who are you?

Anderson. Oh, I'm only the landlord. You haven't paid
   your rent this month, lady.

Madeline. No, I know I haven't. But you wouldn't throw
   me out on a stormy night like this, would you mister?

The scene aptly visualizes Mr. Anderson's proprietary relationship to his employees, who must work, metaphorically, in
a space over which he presides as "landlord" and patriarch.
When Madeline, who has not eaten in some time, comes to
dinner at Anderson's apartment, he offers her a modeling job
in the department store. As she thanks him and tries to leave,
he presses her against the door and kisses her, a fade-out illustrating the film's publicity line that "millions of heartsick girls
will pay *any price* for a job!"[58]

During her first day at work, Madeline is noticed by a male
coworker as she glides to and fro in the bridal boutique,
modeling a wedding gown. He admires her as she stands in
a medium-long shot displaying the gown, looking radiantly
bridelike; the couple quickly fall in love and get married. Thus,
Madeline's first appearance in the store prefigures her proprietary sexualization by its "landlord," while the second indicates
that even though she now has a job, her proper role is that of a
bride. There is hardly a moment in between for her to be seen
as a wage earner in the commercial sphere; both the film's settings and costumes repeatedly code her role as domestic.

In *Skyscraper Souls*, a young woman named Lynn Harding
(Maureen O'Sullivan) works in a modern, monolithic building owned and run by the ruthless developer David Dwight
(again, Warren William). Not only is Dwight a sexual predator, he has a conveniently located penthouse at the top of the
skyscraper. Thus, as in *Employees' Entrance*, William's tyran-

nical boss appropriates the power of a domestic patriarch, since every worker in the building is, literally, in his home. Although married, Dwight has had an ongoing affair with his assistant, Sarah, to whom the young Lynn is secretary. Sarah is maternally protective of Lynn and devoted to Dwight but sadly deprived of legitimacy as either wife or mother. When Dwight convinces the young Lynn to go on holiday with him, Sarah shoots him in order to save Lynn from her own fate. Her bloodied hands held out, stigmata-like, Sarah then leaps from the skyscraper.

Lynn's character is primarily defined in terms of her own confusion about whether to marry for love or money; she is courted by a bank teller whom she initially rejects because of his limited income. She is thus vulnerable to the lure of Dwight's money and corruptible because of her daily presence in his "home" and subsequent exposure to his lifestyle. The vulnerability presumed to follow from Lynn's presence in this masculine sphere is highlighted in a scene in which she has bought a new evening gown for a date with the bank teller. Lynn initially wears a youthful but professional outfit with a white-collar blouse and man's necktie, but Sarah encourages her to try on the new gown in her inner office. While she is changing, Dwight comes into the outer office. Lynn stumbles out in her underwear with her head and arms wedged help-lessly in the clinging dress, and asks Sarah for help. Lynn is mortified when she recovers and sees Dwight, but he responds by asking Lynn to work late and bring a report up to his pent-house that evening, where he is hosting a cocktail party. Wear-ing her new evening gown, Lynn appears at the party and is encouraged by Dwight to try some champagne; she proceeds to get drunk and pass out in his bed. Lynn's seduction and "fall" are thus catalyzed by the fact that she is "exposed" as sexual rather than professional.

The film *Big Business Girl* (1931) offers a similar narra-tive of the conflicts encountered by a working woman who comes up against patriarchal possessiveness at work and at

Loretta Young and Ricardo Cortez in a First National publicity photograph for *Big Business Girl* (1931).

home. The film concerns Claire MacIntyre, nicknamed Mac (Loretta Young). On graduating from college, she postpones marriage to her boyfriend Johnny because she has debts to pay off, and he cannot support her. After pounding the pavement, Mac gets a job at an advertising agency, following a scene in which she is hired because the boss, R. J., admires her legs. She is clever and ambitious, however, and asks to be promoted to copywriter based on an advertisement she has written. Another secretary sympathizes with her, but is skeptical:

Secretary. I used to be terribly ambitious myself. I used
    to try and write copy . . . have visions of grabbing off
    a sweet job at a man's salary. However . . .
Mac. . . . I *know* I can write good advertising copy.
Secretary. Do you *like* working, Mac?
Mac. I'm going to like it when I quit being a slave to
    a typewriter . . . have a job that gives me fine clothes,
    a nice apartment with all the trimmings.

When Mac is given the promotion, we learn after she has left the room that R. J. has offered her a fraction of the salary she deserves.[59] Mac enters her new office and happily tries out her telephone and intercom. By accident, she overhears R. J.'s ongoing discussion of her with his partner, who comments, "even if this piece of copy was an accident, she's worth a hundred twenty-five a week as an office decoration." The cut to Mac's reaction is filled with pathos, as her gestures change from the proud, proprietary exploration of her own office to those of humiliation. Assuming (wrongly) that she has been promoted simply because of her looks, Mac quickly pulls herself together and indicates that she will, accordingly, take full advantage of the situation (she proceeds to "vamp" her boss with cynical detachment).

A subsequent scene indicates that Mac has achieved exactly what she wanted: while dressing for a party, her "fine clothes" are lovingly rendered by lingering close-ups on the details of each item she puts on, as well as on the bulging walk-in closet she selects each garment from. The dressing sequence is extended far beyond its narrative significance and represents a clear instance of the presumed "visual pleasure" attributed to fashion display, as well as narratively indicating the rewards of Mac's determination. But in films like *Skyscraper Souls* and *Big Business Girl,* the function of professional clothing to ward off unwanted sexual attention in the workplace is shown to be ineffective; instead, the working woman is "exposed" in feminine clothing, denying her the ability to control her own professional role or image. The secretary Lynn is seen half-dressed by her employer and then required to work overtime in an evening gown; Mac is followed into her apartment by her boss after a business dinner that required an evening gown. In effect, these characters are made to perform their jobs while dressed for social engagements, and Mac is specifically instructed to doll herself up and flirt with male business clients. The disruption of these characters' professional self-presentation suggests that women will *inevitably* be exposed in the workplace as primarily sexual, since that is the way their bosses see them. Feminine clothing functions to discredit them, acting as a "stigma symbol" that undermines rather than supports their desired status and identity. These women are denied the conventional function of work dress codes to allow for the separation of professional from sexual identity—they are prevented from managing their own social identities.[60]

Feminine sexuality is not always depicted as a disruptive stigma for working women. However, when it is not, the workplace "invisibility" of their femininity is often posed as a romantic problem—as the complete inverse of the sexual harassment scenario. Such films appear to caution viewers that femininity, far from being essential and always visible, can be "lost" by women who take on a professional identity. In *Platinum Blonde* (1931), for example, Loretta Young plays a female reporter called Galagher (like Mac, she loses her feminine first name as part of her adaptation to the workplace) whose male coworker, whom she loves, considers her merely a "pal" until she devises a pretext to appear before him in an evening gown. This representation of femininity as a guise that can be selectively deployed has the distinct advantage of being a matter of image choice on the part of the female worker rather than a sexual essentialism that victimizes her. Like the "makeover," this notion of selective femininity under-

Loretta Young in a Columbia Pictures publicity photograph for *Platinum Blonde* (1931). Courtesy of the Academy of Motion Picture Arts and Sciences.

mines fixed gender roles to some extent by implying that women can calibrate their self-presentation rather than having it determined by traditional roles. The next section will look at films in which both work and self-fashioning are used by women to escape the status and relationships they are born into, and will conclude with a discussion of films in which a woman's freedom to create her identity through consumerism is valorized over her work role.

"Never Again Will You Call Them the Weaker Sex"

Films of the 1930s offer a surprising number of different views on working women, in addition to presenting them as casualties of the depression.[61] Mary Beth Haralovich has suggested that the 1930s produced a "woman's proletarian film" genre, and this is supported by fan magazine references to "working girl" films. But the working women in these films come from a range of class positions. Mac, for example, is a college graduate who must work because of the debt she has incurred by having pampered herself in college with "the best clothes, the best rooms, the best everything." Other working women, however, are motivated by a driving desire to rise from poverty and enjoy material abundance, as in the Crawford film *Possessed* (1931), or to escape exploitation, as in *Mannequin* (1938). Regardless of class background, however, these women must do more than hold down a job to reach their goals; they must re-create themselves through fashion and performance.

In the opening sequence of *Possessed*, Marion (Crawford) stands at a railroad crossing after a long day working at a factory. A luxury train passes slowly, and its brightly lit windows glide by in a moving, cinema-like display. Each window reveals a different facet of the good life, and in the final two windows a couple dance gracefully from one illuminated frame to the other, slowly embracing as the last image disappears from view. Marion stands transfixed as the train comes to a stop and a male passenger drinking champagne strikes up a conversation with her. Eventually he comments, "You know, there's something wrong with you." Marion responds quickly, "There's everything wrong with me—my clothes, my shoes, my hands, the way I talk. But at least I know it." She moves to New York and becomes the mistress of a wealthy man, transforming herself by learning to dress, order elaborate food in French, and play the piano at elegant cocktail parties. When asked by her lover if she has any regrets, she replies that she left school at twelve and "never learned to spell regret." Her labor is rewarded, however, when he marries her and legitimates her new status.

In *Mannequin* (1938), another Crawford film, the heroine Jessie is not interested in upward mobility; her ambition arises from her young husband's refusal to work, a situation that repeats her mother's drudgery as the only worker in the family

Joan Crawford, post-makeover, in an MGM publicity photograph for *Possessed* (1931).

(aside from Jessie). In a poignant scene, Jessie and her mother repeat their nightly routine of preparing dinner for the complaining men, and the mother is suddenly compelled to offer some advice:

> **Mother.** There's some things I've been wanting to tell
> you. . . . You're a woman, Jess, you want some say
> about the life you live. A woman's supposed to lead a
> man's life—her man's life. Well, we're made that way,
> usually. A woman's weakness is *supposed* to fit into a
> man's *strength*. Her respect pays for the security a man
> gives her. That's with most women . . . but not you,
> Jessica, you've got strength of your own. You can do
> things, not just dream about 'em, like (looking down),
> like most women.
>
> **Jessie.** What are you trying to tell me, Ma?
>
> **Mother.** Live your life for yourself, Jessie. Remember what
> it was you hated. Always remember what it is *you* want.
> Get it. Any way you can. Even if you have to get it
> (pause) alone.

During this scene Jessie wears a dark dress with a bright white collar, photographed with diffusion so that it glows like a halo and seems to separate her face from its background of the steam-filled kitchen where her mother works. Following a temporal ellipsis, Jessie reappears in a smart, slightly military dark suit with large gold buttons, having gotten a divorce and a job as a fashion model in a shop. Although she goes on to marry a wealthy industrialist, Jessie's initial transformation is made when she takes her mother's advice not to make the mistake of relying on a man to provide for her. The value of an egalitarian, companionate marriage over women's economic dependence is underscored at the end of the film, when Jessie's new husband loses his fortune and they are both forced to "roll up their sleeves" in shared labor.

Narratives that link women's economic survival to their ability to take control of their lives through work and self-improvement are clearly linked to consumer marketing emphases on identity management. This notion of work as.a means of self-transformation rather than as a productive value in itself suggests that women's movement into the workplace, which in large part paralleled the transition to a consumer economy, was informed by cultural associations very different from the Protestant work ethic. Many women took up paid labor at a cultural moment when what one did was becoming less important than how one lived. Work gave them more freedom to choose how they lived, and the process of creating that lifestyle was part of their essential role in the consumer economy. This role also coded women ambiguously in terms of social identity because they were no longer defined by their relationships to a male provider, nor were they necessarily as identified with their work as men had traditionally been.

Along with the proletarian woman's film, there are a number of films from the 1930s that focus on women whose economic autonomy is linked to a more privileged, bohemian lifestyle. Such women are often artists or performers, as in *The Divorcée* (1930), *Morocco* (1930), and *Ex-Lady* (1933), although the provocative lives of such independent women became less visible following the increased enforcement of the Production Code in 1934. In some of these films, the heroine initially identifies strongly with her work; often, however, this is questioned—not by evidence that she is incapable of performing as well as a man but by the suggestion that such an identity is ultimately unsatisfying. As in films like *Platinum Blonde,* in which the heroine's femininity has vanished because she is overidentified with her work, workaholic women are usually enticed via romance into reasserting their neglected femininity. While such films show an ideological bias against female professionalism, they also use the working woman as a way of contrasting traditional "masculine" capitalism (hard work and self-denial) with a more "feminized," consumerist set of values (self-fulfillment and romance). There are significant exceptions to this pattern, however, most notably *Female*

(1933), in which the heroine's identification with her work is satirized but not convincingly negated.

Female ends ambiguously, with the heroine engaged to be married but still in a dominant role. Alison Drake (Ruth Chatterton) runs the car manufacturing business that she inherited from her father. Her character throughout most of the film offers a parody of the male business tycoon as sexual predator: Alison systematically seduces her male employees by telling them to come to her house for a meeting and using a well-timed routine to get them drunk and into bed. When they fall in love with her, she ships them off to her Montreal office and chooses a new boy from the staff. She tells a friend that she decided long ago to "travel the same open road that men have always traveled" and "treat men exactly the same way that men have always treated women." She lives in a luxurious modern mansion, dresses in elegant clothing, has numerous servants, and appears exceedingly fulfilled by her work: she exclaims, "Oh, but I love it, the battling and the excitement, I don't think I could do without it now."

Alison Drake is unusual in her mixing of a powerful professional role with routine sexual relationships, since professional women were usually portrayed as either romantically deprived or as having to hide their exercise of power so as not to appear too unfeminine. The film also details the way she uses feminine clothing to disarm men who are put off by her power. Such strategies typify magazine advice given to professional women who were in danger of threatening potential suitors. In 1932, *Photoplay*'s advice columnist explained that the "business of charm" was to "make yourself look what you want to be," even if it is just for the evening: "Suppose you are the most efficient business woman that ever lived, no man wants you to rub it in. . . . Shed your competent shell when five o'clock rolls around. Take off your tailored suit, put on a *deceptively feminine* gown" (my emphasis).[62]

But the tactical necessity of acting like a girl was not limited to after-hours interaction with men; it was also described as part of women's work life. Alison Drake has no need to camouflage her power at work (after all, she owns the company), but the same *Photoplay* column suggested that being "deceptively feminine" is often necessary to placate male colleagues. The columnist cited "one of the most successful business women" she knows as saying, "I never let people see me work except when its important, and I always try to do things in such a way that an idea of mine always looks as if it surprised me as much as it has my business associates."[63] Lois Scharf's research indicates that by the mid-1930s female clerical workers were increasingly evaluated by potential employers according to their personality and appearance rather than work abilities, and encouraged to emphasize "feminine," subordinate qualities: "One employment bureau official discovered that she not only had to deprecate the abilities of a female applicant, but she also emphasized the woman's 'ability to take orders and to conform.'"[64]

Given such requirements to be pliant and obsequious toward male colleagues, it is interesting that quite a few films from this period feature women who set out to prove their work abilities in *competition* with men—a scenario particularly common in "girl reporter" films—suggesting that the films may have offered some wish fulfillment to women viewers who felt held back professionally. When a film features a woman who has already proven her ability to work "like a man," however, the narrative often revolves around getting her to readopt her abandoned femininity by falling in love, a plot pattern that was dominant in working-women films by the early 1940s. Rosalind Russell described this pattern retrospectively, saying: "I could order the clothes for my pictures in my sleep. I'd say . . . 'Make me a plaid suit, a striped suit, a grey flannel, and a negligee for the scene in the bedroom when I cry.'"[65] However, romance was not the only cinematic element used to imply that successful working women might be less than fulfilled. Another one was to identify the successful career woman as a workaholic and imply that if a woman did manage to excel, she would probably be repressed and unhappy. In films like *Queen Christina* (1933), *Double Wedding* (1937), and *Ninotchka* (1939) the heroine's "masculine" work ethic is contrasted with a more liberatory, consumerist paradigm of *fun*. In each of these films, a professional woman is revealed to be deeply unhappy in spite of her powerful position. In particular, a contrast is drawn between her ability to exert power over people and her discovery that she no longer wants this power but wants only to be free. As a 1931 advertisement for *Leftover Ladies* exclaimed, "She Wanted Freedom! How Could She Know a Career Meant Bondage?"[66]

The title character of *Queen Christina* (Greta Garbo) longs to travel, to have more time to read, and to be able to enjoy life among the people; these desires are made equally, if not more, significant in her choice to abdicate the throne than is her forbidden romance with a Spaniard. The film has an ambiguous position on heterosexual romance because of Christina's androgyny—her love affair primarily underscores the erotic freedom she feels while disguised as a man. Ironically, Christina's professional role requires a confiningly feminine costume, while dressing as a man is linked to the character's ability to enjoy physical movement (she explores her country on horseback), sensual pleasure (she seduces the Spaniard while dressed in drag), and, most of all, independence and leisure.

Similarly, *Double Wedding* features Myrna Loy as Margit Agnew, a successful fashion designer and owner of a chain of dress shops. Margit wears tailored outfits that identify her more as a spinsterish dressmaker than with the glamour of fashion design. Her clothes represent the fussiness of needlework, such as one jacket with white zigzagging trim like the edge left by pinking shears. Another suit has a bow tie made of clustered string, like a mass of tangled sewing thread tied around her neck. There is a slightly whimsical quality to these outfits, however, in that they exaggerate Margit's buttoned-down character. When she reluctantly discovers she has fallen in love with Charlie Lodge (William Powell), an eccentric, fun-loving painter who lives in a trailer, she suddenly appears in a boy scout–like suit, with a short, dark jacket, dark shirt, white four-in-hand tie, and a jaunty Tyrolean cap. Her male-coded sportswear endows Margit with a boyish freedom for her new life on the road in Charlie's trailer.

In *Ninotchka*, the title character's style as a professional woman is not quite spinsterish. She is simply plain—her drab, uniformlike dress lacks any details associated with either gender. She is characterized as sexless and hyperrational, having repressed all carnal appetites including hunger (she stops eating when she has consumed "a sufficient number of calories for the day"). Although she is an envoy from the Soviet Union, and thus a parody of state-socialist planning, her rationalism and asceticism also align her with Taylorism and Weberian capitalism. While her conversion to capitalism is couched in terms of romance, she is really seduced by fun—the sheer silliness of consumerism, as manifested by a wacky but chic little hat she buys for herself in a moment of weakness. Ninotchka, like Christina and Margit, gives up her masculine work ethic for a feminized realm of self-discovery and -invention that is represented, in part, by the pleasures of fashion and the rejection of restrictive dress codes. Significantly, in a run-in with a former Russian aristocrat, Ninotchka defends her appearance in an elaborate, off-the-shoulder chiffon evening gown with puffed sleeves. When asked if this is "what the factory workers wear at their dances," Ninotchka replies: "Exactly. You see, it would have been very embarrassing for people of my sort to wear low-cut gowns in the old Russia. The lashes of the Cossacks were not very becoming. And you know how vain women are." This comment clearly aligns Ninotchka with the notion that American consumer fashion symbolizes a democratic appropriation of social status and power in opposition to aristocratic elitism and oppression. The film implies that, unlike in the Soviet Union, American factory workers can, indeed, wear evening gowns, and that working women have the right to be just as chic as wealthy ones.

These films supported the notion that women's wage labor could provide access to both material pleasure and a self-determined social identity. Such possibilities were clearly essential to the kinds of constant change and stylistic innovation discussed in chapter 1 as the marketing basis of the consumer economy. Women's labor, though motivated throughout the depression by financial struggle, was also informed in central ways by the precepts of consumer culture. The marketing values of upward mobility and self-transformation that accompanied women's continued movement into the workforce highlighted contradictions between consumerist models of self-invention and the limitations of women's traditional social roles.

CONCLUSION

The 1930s were a decade of conservative anxiety about the cinema, both among religious groups, who pressed for censorship, and social scientists concerned about the medium's effects on viewers. The Payne Fund, for example, commissioned a group of sociologists to study the impact of cinema on American youth. Herbert Blumer's 1933 contribution, *Movies and Conduct*, was seen to validate fears about Hollywood's ability to undermine traditional social norms. In the book's chapter on "Motion Pictures and Unrest," Blumer reported that 22 percent of a sample of 458 high school students had become more dissatisfied with their lives, social constraints, and material circumstances in comparison with the settings and behaviors they regularly saw in Hollywood films (the respondents' class backgrounds are not indicated). Blumer pointed out that "it is interesting to observe in the case of those who spoke of having become dissatisfied as a result of witnessing motion pictures that the percentage of girls was twice as great as the percentage of boys."[1]

In addition to creating "screen shoppers" and promoting a

sense of collective material entitlement, Hollywood films also problematized existing norms of gender, class, and racial difference. Although the "unrest" that Blumer found among teenage moviegoers does not necessarily represent a social critique, these viewers were capable of emulating star performances for their own ends (a girl wrote, for example, "I have one girlfriend that I love a good deal. . . . It is on her that I make use of the different ways of kissing that I see in the movies").[2] This process contradicted the naturalness of social and behavioral categories, substituting for it a sense of the conventionality of those norms. Consumer fashion marketing was closely linked to this process, encouraging the emulation of Hollywood's "theatrical" identities in the name of self-improvement.

As a sign of women's modernity, fashion has symbolized shifts in their social status. For example, fashion historian Valerie Steele has commented that "the social and sexual modernity of the Gibson Girl and the Poiret flapper were, to some extent, more a question of image than reality—but they became more real by virtue of people's growing acceptance of the pose."[3] As in other recent work in gender studies, my emphasis here is on the relative instability of the social encoding of gender but also on the way that consumerism invites people to monitor their own adherence to dress codes and conventions (unlike early sumptuary laws, for example, which were aimed at forcibly preventing the middle class from dressing like the aristocracy).[4] Consumerism thus promotes an ethos of self-formation that makes it, in Don Slater's words, "a privileged site of autonomy, meaning, subjectivity, privacy and freedom," and simultaneously a site of "strategic action by dominating institutions."[5]

It is clear that Hollywood helped to shape the modern "fashion system" and that consumer fashion, in turn, inflected Hollywood's representations of femininity. This relationship, however, needs to be seen not only in terms of how it typifies the cross-promotional reach of the culture industries but also in light of the potential for consumer practices to empower women via "networks of communication and sociability" and a performative "politics of style."[6] As Victoria de Grazia suggests, "the turnover and sheer quantity and variety of consumption practices continuously disrupt conventional boundaries of all kinds, challenging received notions of sovereignty, customary identities, and familiar authority—as well as the conventional distinctions between private and public."[7] Stars typify the ideals promoted by consumer culture and its emphasis on appearances rather than inherited social rank and identity. In the 1930s, consumer culture's promotion of constant change and planned obsolescence not only foregrounded the idea that clothes make the woman but also facilitated the deconstruction of traditional assumptions about class, race, and gender.

As a set of constantly changing style imperatives, consumer femininity directly contradicts traditional notions of "the feminine" as natural and immanent. As Steven Cohan points out in his work on masculinity and stardom, Hollywood stars produce "an effect akin to drag": their embodiment of social ideals is so stylized and theatrical that they effectively denaturalize themselves.[8] Similarly, Andrea Weiss has argued that "the rise of the cinema and especially the Hollywood star system promoted the idea that different roles and styles could be adopted by spectators as well as by actors and actresses, and could signal changeable personalities, multiple identities."[9] Weiss suggests, for example, that the Hollywood star's "theatrical sense of self" was "invaluable to the formation of lesbian identity" in the twentieth century. Drawing on Elizabeth Wilson's theory that fashion is inextricably related to modernity and its fragmentation of traditional, stable identities, Pam Cook suggests that part of the pleasure of cinema is the way that costume invites viewers to "flirt with the loss of self."[10] From such a perspective, consumer fashion and film costume are potentially subversive because they encourage fantasies of self-transformation while drawing attention to the conventional basis of social types and categories.

The Hollywood star system's construction of "symbolic identities," to use Richard DeCordova's term, involves fans in a symbolic economy that is overtly about the *pleasures* of consumerist self-fashioning and conscious "presentation of self in everyday life."[11] The gap between a star's public persona and her or his "real" self was constantly explored in fan magazines in the 1930s, but in ways that emphasized the existence rather than the closure of that gap.[12] The mutability of personality itself became a major theme of popular literature and journalism from the 1920s onward, suggesting that many aspects of social identity might be constructed rather than innate.[13] As historian Richard Sennett makes clear in *The Fall of Public Man,* the notion of social identity as performative rather than immanent did not originate with twentieth-century consumerism. Before the influence of Romanticism, he argues, eighteenth-century social behavior and appearance were consciously performative, drawing on a well-established hierarchy of social roles.

For Sennett, contemporary forms of social role playing are problematic because they are combined with Romantic notions of personal authenticity—the idea that social and private selves must be unified in order for a true, authentic self to be revealed.[14] As Don Slater has argued, this is an impossible task in a society that requires individuals to enact numerous, fragmented social roles on a daily basis. As a result, he argues, "the demand for authenticity, launched by romanticism, entails that in everyday life we are scrutinized not only for our fashionability but also for our consistency (as a mark of our truth)."[15] Conflicting roles must be juggled, while at the same time a consistent, "real" personality is drawn from the behavioral repertoire of our social group. Advertising addresses us as individuals, but consumer marketing is always based on the knowledge that our taste is tailored to our social reference groups and aspirations.

Some cultural theorists have argued that consumer culture has produced a great deal of self-consciousness about the commodification of personality, style, and taste. Dick Hebdige, for example, argues that the subcultural use of style (such as punk fashion) can be a "self conscious commentar[y]" on mainstream values.[16] I would argue that even mainstream consumer fashion relies on a high degree of individual self-consciousness about the relationship between dress codes, social categories, and cultural politics. Most people must conform to workplace and social dress codes that they do not particularly identify with, a situation in direct contradiction to Romantic notions that public and private selves should be integrated. As contemporary work on ethnicity and sexuality has indicated, marginalized social groups in particular may see the notion of private/public self-integration as no more than a myth of normative subjectivity, posing artificial social norms as natural categories of selfhood.

Women are commonly seen as particularly vulnerable to beauty and behavioral norms because of their status as the designated shoppers of American consumerism. Ironically, however, the myth of the rational, "sovereign consumer" (whose demands, according to classical liberal economics, determine what the market will supply) has usually been characterized as male. Marketing discourses have relentlessly described the female shopper as *irrational*—as "the *object* of rational calculation by other forces," like advertising and fashion, rather than a subject who makes calculated choices on her own behalf.[17] This dismissal of female consumers' agency overlooks the range of motives for consumerism and the ways that taste cultures can comment on, rather than simply reinforce, existing social structures. Women can be seen as users of fashion culture rather than victims of it, particularly if participation in such a gendered discourse is not assumed to represent an unquestioning acceptance of gender norms.[18]

On the other hand, the notion that discourses of fashion and gender may have been relevant to women's film viewing in the 1930s does not mitigate the importance of structural questions about who controls communications media or the ways that social and commercial discourses are circumscribed by dominant institutions. This work has attempted to acknowledge *both* the economic basis of the connection between Hollywood and fashion *and* the contested nature of its cultural politics. As Pierre Bourdieu's work points out, the "symbolic struggles" of everyday life are constrained but far from apolitical.[19] My argument has been, in part, that Hollywood's promotion of consumer fashion has not only fueled these struggles but has highlighted the degree to which social power relies on representational codes and categories. By underscoring the performativity of social hierarchies, popular fashion discourses potentially demystified certain power relations rather than simply reifying them within a "system of objects" that can only reproduce itself. This interpretation does not mean that more conservative or "preferred readings" of Hollywood films from this decade are inaccurate, but it suggests that the films were likely to be viewed within a larger context of changing social roles and consumer cultures. Social theories that emphasize the politics of symbolic activity as it occurs in everyday life can help to position cultural and textual analysis closer to the possible interests, pleasures, and strategies that inform both media reception and fashion consumption.

In the attempt to engage such motivations, fashion discourses of the 1930s undermined long-standing social assumptions about class, gender, and ethnicity as essential categories of personhood. It has been argued that the rise of consumer fashion led to a "willingness to commodify sociality," but commodification can also be viewed as making social relations more visible and overt.[20] From this perspective, participation in such a symbolic economy does not imply that the myths of consumer capitalism have been swallowed whole, but that they constitute the medium of contemporary social struggles. Female consumers have been the advance guard on this terrain, although men are increasingly being called on to negotiate similar issues of self-presentation and social identity. In the postindustrial, service-sector workforce, male workers are increasingly judged according to performative as well as productive skills, with a higher value placed on youth and physical capital. As a result, men are now considered a key market for cosmetic surgery, grooming, and fashion products.[21]

Most likely this trend will equalize, to some extent, the performative pressures placed on men and women, putting an end to stereotypes about women's unique susceptibility to advertising ideals and self-modification. As self-fashioning becomes less feminized and more clearly a matter of modern economic and social status, it will continue to raise questions about the legitimacy of both traditional social divisions *and* contemporary market values. The 1930s were a formative decade in the articulation of "post-traditional" identity, and this process was modulated in significant ways by the complexity of women's responses to popular film and fashion culture.

NOTES

Introduction

1. Cf. Claudia B. Kidwell and Margaret C. Christman, *Suiting Everyone: The Democratization of Clothing in America* (Washington, D.C.: Smithsonian Institution Press, 1974); Florence S. Richards, *The Ready-To-Wear Industry 1900–1950* (New York: Fairchild Publications, 1951); Ben Fine and Ellen Leopold, *The World of Consumption* (London: Routledge, 1993).

2. Advertising supplement in *Woman's Way,* Apr. 6, 1929. Throughout the 1920s and 1930s, *Vogue* regularly featured high-profile society matrons and debutantes modeling the latest Parisian couture.

3. Thorstein Veblen, *The Theory of the Leisure Class* (New York: Macmillan, 1899). It is interesting that David Riesman and colleagues' analysis of the "other-oriented" male did not appear until 1950, while it is clear that the social phenomena they describe were omnipresent in media addressing women throughout the 1930s.

4. Erving Goffman, *The Presentation of Self in Everyday Life* (New York: Doubleday, 1959).

5. Winifred Holtby, *Women in a Changing Civilization* (1935; reprint, Chicago: Academy Press, 1978), 118–19, cited in Elizabeth Wilson and Lou Taylor, *Through the Looking Glass: A History of Dress from 1860 to the Present Day* (London: BBC Books, 1989), 84.

6. Wilson and Taylor, *Through the Looking Glass,* 89.

7. Cf. Jürgen Habermas, "The Tasks of a Critical Theory," in *The Polity Reader in Social Theory* (Cambridge: Polity Press, 1994), 143.

8. Kathy Peiss, "Making Up, Making Over: Cosmetics, Consumer Culture, and Women's Identity," in *The Sex of Things: Gender and Consumption in*

Historical Perspective, ed. Victoria de Grazia and Ellen Furlough (Berkeley: University of California Press, 1996), 312.

9. Samuel Goldwyn and Eric Erenbright, "Women Rule Hollywood," *New Movie* 11, 2 (Mar. 1935): 18–19, 53.

10. "Fashions of 1934," *Variety,* Jan. 23, 1934 (clipping; no page number), Academy of Motion Picture Arts and Sciences Margaret Herrick Library.

11. Dorothy Donnell, "Are You a Screen Shopper?" *Motion Picture Magazine,* Sept. 1930, 70.

12. Cf. "Voice Lessons," *Premiere,* Women in Hollywood Special Issue, 1996.

13. Tino Balio, *Grand Design: Hollywood as a Modern Business Enterprise, 1930–1939* (Berkeley: University of California Press, 1995), 146.

14. Don Slater, *Consumer Culture and Modernity* (Oxford: Polity Press, 1997), 29–30.

15. Pierre Bourdieu, *Distinction: A Social Critique of the Judgment of Taste,* trans. Richard Nice (Cambridge: Harvard University Press, 1984), 253.

16. Ibid.

17. Frederick Wasser, "Is Hollywood America? The Trans-Nationalization of the American Film Industry," *Critical Studies in Mass Communication* 12, 4 (Dec. 1995): 428.

18. Peter Wollen, "Strike a Pose," *Sight and Sound* 5, 3 (Mar. 1995): 14.

19. Neal Gabler, *An Empire of Their Own: How the Jews Invented Hollywood* (New York: Doubleday, 1988), 5, 35.

20. Charlotte Herzog and Jane Gaines, " 'Puffed Sleeves before Tea Time': Joan Crawford, Adrian and Women Audiences," in *Stardom: Industry of Desire,* ed. Christine Gledhill (London: Routledge, 1991), 86; they cite "Our Dancing Lady," *Silver Screen* 3, 12 (Oct. 1933): 49.

21. Alice Kessler-Harris, *Out to Work: A History of Wage-Earning Women in the United States* (New York: Oxford University Press, 1982), 229, 256; Lois Scharf, *To Work and to Wed: Female Employment, Feminism, and the Great Depression* (Westport, Conn.: Greenwood Press, 1980), 100–101.

22. I use the term *techniques of the self* in the senses derived from Marcel Mauss's concept of "technologies of the body" (which Jennifer Craik has linked to fashion) and Michel Foucault's concept of "a break with one's past identity" and a "symbolic, ritual, and theatrical" or verbal self-reconstitution. Michel Foucault, "Technologies of the Self," in *Technologies of the Self: A Seminar with Michel Foucault,* ed. L. Martin, H. Gutman, and P. Hutton (London: Tavistock, 1988), 42–43; Jennifer Craik, *The Face of Fashion: Cultural Studies in Fashion* (London, Routledge, 1994).

23. Chris Schilling, *The Body and Social Theory* (London: Sage, 1993), 140.

24. Angela Partington, "Popular Fashion and Working-Class Affluence," in *Chic Thrills: A Fashion Reader,* ed. Juliet Ash and Elizabeth Wilson (Berkeley: University of California Press, 1993), 157.

25. Bernard Barber and Lyle S. Lobel, " 'Fashion' in Women's Clothes and the American Social System," in *Class, Status and Power,* ed. Reinhard Bendix and S. M. Lipset (The Free Press of Glencoe, 1961), 326, 329.

26. Satch LaValley, "Hollywood and Seventh Avenue: The Impact of Period Films on Fashion," in *Hollywood and History: Costume Design in Film,* ed. Edward Maeder (New York: Thames and Hudson; Los Angeles: Los Angeles County Museum of Art, 1987).

27. Roland Marchand, *Advertising the American Dream* (Berkeley: University of California Press, 1985), 197.

28. "The Unseen Label," *Vogue* 76, 9 (Oct. 1930): 66.

29. Jane Mulvagh, *Vogue History of Twentieth-Century Fashion* (London: Viking Penguin, 1988), 134, 186–87.

30. Mike Featherstone, *Consumer Culture and Postmodernism* (London: Sage, 1991), 20.

31. Cited in Georgina Howell, *In Vogue: Seventy-five Years of Style* (London: Condé Nast Books, 1991), 72.

32. Elizabeth Wilson, *Adorned in Dreams: Fashion and Modernity* (London: Virago, 1985), 124.

33. Ella Shohat, "Gender and Culture of Empire: Toward a Feminist Ethnography of the Cinema," *Quarterly Review of Film and Video* 13, 1–3 (1991): 68.

34. Cf. Rebecca Bell-Metereau, *Hollywood Androgyny* (New York: Columbia University Press, 1993).

1. Consumer Fashion and Class

1. Claudia B. Kidwell and Margaret C. Christman, *Suiting Everyone: The Democratization of Clothing in America* (Washington, D.C.: Smithsonian Institution Press, 1974), 149.

2. William Leach, *Land of Desire: Merchants, Power, and the Rise of a New American Culture* (New York: Vintage Books, 1993), 300; Christopher Breward, *The Culture of Fashion: A New History of Fashionable Dress* (Manchester: Manchester University Press, 1995), 181–225; Kidwell and Christman, *Suiting Everyone*, passim; Stephen Norwood, *Labor's Flaming Youth: Telephone Operators and Worker Militancy, 1878–1923* (Urbana: University of Illinois Press, 1990), 13.

3. Robert S. Lynd and Helen Merrell Lynd, *Middletown, A Study in Contemporary American Culture* (New York: Harcourt, Brace and Company, 1929), 161. For a description of eighteenth- and early-nineteenth-century uses of fashion to distinguish between classes and occupations, see Richard Sennett, *The Fall of Public Man: On the Social Psychology of Capitalism* (New York: Vintage, 1978), 64–72.

4. Christine Frederick, *Selling Mrs. Consumer* (New York: The Business Bourse, 1929), 50.

5. Frank R. Coutant, "Where Are We Bound in Marketing Research?" *The Journal of Marketing* 1, 1 (July 1936): 28–34; Leach, *Land of Desire*, 300.

6. Kidwell and Christman, *Suiting Everyone*, 137, 143; Ben Fine and Ellen Leopold, *The World of Consumption* (London: Routledge, 1993), 95; Kidwell and Christman, *Suiting Everyone*, 165, 175; Florence S. Richards, *The Ready-To-Wear Industry 1900–1950* (New York: Fairchild Publications, 1951), 21; Frederick, *Selling Mrs. Consumer*, 109.

7. Leach, *Land of Desire*, 94.

8. Fine and Leopold, *The World of Consumption*, 170.

9. Roland Marchand, *Advertising the American Dream: Making Way for Modernity, 1920–1940* (Berkeley, Calif.: University of California Press, 1985), 121.

10. Frederick, *Selling Mrs. Consumer*, 251, 17; cited in Marchand, *Advertising the American Dream*, 66.

11. Michael B. Miller, *The Bon Marché: Bourgeois Culture and the Department Store, 1869–1920* (Princeton, N.J.: Princeton University Press, 1981), 186; David Chaney "The Department Store as a Cultural Form," *Theory Culture and Society* 1, 3 (1983): 28; Elaine S. Abelson, *When Ladies Go a Thieving: Middle Class Shoplifters in the Victorian Department Store* (Oxford: Oxford University Press, 1989), 21; Leach, *Land of Desire*, 31.

12. Cited in Neil Harris, "The Drama of Consumer Desire," in *Yankee Enterprise: The Rise of the American System of Manufactures,* ed. O. Mayr and R. Post (Washington, D.C.: Smithsonian Institution Press, 1981), 194; Miller, *The Bon Marché,* 197–206; Leslie Camhi, "Stealing Femininity: Department Store Kleptomania as Sexual Disorder," *differences: A Journal of Feminist Cultural Studies* 5, 1 (1993): 26–45; Nancy Green, "Art and Industry: The Language of Modernization in the Production of Fashion," *French Historical Studies* 18, 3 (spring 1994): 735.

13. Frederick, *Selling Mrs. Consumer,* 43.

14. Cited in T. J. Jackson Lears, *Fables of Abundance: A Cultural History of Advertising in America* (New York: Basic Books, 1994), 225.

15. Frederick, *Selling Mrs. Consumer,* 46, 21; Marchand, *Advertising the American Dream,* 66; Lears, *Fables of Abundance,* 230.

16. Harris, "The Drama of Consumer Desire," 212.

17. Jackson Lears notes that economist Simon Patten (1852–1922), one of the first to declare an American "era of abundance," was at pains to counter entrenched Protestant fears that an end to material scarcity would morally corrupt the working class. Patten, in Lear's words, emphasized that consumer goods would "keep people striving for more things as they struggled to maintain an ever-rising standard of living." In 1925, George Frederick echoed Patten when he emphasized the ability of advertising to inspire workers "to work harder to get the latest model." Lears, *Fables of Abundance,* 113–14, 227.

18. Frieda Wiegand McFarland, *Good Taste in Dress* (Peoria, Ill.: Manual Arts Press, 1936), 71.

19. Margaretta Byers with Consuelo Kamholz, *Designing Women: The Art, Technique, and Cost of Being Beautiful* (New York: Simon and Schuster, 1938), 116.

20. David Chierichetti, *Hollywood Costume Design* (New York: Harmony Books, 1976), 14; "Adhere to Your Type Religiously If You Would Be Smartly Gowned," *Screen News* 4, 47 (Nov. 28, 1925): 12; Paul Nystrom, *The Economics of Fashion* (New York: Roland Press, 1928), 480; Elizabeth Wilson, *Adorned in Dreams: Fashion and Modernity* (London: Virago, 1985), 124.

21. Nystrom, *The Economics of Fashion,* 480, 476.

22. Frederick, *Selling Mrs. Consumer,* 25; Margaret Story, *Individuality and Clothes* (New York: Funk and Wagnalls Co., 1930), 13–38.

23. McFarland, *Good Taste in Dress,* 74–75; Georgina Howell, *In Vogue: Seventy-five Years of Style* (London: Condé Nast Books, 1991), 72; Maureen Turim, "Fashion Shapes: Film, the Fashion Industry, and the Image of Women," *Socialist Review* 13, 5 (1983): 79–97; Kathy Peiss, "Making Up, Making Over: Cosmetics, Consumer Culture, and Women's Identity," in *The Sex of Things: Gender and Consumption in Historical Perspective,* ed. Victoria de Grazia and Ellen Furlough (Berkeley: University of California Press, 1996), 311–36.

24. This distinction should not be confused with an earlier shift from the Enlightenment belief in "natural character," which is defined by Richard Sennett

as the "common thread running through mankind" that could only be affected through the individual moderation of desires, to the nineteenth-century notion of the "direct expression of the 'inner' self." By the early twentieth century, Susman suggests, the definition of this "inner self" in terms of moral character was overshadowed by the concept of "personality," a more behavioral representation of the self. Cf. Sennett, *The Fall of Public Man,* 152–53.

25. Cf. T. J. Jackson Lears, "From Salvation to Self-Realization: Advertising and the Roots of the Consumer Culture, 1880–1930," in *The Culture of Consumption: Critical Essays in American History, 1880–1980,* ed. Richard W. Fox and T. J. Jackson Lears (New York: Pantheon Books, 1983), 1–38.

26. Charles W. Morris, introduction to *Mind, Self, and Society,* by George H. Mead, ed. C. W. Morris (Chicago: University of Chicago Press, 1934), v; John P. Hewitt, *Self and Society: A Symbolic Interactionist Social Psychology,* 3d ed. (Boston: Allyn and Bacon, 1984), 1–22.

27. P. F. Valentine, "What Is Personality?" *Scientific American* 15, 4 (Apr. 1937): 238–39.

28. "How's Your Personality?" *Saturday Evening Post* 206 (Sept. 16, 1933): 36; "Measurement of Personality," *Science* 80 (Dec. 28, 1934): 605–8; "A Workable Cue to Happiness and Personality," *Reader's Digest* 30, 182 (June 1937): 1–5; "Personality Can Be Acquired," *Reader's Digest* 29, 176 (Dec. 1936): 1–4; "Building a Personality," *Reader's Digest* 30 (May 1937): 79–81, rpt. from *Physical Culture,* 1931; "I'm a New Woman," *Reader's Digest* 36, 218 (June 1940): 9–11, rpt. from *The Forum,* 1940; William S. Walsh, *Cultivating Personality* (New York: E. P. Dutton and Co., 1930); Sadie Rae Shellow, *How to Develop Your Personality* (New York: Harper, 1932); Arthur G. Melvin, *Building Personality* (New York: John Day Co., 1934); Mildred Graves Ryan, *Your Clothes and Personality* (New York: D. Appleton-Century Co., 1937); Margaret E. Bennett and Harold C. Hand, *Designs for Personality* (New York: McGraw Hill, 1938).

29. Kay Austin, *What Do You Want for $1.98?: A Guide to Intelligent Shopping* (New York: Carrick and Evans, 1938), 25.

30. Fenja Gunn, *The Artificial Face: A History of Cosmetics* (Newton Abbot: David and Charles, 1973), 128, 139; Lillian Russell, "Beauty as a Factor in Success on the Stage," *Woman Beautiful* 4 (Apr. 1910): 39.

31. Jeanne Allen, "The Film Viewer as Consumer," *Quarterly Review of Film Studies* 5, 4 (fall 1980): 488; Nan Enstad, "Dressed for Adventure: Working Women and Silent Movie Serials in the 1910s," *Feminist Studies* 21, 1 (spring 1995): 74; Prudence Glynn, *In Fashion: Dress in the Twentieth Century* (New York: Oxford University Press, 1978), 73. On tie-ins more generally, see Janet Staiger, "Announcing Wares, Winning Patrons, Voicing Ideals: Thinking about the History and Theory of Film Advertising," *Cinema Journal* 29, 3 (spring 1990): 10–14; Margaret Farrand Thorp, *America at the Movies* (New Haven, Conn.: Yale University Press, 1939), 246–47.

32. Cited in Elizabeth Leese, *Costume Design in the Movies* (New York: Ungar, 1978), 10–11; also see Peter Wollen, "Strike A Pose," *Sight and Sound* 5, 3 (Mar. 1995): 12; Lucy Davis, "The Girl on the Cover," *Photoplay* 7, 2 (Jan. 1915): 35–37; Grace Corson, "Screen Inspired Readymades," *Photoplay* 27, 6 (May 1925): 49–53.

33. Howard Mandelbaum and Eric Myers, *Screen Deco* (New York: St. Martin's, 1985), 32–34.

34. Donald Albrecht, *Designing Dreams: Modern Architecture in the Movies* (London: Thames and Hudson; New York: Harper and Row, 1986), 7, 40.

35. David Bordwell, Janet Staiger, and Kristin Thompson, *The Classical Hollywood Cinema: Film Style and Mode of Production to 1960* (New York: Columbia University Press, 1985), 355.

36. J. Walter Thompson Collection, Staff Meeting Files, May 12, 1930, at the John Hartman Center for Sales, Advertising and Marketing History, Duke University.

37. Dorothy Donnell, "Are You a Screen Shopper?" *Motion Picture*, Sept. 1930, 70.

38. Charles Eckert, "The Carole Lombard in Macy's Window," in *Fabrications: Costume and the Female Body,* ed. Jane Gaines and Charlotte Herzog (New York: Routledge, 1990), 115.

39. Charlotte Herzog and Jane Gaines, "'Puffed Sleeves before Tea Time': Joan Crawford, Adrian and Women Audiences," in *Stardom: Industry of Desire,* ed. Christine Gledhill (London: Routledge, 1991), 78.

40. Cf. "Actress Designs Own Gowns for Screen Appearances," *Screen News* 3, 36 (Sept. 6, 1924): 10; "Barbara Coming West with Own Personal Modiste," *Screen News* 2, 40 (Oct. 6, 1923): 2. Studios required even star performers to supply their own modern costumes until the late teens; cf. Frances Agnes, *Motion Picture Acting* (New York: Reliance Newspaper Syndicate, 1913), 76–77; Lillian Conlon, "My Lady Favorite's Wardrobe De Luxe," *Motion Picture Classic* 3, 1 (Sept. 1916): 53.

41. Howell, *In Vogue,* 72; Cecil Beaton, "Hollywood Goes Refined," *Vogue* 77, 12 (June 15, 1931): 34–35.

42. Harold Seton, "The Verdict of the Vanderbilts," *Motion Picture Magazine* 27 (Feb. 1924): 27–28.

43. Herzog and Gaines, "'Puffed Sleeves before Tea Time,'" 89; Eleanor Barry "You'll Be in Hollywood Yet," *Harper's Bazaar* 2668 (Feb. 1935): 39–43; see also "Made in Hollywood," *Vogue* 87, 11 (June 1, 1936): 102.

44. Katherine Albert, "Hollywood Leads Paris in Fashions!" *Photoplay* 36, 6 (Nov. 1929): 56–57, 139.

45. William P. Gains, "Hollywood Snubs Paris: Movie Capital Is Self-Reliant as a Style Center," *Photoplay* 45, 5 (Apr. 1934): 78–79, 107.

46. Cf. Adelia Bird, "Dresses You Could Really Wear," *Modern Screen* 10, 3 (Feb. 1935): 56–58, 80; Janet Dare, "The $25-a-Week Girl Can Dress Well, Too!" *Movie Classic* 8, 6 (Aug. 1935): 50–51; "Practical Styles in Crawford Pix," *MGM Studio News* 11, 2 (Aug. 8, 1935): n.p.

47. Lois Shirley, "Your Clothes Come from Hollywood," *Photoplay* 35, 3 (Feb. 1929): 70–71.

48. Virginia T. Lane, "Fashions: Yesterday, Today and Tomorrow," *Motion Picture* 51, 1 (Feb. 1936): 45; Virginia T. Lane "Adding Common Sense to Glamor," *Modern Screen* 9, 1 (Dec. 1934): 56–57, 58, 101.

49. Margery Wells, "Screen Stars' Dresses and Hats for You, and You, and You," *Modern Screen* 7, 6 (May 1934): 72–73.

50. Research by Charlotte Herzog and Jane Gaines has cast doubt on the number of Cinema Fashions Shops that Waldman actually opened, since they were unable to substantiate the numbers published in *Fortune.* See Herzog and Gaines, "'Puffed Sleeves before Tea-Time,'" 88; Press Book, *Imitation of Life,* dir. John M. Stahl, Universal, 1934; "Cinema Fashions," *Fortune* 15, 1 (Jan. 1937): 44.

51. Advertisements in *Photoplay* 43, 2 (Jan. 1933): 62–67; *Photoplay* 43, 3 (Mar. 1933): 64–69.

52. *Saturday Evening Post,* May 18, 1935, n.p., clipping, Academy of Motion Picture Arts and Sciences Library.

53. Paramount Studios press release 1938, Academy of Motion Picture Arts and Sciences Margaret Herrick Library, Travis Banton files.

54. "Adrian and Woody, pt. 1," *Mode Historique* (winter 1982): 1–3.

55. "Hollywood," *Harper's Bazaar,* 2713 (Sept. 1, 1938): 106–7; "Dresses You Could Really Wear," *Modern Screen* 10, 3 (Feb. 1935): 56–58; "Classic Stresses Practical Dresses—That Are Easy to Make," *Movie Classic* 9, 5 (Jan. 1936): 49.

56. Cf. Peggy Hopkins Joyce, "U.S. Garb Best," and "Chicago Society Leader Here to Take Hollywood Styles Back to Midwest," unidentified newspaper clippings, 1933, Academy of Motion Picture Arts and Sciences Margaret Herrick Library.

57. Eckert, "The Carole Lombard in Macy's Window," 33.

58. Herzog and Gaines, "'Puffed Sleeves before Tea-Time,'" 82, 87–88.

59. Ibid., 83.

60. Dorothy Spensley, "The Most Copied Girl in the World," *Motion Picture Magazine* 53, 4 (May 1937): 30–31; cf. "Each of Crawford's Films Leaves Its Mark on Fashions," *MGM Studio News* 2, 13 (Sept. 24, 1935): n.p.

61. Madame Sylvia, "If You Would Have a Figure Like Harlow," *Modern Screen* 11, 6 (Nov. 1935).

62. Lane, "Adding Common Sense to Glamor," 56–58.

63. Richard W. Pollay, "The Subsiding Sizzle: A History of Print Advertising, 1900–1980," *Journal of Marketing* 49, 3 (1985): 29; Marchand, *Advertising the American Dream,* 14, 52–53, 97–99; J. Walter Thompson Collection, Staff Meeting Files, "The Federal Trade Commission and the Tainted Testimonial," Aug. 4, 1931, at the John Hartman Center for Sales, Advertising and Marketing History, Duke University.

64. Marchand, *Advertising the American Dream,* 948.

65. Donnell, "Are You a Screen Shopper?" 71.

66. "The Inside of the Testimonial Racket," *Advertising and Selling* 16, 5 (Jan. 7, 1931): 56.

67. "Glenda Golden" appears to have been a fictional star of the 1930s. She is, for example, the gold-digging chorus girl who is referred to but never actually seen in Frank Capra's film *Platinum Blonde* (1931).

68. The "Sheer Silk" and "Kissable Lipstick" advertisements border on product placement, since they are identical to real ads run in *Photoplay* for "Real Silk" stockings and "Kissproof" lipstick.

69. Audrey Rivers, "Connie Bennett's Huge Salary Starts Trouble," *Movie Classic* 1, 4 (Dec. 1931): 43; Bennett also came from an elite stage family and was one of only a few Hollywood actresses to be regularly featured in *Vogue* in the early 1930s.

70. Rose Colefax, letter captioned "What Price Hollywood," *Photoplay* 41, 4 (Sept. 1932): 12.

71. Carolyn Van Wyck, "Finding Your Type in the Stars," *Photoplay* 44, 5 (Oct. 1933): 94.

72. Adele W. Fletcher, "Stop Making Excuses! You Can Learn to Dress," *Modern Screen* 9, 1 (Dec. 1934): 56.

73. Adele W. Fletcher, "Glamor Is Not a Gift," *Modern Screen* 10, 6 (May 1935): 28.

74. Ruth Biery, "The New 'Shady Dames' of the Screen," *Photoplay* 42, 3 (Aug. 1932): 28.

75. Neva O'Hammer, letter, *Photoplay* 42, 5 (Oct. 1932): 16.

76. Herzog and Gaines, "'Puffed Sleeves before Tea Time,'" 84–86.

77. Ibid., 86; they cite "Our Dancing Lady," *Silver Screen* 3, 12 (Oct. 1933): 49.

78. "If Winter Comes," *Photoplay* 35, 1 (Dec. 1928): 60–61; photo caption, *Photoplay* 37, 1 (Dec. 1929): 85.

79. Richard W. Pollay, "The Subsiding Sizzle," 31; cf. Katherine Albert, "Granddaughter of an Empress: Hollywood Was Harboring Royalty and Didn't Know It," *Photoplay* 40, 4 (Sept. 1931): 28–29; Basil Lee, "The Real First Lady of Films," *Photoplay* 46, 2 (July 1934): 28–29.

80. "Who Is Hollywood's Social Leader?" *Photoplay* 39, 1 (Dec. 1930): 32–33.

81. Reginald Taviner, "Can Hollywood 'Take It'?" *Photoplay* 44, 1 (June 1933): 38–39.

82. Judith Mayne, *Directed by Dorothy Arzner* (Bloomington: Indiana University Press, 1994), 74.

83. Ibid., 106.

84. See Charlotte Herzog's description of this pattern in "Powder Puff Promotion: The Fashion Show in the Film," in *Fabrications: Costume and the Female Body,* ed. Jane Gaines and Charlotte Herzog (New York: Routledge, 1990), 134–59.

85. Lea Jacobs, *The Wages of Sin: Censorship and the Fallen Woman Film 1928–1942* (Madison: University of Wisconsin Press, 1991), 52.

86. Jack Jamison, "The City of Forgotten Nobles: Real Titled Folk of Old World's Aristocracy Are Lost in Shuffle of Hollywood's Reel Personalities," *Photoplay* 45, 5 (Apr. 1934): 74–75; "Brief Reviews," *Photoplay* 35, 1 (Dec. 1928): 8.

87. In 1930, Paramount invited Dietrich from Germany and gave her a Garbo makeover; in 1931, Warner's "contribution to the Dietrich-Garbo glamor school" was Lil Dagover; in 1931, Sari Maritza was briefly known as the star who "wears Paris gowns, speaks the most cultured British, had a Hungarian mother and was born in China"; while Tala Birell was described as "a Viennese with a Polish Mother, [who] speaks German, French, English and Polish"; "The New Exotics," *Photoplay* 41, 6 (May 1932): 74.

88. Jane Mulvagh, *Vogue History of Twentieth-Century Fashion* (London: Viking Penguin, 1988), 125.

89. Richard Dyer, *Stars* (London: British Film Institute, 1979), 36.

2. Style as Spectacle

1. Richard Dyer, "Entertainment and Utopia," in *Movies and Methods,* vol. 2, ed. Bill Nichols (Berkeley: University of California Press, 1985), 220–32.

2. Charles and Mirella Jona Affron, *Sets in Motion: Art Direction and Film Narrative* (New Brunswick, N.J.: Rutgers University Press, 1995), 145, 144.

3. Charlotte Herzog and Jane Gaines, "'Puffed Sleeves before Tea-Time':

Joan Crawford, Adrian and Women Audiences," in *Stardom: Industry of Desire*, ed. Christine Gledhill (London: Routledge, 1991), 81.

4. Jane Mulvagh, *Vogue History of Twentieth-Century Fashion* (London: Viking Penguin, 1988), 123.

5. Cf. Charlotte Herzog's description of this pattern in "Powder Puff Promotion: The Fashion Show in the Film," in *Fabrications: Costume and the Female Body*, ed. Jane Gaines and Charlotte Herzog (New York: Routledge, 1990), 134–59; for a discussion of early film spectacles, see Tom Gunning, "The Cinema of Attractions: Early Film, Its Spectator and the Avant-Garde," *Wide Angle* 8, 3–4 (1986): 63–70.

6. Richard Dyer, *Stars* (London: BFI Publishing, 1979); Barry King, "Articulating Stardom," in *Stardom: Industry of Desire*, ed. Christine Gledhill (London: Routledge, 1991), 176; James Naremore, *Acting in the Cinema* (Berkeley: University of California Press, 1988).

7. Alan Williams, *Republic of Images: A History of French Filmmaking* (Cambridge: Harvard University Press, 1992), 80.

8. Charles and Mirella Affron, *Sets in Motion*, 90–93.

9. Pam Cook, *Fashioning the Nation: Costume and Identity in British Cinema* (London: BFI Publishing, 1996), 52–53; cf. Stella Bruzzi, *Undressing Cinema* (London: BFI Publishing, 1997).

10. Tino Balio, *Grand Design: Hollywood as a Modern Business Enterprise, 1930–1939* (New York: Charles Scribner's Sons, 1993), 180.

11. Peter Wollen, "Strike A Pose," *Sight and Sound* 5, 3 (Mar. 1995): 12; "Showing Gowns on Living Models," *Merchants' Record and Show Window* 25 (Nov. 1909): 39, cited in William Leach, *Land of Desire: Merchants, Power and the Rise of a New American Culture* (New York: Viking Books, 1993), 95, 102.

12. Leach, *Land of Desire*, 103.

13. Gaylyn Studlar, *This Mad Masquerade: Stardom and Masculinity in the Jazz Age* (New York: Columbia University Press, 1996), 108, 283.

14. Wollen, "Strike A Pose," 12.

15. Florenz Ziegfeld, "Showman's Shifting Sands," *Ladies' Home Journal* June 1923: 23, cited in Rosaline Stone, *The Ziegfeld Follies: A Study of Theatrical Opulence from 1907 to 1931* (Ann Arbor: University of Michigan Press, 1985), 150.

16. "Dress and the Picture," *Moving Picture World* 7, 2 (July 9, 1910): 73–74.

17. Cited in Elizabeth Leese, *Costume Design in the Movies* (New York: Dover Publications, 1991), 9.

18. Hugh Hoffman, "New York Fashion Show in Pictures," *Moving Picture World* 18, 1 (Oct. 4, 1913): 32.

19. Leese, *Costume Design in the Movies*, 11.

20. *Vogue*, Oct. 27, 1930: 16h.

21. Leach, *Land of Desire*, 95, 309; Lazare Teper, *The Women's Garment Industry: An Economic Analysis* (New York: International Ladies' Garment Workers' Union, Educational Dept., 1937), 31–32.

22. Press book for *Fashions of 1934*, 24.

23. For a detailed description of this sequence, see Herzog, "Powder Puff Promotion," 137–50.

24. This is pointed out by Martin Rubin, who also offers a comparison of the early Berkeley backstage musicals and the integrated style of the Mark

Sandrich films with Astaire and Rogers; cf. Martin Rubin, *Showstoppers: Busby Berkeley and the Tradition of Spectacle* (New York: Columbia University Press, 1993), 40–41.

25. Rick Altman, *The American Film Musical* (Bloomington: Indiana University Press, 1987), 204, 234.

26. Florenz Ziegfeld, "What Becomes of the *Ziegfeld Follies* Girls?" *Pictorial Revue* May 1925: 13; cited in Stone, *The Ziegfeld Follies*, 81.

27. Geraldine Maschio, *The Ziegfeld Follies: Form, Content, and Signification of an American Revue* (Ann Arbor: University of Michigan Press, 1981), 22–26.

28. Stone, *The Ziegfeld Follies*, 147.

29. Lady Lucile Duff Gordon, *Discretions and Indiscretions* (New York: Stokes, 1932), cited in Susan Perez Prichard, *Film Costume: A Bibliography* (Metuchen, N.J.: Scarecrow Press, 1981), 115.

30. Maschio, *The Ziegfeld Follies*, 74–75; Stone, *The Ziegfeld Follies*, 204.

31. Stone, *The Ziegfeld Follies*, 149.

32. Armando Riverol, *Live from Atlantic City: The History of the Miss America Pageant before, after and in Spite of Television* (Bowling Green, Ohio: Bowling Green State University Popular Press, 1992), 14–19, 26–33.

33. Cf. Mikhail Bakhtin, *Rabelais and His World,* trans. Helene Iswolsky (Cambridge: MIT Press, 1968).

34. Bob Pike and Dave Martin, *The Genius of Busby Berkeley* (Reseda, Calif.: Creative Film Society, 1973), 64; cited in Paula Rabinowitz, "Commodity Fetishism: Women in Gold Diggers of 1933," *Film Reader 5* (1982): 147.

35. Rabinowitz, "Commodity Fetishism," 143, 144.

36. Stone, *The Ziegfeld Follies*, 210.

37. Critiques of these films are also frequently based on a separation of musical numbers from both narrative context and star intertext; cf. Rabinowitz, "Commodity Fetishism," 147; Lucy Fischer, *Shot/Countershot: Film Tradition and Women's Cinema* (Princeton, N.J.: Princeton University Press, 1989), 143–44.

38. Fischer, *Shot/Countershot,* 137.

39. In an accurate depiction of the gendered division of garment labor, men's hands operate the tools, while women are seen hunched over tables doing handwork in a brief long shot of the "dress factory."

40. Jeanne Allen, "The Film Viewer as Consumer," *Quarterly Review of Film Studies* 5, 4 (fall 1980): 495.

41. "Cinema Fashions," *Fortune* 15, 1 (Jan. 1937): 44.

42. Mulvagh, *Vogue History of Twentieth-Century Fashion,* 184.

43. Cf. Angela Partington, "Popular Fashion and Working-Class Affluence," in *Chic Thrills: A Fashion Reader,* ed. Juliet Ash and Elizabeth Wilson (Berkeley: University of California Press, 1993), 145–61.

44. Herzog, "Powder Puff Promotion," 155.

45. Sample advertisement, *Fashions of 1934* press book, n.p.

46. Richard Sennett, *The Fall of Public Man: On the Social Psychology of Capitalism* (New York: Vintage, 1978), 176.

47. Ibid., 174, 175–76.

48. Roberta Pearson, *Eloquent Gestures: The Transformation of Performance Style in the Griffith Biograph Films* (Berkeley: University of California Press, 1992), 21–37.

49. Jane Gaines, "Costume and Narrative: How Dress Tells the Woman's

Story," in *Fabrications: Costume and the Female Body,* ed. Jane Gaines and Charlotte Herzog (New York: Routledge, 1990), 181, 186, 188.

50. "Producers Aim Classics," *Motion Picture Herald,* Aug. 15, 1936, 13; cited in Balio, *Grand Design,* 179; Balio, *Grand Design,* 180.

51. Sumiko Higashi, *Cecil B. DeMille and American Culture: The Silent Era* (Berkeley: University of California Press, 1994), 145; Balio, *Grand Design,* 189, 179.

52. Satch LaValley, "Hollywood and Seventh Avenue: The Impact of Period Films on Fashion," *Hollywood and History: Costume Design in Film,* ed. Edward Maeder (New York: Thames and Hudson; Los Angeles County Museum of Art, 1987), 87.

53. Cook, *Fashioning the Nation,* 7, 46–47, 61.

54. Sue Harper, *Picturing the Past: The Rise and Fall of the British Costume Film* (London: BFI Publishing, 1994), 132.

55. Cf. Susan Perez Prichard, *Film Costume: An Annotated Bibliography* (Metuchen, N.J.: Scarecrow Press, 1981), 483–563.

56. Vivian Sobchack, "'Surge and Splendor': A Phenomenology of the Hollywood Historical Epic," *Representations* 29 (winter 1990): 29.

57. "Facts That Make 'Antoinette' Most Fabulous Picture Screen Ever Attempted," *MGM Studio News* 5, 2 (Mar. 23, 1938): n.p.; "Heavy Costumes," *MGM Studio News* 5, 6 (Aug. 15, 1938): n.p.; "Royal Robe Uses 2,500 Ermine Pelts," *MGM Studio News* 5, 6 (Aug. 15, 1938): n.p.; "Shearer Gowns Set New Record," *MGM Studio News* 4 (Dec. 24, 1937): n.p.; Cal York, "Close-Ups and Long Shots," *Photoplay* 44, 4 (Sept. 1933): 94.

58. Ben Fine and Ellen Leopold, *The World of Consumption* (London: Routledge, 1993), 102.

59. Sobchack, "'Surge and Splendor,'" 36.

60. Helen Dale, "Two Queens Were Born in Sweden," *Photoplay* 44, 5 (Oct. 1933): 28–29.

61. James Reid, "How Hepburn Is 'Queening' It," *Motion Picture* 51, 6 (July 1936): 66–67.

62. Ruth Rankin, "They're All Queening It," *Photoplay* 45, 1 (Dec. 1933): 34–35.

63. Both quotations are cited in LaValley, "Hollywood and Seventh Avenue," 80, 78.

64. Kathleen Howard, "Fashion Letter for November," *Photoplay* 50, 5 (Nov. 1936): 90.

65. Cal York, "Close-Ups and Long Shots," *Photoplay* 44, 6 (Nov. 1933): 25.

66. Louise Duggan, "Hot from Paris: Mlle. Chanel Tells Hollywood and You How to Dress," *Motion Picture Classic* 33, 4 (June 1931): 29; "Going Hollywood in Fashion," *Photoplay* 41, 2 (Jan. 1932): 110; Seymour, "Fashion Foibles," *Photoplay* 41, 1 (Dec. 1931): 118.

67. Balio, *Grand Design,* 207; Anne Hollander, "Movie Clothes: More Real Than Life," *New York Times Magazine,* Dec. 1, 1974: 68, 70–71; LaValley, "Hollywood and Seventh Avenue," 78.

68. W. Robert LaVine, *In a Glamorous Fashion: The Fabulous Years of Hollywood Costume Design* (New York: Charles Scribner's Sons, 1980), 92–93.

69. Adrian, "Garbo as Camille," *Vogue,* Nov. 15, 1936: 70.

70. Seymour, "Little Tricks That Make Hollywood Fashions Individual," *Photoplay* 41, 4 (Sept. 1932): 104.

71. For a discussion of the probable inaccuracy of Waldman's claim, see Herzog and Gaines, "'Puffed Sleeves before Tea-Time,'" 88.

72. Gaines, "Costume and Narrative," 180.

73. See chapter 4 for a more detailed discussion of these fashion trends.

74. Photo caption for *Today We Live, Photoplay* 43, 2 (Jan. 1933): 80; Seymour, "Little Tricks That Make Hollywood Fashions Individual," 104; publicity photo caption for *Letty Lynton,* Academy of Motion Picture Arts and Sciences Library.

75. Jane Gaines has proposed a very different reading of this metallic dress, arguing that its "textural rigidity" signifies Letty's "heartlessness" and transformation into a murderess. This is a very plausible reading if Letty's actions are seen as purely selfish and immoral; it seems to me, however, that the film's narrative and formal elements work hard against such a reading, since she is allowed to go entirely unpunished for the killing.

3. Hollywood Exoticism

1. Kathy Peiss, "Making Faces: The Cosmetics Industry and the Cultural Construction of Gender, 1890–1930," *Genders* 7 (spring 1990): 164.

2. David Palumbo-Liu, "The Bitter Tea of Frank Capra," *positions* 3, 3 (1995): 782.

3. Ella Shohat, "Gender and Culture of Empire: Toward a Feminist Ethnography of the Cinema," *Quarterly Review of Film and Video* 13, 1–3 (1991): 68.

4. Cf. Gaylyn Studlar, *This Mad Masquerade: Stardom and Masculinity in the Jazz Age* (New York: Columbia University Press, 1996).

5. Feature film entry for *Imitation of Life, The AFI Catalog of Motion Pictures Produced in the U.S.: Feature Films, 1931–1940,* exec. ed. Patricia King Hanson, assoc. ed. Alan Gevinson (Berkeley, Calif.: University of California Press, 1993), 1013; Susan Courtney, "(De)Coding Hollywood's Fantasy of Miscegenation," paper given at the Society for Cinema Studies Conference, Dallas, Tex., Mar. 1996.

6. McKinney's mother is also described as a woman "of light skin, who might have Spanish blood"; Herbert Howe, "A Jungle Lorelei," *Photoplay* 36, 1 (June 1929): 118–19.

7. Ella Shohat and Robert Stam, *Unthinking Eurocentrism: Multiculturalism and the Media* (London: Routledge, 1994), 189, 224, 220.

8. Arthur Marwick, *Beauty in History: Society, Politics, and Personal Appearance c. 1500 to the Present* (London: Thames and Hudson, 1988), 70.

9. Gilbert Vail, *A History of Cosmetics in America* (New York: Toilet Goods Association, 1947), 77–78, 87, 98–99; Kate de Castelbajac, *The Face of the Century: One Hundred Years of Makeup and Style* (New York: Rizzoli, 1995), 12.

10. De Castelbajac, *The Face of the Century,* 46.

11. Peiss, "Making Faces," 147; Lois Banner, *American Beauty: A Social History through Two Centuries of the American Idea, Ideal, and Image of the Beautiful Woman* (New York: Knopf, 1983), 214.

12. Mark H. Haller, *Eugenics: Hereditarian Attitudes in American Thought* (New Brunswick, N.J.: Rutgers University Press, 1963), 153.

13. Marwick, *Beauty in History,* 245; Banner, *American Beauty,* 207, 217.

14. Fenja Gunn, *The Artificial Face: A History of Cosmetics* (Newton Abbot:

David and Charles, 1973), 128, 139; Lillian Russell, "Beauty as a Factor in Success on the Stage," *Woman Beautiful* 4 (Apr. 1910): 39.

15. Vail, *A History of Cosmetics in America,* 102.

16. Helena Rubenstein, *My Life for Beauty* (London: Bodley, Head, 1964), 58–59.

17. Fred E. Basten with Robert Salvatore and Paul A. Kaufman, *Max Factor's Hollywood: Glamour, Movies, Make-Up* (Santa Monica, Calif.: General Publishing Group, 1995), 34, 90.

18. Alicia Annas, "The Photogenic Formula: Hairstyles and Makeup in Historical Films," in *Hollywood and History: Costume Design in Film* (London: Thames and Hudson; Los Angeles County Museum of Art, 1987), 55–56.

19. De Castelbajac, *The Face of the Century,* 75.

20. Ruth Biery, "The New 'Shady Dames' of the Screen," *Photoplay* 42, 3 (Aug. 1932): 28; in letters to the editor, fans reportedly "liked 'Letty Lynton' but wished Joan wouldn't use so much eye and mouth make-up"; "The Audience Talks Back," *Photoplay* 42, 3 (Aug. 1932): 6–7.

21. Jeanette Eaton, "The Cosmetic Urge," *Harper's Magazine* 162 (Feb. 1931): 323.

22. Cf. Carolyn van Wyck, "Photoplay's Own Beauty Shop," *Photoplay* 41, 5 (Apr. 1932): 55.

23. Dorothy Manners, "These Stars Changed Their Faces—And So Can You!" *Motion Picture* 45, 5 (June 1933): 32–33.

24. Carolyn van Wyck, "Friendly Advice on Girls' Problems: What Any Girl Can Do with Make-Up," *Photoplay* 38, 3 (Aug. 1930): 18, 116.

25. Max Factor advertisement, *Photoplay* 38, 3 (Aug. 1930): 101.

26. Adele Whitely Fletcher, "Miracle Men at Work to Make You Lovelier," *Photoplay* 53, 7 (July 1939): 26.

27. Carolyn van Wyck "Photoplay's Own Beauty Shop," *Photoplay* 53, 1 (Jan. 1939): 66.

28. Basten, *Max Factor's Hollywood,* 80; Roland Marchand, *Advertising the American Dream: Making Way for Modernity, 1920–1940* (Berkeley: University of California Press, 1985), 132–40; advertisement, *Photoplay* 53, 9 (Sept. 1939): 77.

29. Marie du Bois, "What Is Sun-Tan Doing to Cosmetics?" *Advertising and Selling* 13, 4 (June 12, 1929): 19.

30. De Castelbajac, *The Face of the Century,* 44; advertisement in *Photoplay* 36, 1 (June 1929): 76; advertisement, *Photoplay* 36, 3 (Aug. 1929): 105.

31. Dorothy Spensley, "The Most Copied Girl in the World," *Motion Picture* 53, 4 (May 1937): 30–31.

32. Peiss, "Making Faces," 160.

33. In her early career, Myrna Loy's heavy-lidded eyes and round face inspired producers to cast her in a series of "native" roles, including Chinese, Malay, Hindu, Egyptian, and French African women. In 1936, however, a *Photoplay* caption noted that whereas "[s]he used to play slant-eyed Oriental seductress roles, today she is the ideal screen wife."

34. Photograph caption, *Photoplay* 36, 2 (July 1929): 22.

35. Edward Sakamoto, "Anna May Wong and the Dragon-Lady Syndrome," *Los Angeles Times,* July 12, 1987: n.p.

36. Palumbo-Liu, "The Bitter Tea of Frank Capra," 761.

37. "New Pictures," *Photoplay* 35, 6 (May 1929): 21.

38. Denise Caine, "Beauty Is Kin Deep!" *Motion Picture* 54, 2 (Sept. 1937): 51.

39. Cited in Studlar, *This Mad Masquerade,* 163; Palumbo-Liu, "The Bitter Tea of Frank Capra," 761.

40. Thomas Cripps, *Slow Fade to Black: The Negro in American Film, 1900–1942* (New York: Oxford University Press, 1977), 94.

41. Ruth Vasey, "Foreign Parts: Hollywood's Global Distribution and the Representation of Ethnicity," *American Quarterly* 44, 4 (Dec. 1992): 625.

42. "U.S.' Overseas Panickers," *Variety* 112, 3 (Sept. 26, 1933): 3.

43. Kristin Thompson, *Exporting Entertainment: America in the World Film Market 1907–34* (London: BFI Publishing, 1985), 162.

44. Vasey, "Foreign Parts," 625.

45. David Selznick is said to have run Selznick International Pictures on this premise; Thomas Schatz, *The Genius of the System: Hollywood Filmmaking in the Studio Era* (New York: Pantheon, 1988), 178.

46. Cited in David Bordwell, Janet Staiger, and Kristin Thompson, *The Classical Hollywood Cinema: Film Style and Mode of Production to 1960* (New York: Columbia University Press, 1985), 355.

47. Cited in Fred Basten, *Glorious Technicolor* (New York: A. S. Barnes, 1980), 27.

48. Bordwell, Staiger, and Thompson, *The Classical Hollywood Cinema,* 356.

49. Virginia T. Lane, "Steffi Is a Perfect Type for Color," *Motion Picture* 52, 1 (Aug. 1936): 43.

50. Photograph caption, *Photoplay* 36, 1 (June 1929): 22; "Two New Exotics," *Photoplay* 41, 6 (May 1932): 74; photograph caption, *Motion Picture* 27, 3 (Apr. 1924): 21.

51. Madame Sylvia, "Garbo's Glamor . . . Mystery or Misery?" *Photoplay* 50, 6 (Dec. 1936): 56–57.

52. Vasey, "Foreign Parts," 629.

53. Advertisement in *Vogue,* Dec. 1, 1932: 3; "The Javanese influence," *Vogue,* Jan. 1, 1933: 28; advertisement in *Vogue,* Dec. 1, 1934: 117; advertisement in *Vogue,* Jan. 1, 1935: 79; *Vogue,* June 1, 1935: 44.

54. Advertisement in *Photoplay* 48, 7 (Dec. 1935): 110.

55. Advertisement in *Photoplay* 52, 10 (Oct. 1938): 90.

56. Ruth Waterbury, "Close Ups and Long Shots," *Photoplay* 52, 6 (June 1938): 13; Sara Hamilton, "Hedy Wine," *Photoplay* 52, 10 (Oct. 1938): 21.

57. Advertisement in *Photoplay* 52, 10 (Oct. 1938): 21; Basten, *Max Factor's Hollywood,* 139, 163; advertisement in *Photoplay* 52, 9 (Sept. 1938): 77; Carolyn van Wyck, "Photoplay's Beauty Shop," *Photoplay* 53, 11 (Nov. 1939): 10–11; Barbara Hayes, "Hedy Lamarr vs. Joan Bennett," *Photoplay* 53, 11 (Nov. 1939): 18–19.

58. Basten, *Max Factor's Hollywood,* 147.

59. Jan Fisher, "If You Want to Be a Glamorous Beauty," *Photoplay* 51, 11 (Nov. 1937): 5; Carolyn van Wyck, "Photoplay's Beauty Shop," *Photoplay* 52, 3 (Mar. 1938): 8.

60. The marketing strategy of encouraging women to buy different lipsticks to match their dresses began in 1931. Cf. Carolyn van Wyck, "Friendly Advice of Girls' Problems: New Make-Up Theory," *Photoplay* 40, 4 (Sept. 1931): 16; Carolyn van Wyck, "Photoplay's Beauty Shop," *Photoplay* 52, 1 (Jan. 1938): 60.

61. Several silent Tarzan films were made, but the first sound version was

released in 1932 with Johnny Weissmuller, who starred in the ongoing series until 1949.

62. Robert Littell, "Every One Likes Chocolate," *Vogue*, Nov. 1, 1936: 127.

63. Cf. James Naremore's discussion of *Cabin in the Sky* (1943) in *The Films of Vincente Minnelli* (New York: Cambridge University Press, 1993), 51–70.

64. Ana M. López, "Are All Latins from Manhattan? Hollywood, Ethnography and Cultural Colonialism," in *Mediating Two Worlds: Cinematic Encounters in the Americas,* ed. John King, Ana M. López, and Manuel Alvarado (London: BFI Publishing, 1993), 71.

65. "You Might Go to: Hawaii," *Vogue*, May 15, 1936: 66

66. Peiss, "Making Faces," 159; Vail, *A History of Cosmetics in America,* 74–78.

67. Reina Lewis, *Gendering Orientalism: Race Femininity and Representation* (New York: Routledge, 1996), 72.

68. Ibid., 113.

69. William Leach, *Land of Desire: Merchants, Power, and the Rise of a New American Culture* (New York: Vintage Books, 1993), 109.

70. Ibid., 110.

71. Richard Martin and Harold Koda, *Orientalism: Visions of the East in Western Dress* (New York: Metropolitan Museum of Art, 1994), 15, 35, 53, 73.

72. Leach, *Land of Desire,* 105.

73. Peter Wollen, *Raiding the Icebox: Reflections on Twentieth Century Culture* (London: Verso, 1993), 2.

74. Advertisement, *Vogue,* Apr. 1, 1936: 109.

75. Advertisement, *Vogue,* July 1, 1936: 82.

76. "China Influences the Young Modern," *Photoplay* 50, 2 (Aug. 1936): 64–65.

77. Jane Mulvagh, *Vogue History of Twentieth-Century Fashion* (London: Viking Penguin, 1988), 112.

78. "Schiaparelli among the Berbers," *Vogue,* Aug. 15, 1936: 44–45.

79. Frances Hughes, "Crystal Gazing into Fall's Fashion Futures," *Photoplay* 53, 8 (Aug. 1939): 65.

80. Photograph and caption, *Photoplay* 50, 1 (July 1935): 71.

4. Suitably Feminine

1. Elizabeth Wilson, *Adorned in Dreams: Fashion and Modernity* (London: Virago, 1985), 162.

2. The phrase "ladies with legs" is from the title of Mary Ann Powell's thesis, "Ladies with Legs: An Historical Survey of the Social Acceptability of Pants on Women 1851–1976" (master's thesis, University of Texas at Austin, 1977).

3. Leonard Hall, "The Perils of Marlene," *Photoplay* 39, 6 (May 1931): 37; photograph of Marlene Dietrich en route to the United States, *Motion Picture* 39, 6 (July 1930): 16.

4. Photograph and caption with Amelia Earhart, *Photoplay* 43, 6 (May 1933): 37; photograph with Dorothea Wieck, *Photoplay* 44, 2 (July 1933): 90.

5. Rosalind Shaffer, "Marlene Dietrich Tells Why She Wears Men's Clothes!" *Motion Picture* 45, 3 (Apr. 1933): 54–55.

6. Jack Smalley, "It Takes a Sherlock Holmes to Tell the Stars off the

Screen," *Motion Picture* 48, 6 (Jan. 1935): 45; Harry D. Wilson, "Why Garbo Plays Dumb," *Motion Picture* 42, 1 (Aug. 1931): 27.

7. Shaffer, "Marlene Dietrich Tells Why She Wears Men's Clothes!" 70, 54.

8. Ibid., 54.

9. Sybil DelGaudio, *Dressing the Part: Sternberg, Dietrich, and Costume* (Rutherford, N.J.: Fairleigh Dickinson University Press, 1993): 104–6; cf. Jack Babuscio, *Camp Grounds: Style and Homosexuality* (Amherst: University of Massachusetts Press, 1993): 30–32.

10. Andrea Weiss, *Vampires and Violets: Lesbians in Film* (New York: Penguin Books, 1993), 32.

11. Ibid., 42.

12. Unidentified newspaper clipping, Feb. 11, 1933, in the Academy of Motion Picture Arts and Sciences Margaret Herrick Library.

13. Photograph of Marlene Dietrich with husband and daughter, *Photoplay* 43, 2 (Jan. 1933): 110.

14. Valerie Steele, *Fashion and Eroticism* (New York: Oxford University Press, 1985), 227.

15. Ibid., 224–25.

16. Between Amelia Bloomer and Paul Poiret, a number of important fashion changes were initiated, most notably the replacement of the corset with the brassiere. A general narrowing of the female silhouette took place in the Edwardian era, which emphasized an S curve rather than the Victorian hourglass shape; this shape was popularized in the drawings of Charles Dana Gibson as the "Gibson Girl" look, which abandoned crinolines and hoops for a flared skirt worn with a "pouter-pigeon" blouse (called a shirtwaist) and, often, a "man-tailored" jacket and bow tie. Between 1892 and 1908, however, the Empire silhouette (with a high waist and straight skirt) began to compete with the S shape. This avant-garde look was used by both Isadora Duncan and Mario Fortuny in their fluid, neo-Greek dresses (1912–13), and it became the basis for Poiret's "corsetless" designs. Such outfits were, in fact, usually worn with a girdlelike boneless corset and a brassiere. With this high-breasted, narrow silhouette the brassiere-plus-girdle combination became the new foundation of mainstream women's fashion. Steele, *Fashion and Eroticism,* 226; Barbara Burman Baines, *Fashion Revivals from the Elizabethan Age to the Present Day* (London: B. T. Batsford Ltd., 1981), 54–59.

17. Cited in Maurine Weiner Greenwald, *Women, War, and Work: The Impact of World War I on Women Workers in the United States* (Ithaca, N.Y.: Cornell University Press, 1980), 127.

18. Powell, "Ladies with Legs," 137–38; Agnes Rogers, *Women Are Here to Stay* (New York: Harper and Bros., 1949), 83.

19. Alison Adburgham, *A Punch History of Manners and Modes, 1841–1940* (London: Hutchinson, 1961), 263.

20. Marjorie Garber, "Strike a Pose," *Sight and Sound* 2, 5 (Sept. 1992): 25.

21. Marjorie Garber, *Vested Interests: Cross-Dressing and Cultural Anxiety* (New York: HarperCollins, 1993), 17.

22. Cited in Barbara Schreier, "Sporting Wear," in *Men and Women: Dressing the Part,* ed. Claudia B. Kidwell and Valerie Steele (Washington, D.C.: Smithsonian Institution Press, 1989), 112.

23. Cited in Powell, "Ladies with Legs," 52.

24. Joan Riviere, "Womanliness as a Masquerade," in *Formations of*

Fantasy, ed. Victor Burgin, James Donald, and Cora Kaplan (London: Routledge, 1989), 38.

25. Cf. Judith Butler, *Gender Trouble* (New York: Routledge, 1990); Judith Butler, *Bodies That Matter: On the Discursive Limits of "Sex"* (New York: Routledge, 1993), 12–16; J. L. Austin, *How to Do Things with Words*, ed. J. O. Urmson and Marina Sbisà (Cambridge: Harvard University Press, 1955).

26. Butler, *Bodies That Matter*, 224, 230.

27. Butler, *Gender Trouble*, 34.

28. Steele, *Fashion and Eroticism*, 48.

29. Lee Hall, *Common Threads* (Boston: Little, Brown and Company, 1992), 85; Valerie Steele, "Dressing for Work," in *Men and Women: Dressing the Part*, ed. Claudia B. Kidwell and Valerie Steele (Washington, D.C.: Smithsonian Institution Press, 1989), 83.

30. Schreier, "Sporting Wear," 99.

31. Margaret A. Lowe, "From Robust Appetites to Calorie Counting: The Emergence of Dieting among Smith College Students in the 1920s," *Journal of Women's History* 7, 4 (winter 1995): 42.

32. Katherine Albert, "Diet—The Menace of Hollywood," *Photoplay* 35, 2 (Jan. 1929): 30; "Eat and Be Merry," *Photoplay* 36, 3 (Aug. 1929): 72, 106–7; Bert Ennis, "Meteor Called La Marr," *Motion Picture* 37, 1 (Sept. 1929): 40, 95.

33. Sylvia, "Beauty Is Made, Not Born," *Photoplay* 43, 2 (Jan. 1933): 70.

34. Pat Wallace, "These Film Fashions," *Picturegoer* 18, 105 (Sept. 1929): 50, 52, 54; Pat Wallace, "Moods and Modes," *Picturegoer* 19, 111 (Mar. 1930): 44–45.

35. "News! Views! Gossip!—Of Stars and Studios," *Photoplay* 39, 2 (Jan. 1931): 96; Seymour, "Seymour Says—Plot Your Summer Fashions by the Stars!" *Photoplay* 40, 1 (June 1931): 55; photograph of Frances Dee and Wynne Gibson, *Photoplay* 40, 2 (July 1931): 131; photographs of Mae Clark and June MacCloy, *Photoplay* 40, 3 (Aug. 1931): 12, 121.

36. "Artists, Showmen and Psychologists—They All View with Alarm the Strange Spectacle of Women in Trousers," unidentified newspaper clipping, ca. 1933, Academy of Motion Picture Arts and Sciences Library.

37. Floyd Simonton, unidentified newspaper clipping, ca. 1933, Academy of Motion Picture Arts and Sciences Library.

38. Ruth Biery, "Clothes Habits of Hollywood," *Photoplay* 39, 6 (May 1931): 72–73, 120; Harrison Carroll interview with Adrian, King Features Syndicate, 1933, printed in unidentified newspaper clipping, Academy of Motion Picture Arts and Sciences Library; report on International Association of Clothing Designers edict, unidentified newspaper clipping, 1933, Academy of Motion Picture Arts and Sciences Library.

39. Harry D. Wilson, "Hollywood's Newest Fad," *Motion Picture* 42, 1 (Aug. 1931): 44–45; "Good-By [sic] Skirts, Hello Pants," *Motion Picture* 42, 2 (Sept 1931): 50–51; "Forms of Relaxation," *Motion Picture* 51, 5 (June 1936): 41; photograph of Pauline Starke, *Photoplay* 42, 3 (Aug. 1932): 91; Powell, "Ladies with Legs," 183.

40. Weiss, *Vampires and Violets*, 33.

41. "College Girls in Men's Clothing," *Life* 9 (Sept. 30, 1940): 40–42.

42. Jane Cobb, "Girls Will Be Boys," *New York Times Magazine*, Nov. 3 1940: 10.

43. Katherine Albert, "Hollywood Leads Paris in Fashions!" *Photoplay* 36, 6 (Nov. 1929): 56–57, 138.

44. Laura Blayney, "Paris Answers Hollywood," *Motion Picture* 46, 5 (Dec. 1933): 45.

45. Dorothy Donnell, "Sex Appeal and the Clothes You Wear," *Motion Picture* 47, 2 (Mar. 1934): 28–29.

46. Advertisements, Photoplay 40, 1 (June 1931): 84; *Motion Picture* 42, 1 (Aug. 1931): back cover.

47. *Harper's Bazaar,* Nov. 1930: 91.

48. Claudia Brush Kidwell, "Gender Symbols or Fashionable Details?" in *Men and Women: Dressing the Part,* ed. Claudia B. Kidwell and Valerie Steele (Washington, D.C.: Smithsonian Institution Press, 1989), 124.

49. "The White Collar Girl: Research Notes for 'Kitty Foyle,'" *Life* 13, 13 (Mar. 25, 1940): 81.

50. Advertisement in *Photoplay* 37, 6 (May 1930): back cover.

51. Cited in Steele, "Dressing for Work," 84.

52. Ruth Shonle Cavan and Katherine Howland Ranck, *The Family and the Depression: A Study of One Hundred Chicago Families* (Chicago: University of Chicago Press, 1938), 161–70.

53. Ibid., 164.

54. Alice Kessler-Harris, *Out to Work: A History of Wage-Earning Women in the United States* (New York: Oxford University Press, 1982), 229, 256.

55. Constance Balides, "Scenarios of Exposure in the Practice of Everyday Life: Women in the Cinema of Attractions," *Screen* 34, 1 (spring 1993): 32.

56. Greenwald, *Women, War, and Work,* 99.

57. Cited in Mary Beth Haralovich, "The Proletarian Woman's Film of the 1930s: Contending with Censorship and Entertainment," *Screen* 31, 2 (summer 1990): 181–82.

58. Cited in ibid., 182.

59. In a prior scene, R. J. mentions that he is working on a campaign to sell cars "from the woman's angle," suggesting that Mac is being hired to write advertising aimed at women.

60. Erving Goffman, *Stigma: Notes on the Management of Spoiled Identity* (Middlesex: Penguin Books, 1968), 59.

61. The quotation in the heading is from the press book for *Female* (First National microfiche, 1930), 14.

62. Carolyn Van Wyck, "Helpful Advice on Girls' Problems," *Photoplay* 41, 2 (Jan. 1932): 70–71.

63. Ibid., 71.

64. Lois Scharf, *To Work and to Wed: Female Employment, Feminism, and the Great Depression* (Westport, Conn.: Greenwood Press, 1980), 100–101.

65. Rosalind Russell and Chris Chase, *Life Is a Banquet* (New York: Random House, 1977), 112–13.

66. Advertisement for *Leftover Ladies, Photoplay* 41, 1 (Dec. 1931): 16.

Conclusion

1. Herbert Blumer, *Movies and Conduct* (New York: Macmillan Company, 1933), 156–57.

2. Ibid., 45.

3. Valerie Steele, *Fashion and Eroticism* (New York: Oxford University Press, 1985), 248.

4. Christopher Breward, *The Culture of Fashion* (Manchester: Manchester University Press, 1995), 54–55.

5. Don Slater, *Consumer Culture and Modernity* (Cambridge: Polity Press, 1997), 31.

6. Victoria de Grazia, "Empowering Women as Citizen-Consumers," in *The Sex of Things: Gender and Consumption in Historical Perspective*, ed. Victoria de Grazia and Ellen Furlough (Berkeley: University of California Press, 1996), 275–76.

7. Ibid., 279.

8. Steven Cohan, "The Spy in the Grey Flannel Suit: Gender Performance and the Representation of Masculinity in *North by Northwest*," in *The Masculine Masquerade: Masculinity and Representation*, ed. Andrew Perchuk and Helaine Posner (Cambridge: MIT Press, 1995), 59.

9. Andrea Weiss, *Vampires and Violets: Lesbians in Film* (New York: Penguin Books, 1993), 28.

10. Pam Cook, *Fashioning the Nation: Costume and Identity in British Cinema* (London: BFI Publishing, 1996), 45.

11. Erving Goffman, *The Presentation of Self in Everyday Life* (New York: Doubleday, 1959).

12. Richard Dyer, *Only Entertainment* (London: Routledge, 1992), 65.

13. Cf. Warren Susman, *Culture as History: The Transformation of American Society in the Twentieth Century* (New York: Pantheon, 1984), 279.

14. Richard Sennett, *The Fall of Public Man: On the Social Psychology of Capitalism* (New York: Vintage, 1978).

15. Slater, *Consumer Culture and Modernity*, 95.

16. Dick Hebdige, *Subculture: The Meaning of Style* (London: Methuen, 1979), 107.

17. Slater, *Consumer Culture and Modernity*, 55; cf. John Berger, *Ways of Seeing* (London: BBC/Penguin Books, 1972), 45–64; Judith Williamson, *Decoding Advertisements: Ideology and Meaning in Advertising* (London: Boyars, 1978).

18. Cf. Arjun Appadurai, ed., *The Social Life of Things: Commodities in Cultural Perspective* (Cambridge: Cambridge University Press, 1986); Daniel Miller, *Material Culture and Mass Consumption* (Oxford: Basil Blackwell, 1987).

19. Pierre Bourdieu, *Distinction: A Social Critique of the Judgement of Taste*, trans. Richard Nice (Cambridge: Harvard University Press, 1984), 253.

20. Joanne Finkelstein, *The Fashioned Self* (Philadelphia: Temple University Press, 1991), 187.

21. Amy Spindler, "It's a Face-Lifted, Tummy-Tucked Jungle Out There: Fearing the Ax, Men Choose the Scalpel," *New York Times,* June 9, 1996, sec. 3: 1, 9.

FILMOGRAPHY

The following list includes films that formed a larger survey and contributed to my reading of representative films discussed in the text. Only the films' female stars are listed.

Algiers. Dir. John Cromwell. Perf. Hedy Lamarr. Walter Wanger. 1938.

Alice Adams. Dir. George Stevens. Perf. Katharine Hepburn. RKO. 1935.

Ann Vickers. Dir. John Cromwell. Perf. Irene Dunne. RKO. 1933.

Anna Karenina. Dir. Clarence Brown. Perf. Greta Garbo. MGM. 1935.

Arise My Love. Dir. Mitchell Leisen. Perf. Claudette Colbert. Paramount. 1940.

Artists and Models. Dir. Raoul Walsh. Perf. Ida Lupino. Paramount. 1937.

Artists and Models Abroad. Dir. Mitchell Leisen. Perf. Joan Bennett, Mary Boland. Paramount. 1938.

As You Desire Me. Dir. George Fitzmaurice. Perf. Greta Garbo. MGM. 1931.

Baby Face. Dir. Alfred E. Green. Perf. Barbara Stanwyck. Warner Bros. 1933.

Bachelor Mother. Dir. Garson Kanin. Perf. Ginger Rogers. RKO. 1939.

The Barretts of Wimpole Street. Dir. Sidney Franklin. Perf. Norma Shearer, Maureen O'Sullivan. MGM. 1934.

Beauty for the Asking. Dir. Glen Tryon. Perf. Lucille Ball. RKO. 1939.

Becky Sharp. Dir. Rouben Mamoulian. Perf. Miriam Hopkins. RKO. 1935.

Belle of the Nineties. Dir. Leo McCarey. Perf. Mae West. Paramount. 1934.

Big Business Girl. Dir. William A. Seiter. Perf. Loretta Young. First National. 1931.

Bird of Paradise. Dir. King Vidor. Perf. Dolores Del Rio. RKO. 1932.

The Bitter Tea of General Yen. Dir. Frank Capra. Perf. Barbara Stanwyck. Columbia. 1932.

Blonde Venus. Dir. Josef von Sternberg. Perf. Marlene Dietrich. Paramount. 1932.

The Blue Angel. Dir. Josef von Sternberg. Perf. Marlene Dietrich. UFA. 1930.

Bluebeard's Eighth Wife. Dir. Ernst Lubitsch. Perf. Claudette Colbert. Paramount. 1938.

Bombshell. Dir. Victor Fleming. Perf. Jean Harlow. MGM. 1933.

Bought. Dir. Archie Mayo. Perf. Constance Bennett. Warner Bros. 1931.

The Bride Walks Out. Dir. Leigh Jason. Perf. Barbara Stanwyck. RKO. 1936.

The Bride Wore Red. Dir. Dorothy Arzner. Perf. Joan Crawford. Paramount. 1937.

Broadway Melody of 1936. Dir. Roy Del Ruth. Perf. Eleanor Powell. MGM. 1935.

By Candlelight. Dir. James Whale. Perf. Elissa Landi. Universal. 1933.

Camille. Dir. George Cukor. Perf. Greta Garbo. MGM. 1937.

Christopher Strong. Dir. Dorothy Arzner. Perf. Katharine Hepburn. RKO. 1933.

Cleopatra. Dir. Cecil B. De Mille. Perf. Claudette Colbert. Paramount. 1934.

Colleen. Dir. Alfred E. Green. Ruby Keeler, Joan Blondell. Warner Bros. 1936.

La Cucaracha. Dir. Lloyd Corrigan. Perf. Steffi Duna. Pioneer Pictures Corporation. 1934.

Dames. Dir. Ray Enright. Perf. Joan Blondell, Ruby Keeler. Warner Bros. 1934.

Dance Fools, Dance. Dir. Harry Beaumont. Perf. Joan Crawford. MGM. 1931.

Dance Girl, Dance. Dir. Dorothy Arzner. Perf. Maureen O'Hara, Lucille Ball. RKO. 1940.

Dancing Lady. Dir. Robert Leonard. Perf. Joan Crawford. MGM. 1933.

The Dancing Pirate. Dir. Lloyd Corrigan. Perf. Steffi Duna, Rita Hayworth. Pioneer Picture Corporation. 1935.

Dangerous. Dir. Alfred E. Green. Perf. Bette Davis. Warner Bros. 1935.

Desire. Dir. Frank Borzage. Perf. Marlene Dietrich. Paramount. 1936.

Destry Rides Again. Dir. Joseph Pasternak. Perf. Marlene Dietrich. Universal. 1939.

The Devil Is a Woman. Dir. Josef von Sternberg. Perf. Marlene Dietrich. Paramount. 1935.

Dinner at Eight. Dir. George Cukor. Perf. Jean Harlow, Marie Dressler, Billie Burke. MGM. 1933.

The Divorcée. Dir. Robert Leonard. Perf. Norma Shearer. MGM. 1930.

Dodge City. Dir. Michael Curtiz. Perf. Olivia de Havilland. Warner Bros. 1939.

Double Wedding. Dir. Richard Thorpe. Perf. Myrna Loy. MGM. 1937.

Down Argentine Way. Dir. Irving Cummings. Perf. Carmen Miranda, Betty Grable. 20th Century Fox. 1940.

The Easiest Way. Dir. Jack Conway. Perf. Constance Bennett. MGM. 1931.

East Is West. Dir. Monta Bell. Perf. Lupe Velez. Universal Pictures. 1930.

Easy Living. Dir. Mitchell Leisen. Perf. Jean Arthur. Paramount. 1937.

Employees' Entrance. Dir. Roy Del Ruth. Perf. Loretta Young. Warner Bros. 1933.

Evangeline. Dir. Edwin Carewe. Perf. Dolores del Rio. Edwin Carewe Productions. 1929.

Every Day's a Holiday. Dir. Edward Sutherland. Perf. Mae West. Paramount. 1937.

Ex-Lady. Dir. Robert Florey. Perf. Bette Davis. Warner Bros. 1933.

Fashions of 1934. Dir. William Dieterle. Perf. Bette Davis. Warner Bros. 1934.

Female. Dir. Michael Curtiz. Perf. Ruth Chatterton. Warner Bros. 1933.

Fifth Avenue Girl. Dir. Gregory La Cava. Perf. Ginger Rogers. RKO. 1939.

Fig Leaves. Dir. Howard Hawks. Perf. Olive Borden, Phyllis Haver. Fox Film Corporation. 1926.

Flying Down to Rio. Dir. Thornton Freeland. Perf. Dolores Del Rio, Ginger Rogers. RKO. 1933.

Folies Bergère. Dir. Roy Del Ruth. Perf. Merle Oberon, Ann Sothern. 20th Century. 1935.

A Free Soul. Dir. Clarence Brown. Perf. Norma Shearer. MGM. 1931.

Front Page Woman. Dir. Michael Curtiz. Perf. Bette Davis. Warner Bros. 1935.

The Gang's All Here. Dir. Busby Berkeley. Perf. Carmen Miranda, Alice Faye. 20th Century Fox. 1943.

The Garden of Allah. Dir. Richard Boleslawski. Perf. Marlene Dietrich. Selznick IP. 1936.

The Girl from Mexico (Mexican Spitfire). Dir. Leslie Goodwins. Perf. Lupe Velez. RKO. 1938.

Glorifying the American Girl. Dir. Millard Webb, John Harkrider. Perf. Mary Eaton. Paramount. 1929.

Goin' to Town. Dir. Alexander Hall. Perf. Mae West. Paramount. 1935.

Gold Diggers of 1933. Dir. Mervyn Le Roy. Perf. Joan Blondell, Aline MacMahon, Ruby Keeler. Warner Bros. 1933.

Gold Diggers of 1935. Dir. Busby Berkeley. Perf. Gloria Stuart, Alice Brady. Warner Bros. 1935.

The Golden Arrow. Dir. Alfred E. Green. Perf. Bette Davis. Warner Bros. 1936.

The Goldwyn Follies. Dir. George Marshall. Perf. Vera Zorina. Goldwyn. 1938.

Gone with the Wind. Dir. Victor Fleming. Perf. Vivien Leigh. MGM/Selznick. 1939.

The Good Earth. Dir. Sidney Franklin. Perf. Luise Rainer. MGM. 1937.

The Gorgeous Hussy. Dir. Clarence Brown. Perf. Joan Crawford. MGM. 1936.

The Great Ziegfeld. Dir. Robert Leonard. Perf. Myrna Loy. MGM. 1936.

The Greeks Had a Word for Them. Dir. Lowell Sherman. Perf. Joan Blondell, Madge Evans, Ina Claire. United Artists. 1932.

The Half Naked Truth. Dir. Mervyn LeRoy. Perf. Lupe Velez. Warner Bros. 1933.

Hallelujah! Dir. Charles Vidor. Perf. Nina Mae McKinney. MGM. 1929.

Hands across the Table. Dir. Mitchell Leisen. Perf. Carole Lombard. Paramount. 1935.

Her Jungle Love. Dir. George Archainbaud. Perf. Dorothy Lamour. Paramount. 1938.

Hips, Hips, Hooray. Dir. Mark Sandrich. Perf. Ruth Etting, Thelma Todd. RKO. 1934.

Hired Wife. Dir. William Seiter. Perf. Rosalind Russell. Universal. 1940.

His Girl Friday. Dir. Howard Hawks. Perf. Rosalind Russell. Columbia. 1940.

Holiday. Dir. George Cukor. Perf. Katharine Hepburn. Columbia. 1938.

Hollywood—Style Center of the World. Loews, Inc. 1939.

Honolulu. Dir. Edward Buzzell. Perf. Eleanor Powell. MGM. 1938.

Hot Pepper. Dir. John Blystone. Perf. Lupe Velez. 20th Century Fox. 1933.

The Hurricane. Dir. John Ford. Perf. Dorothy Lamour. Goldwyn. 1937.

I'm No Angel. Dir. Wesley Ruggles. Perf. Mae West. Paramount. 1933.

Idiot's Delight. Dir. Clarence Brown. Perf. Norma Shearer. MGM. 1939.

Imitation of Life. Dir. John Stahl. Perf. Claudette Colbert, Louise Beavers. Universal. 1934.

In Caliente. Dir. Lloyd Bacon. Perf. Dolores Del Rio. Warner Bros. 1935.

In Person. Dir. William A. Seiter. Perf. Ginger Rogers. RKO. 1935.

Jezebel. Dir. William Wyler. Perf. Bette Davis. Warner Bros. 1938.

Jungle Princess. Dir. William Thiele. Perf. Dorothy Lamour. Paramount. 1936.

King of Chinatown. Dir. Nick Grinde. Perf. Anna May Wong. Paramount. 1939.

Kitty Foyle. Dir. Sam Wood. Perf. Ginger Rogers. RKO. 1940.

Kongo. Dir. William Cowen. Perf. Lupe Velez. MGM. 1932.

Lady of the Tropics. Dir. Jack Conway. Perf. Hedy Lamarr. MGM. 1939.

The Last of Mrs. Cheyney. Dir. Sidney Franklin. Perf. Norma Shearer. MGM. 1929.

The Last of Mrs. Cheyney. Dir. Richard Boleslawski. Perf. Joan Crawford. MGM. 1937.

Letty Lynton. Dir. Clarence Brown. Perf. Joan Crawford. MGM. 1932.

Little Women. Dir. George Cukor. Perf. Katharine Hepburn, Joan Bennett. RKO. 1933.

Lost Horizon. Dir. Frank Capra. Perf. Jane Wyatt. Columbia. 1937.

Madam Satan. Dir. Cecil B. De Mille. Perf. Kay Johnson. MGM. 1930.

Madame Du Barry. Dir. William Dieterle. Perf. Dolores Del Rio. Warner Bros. 1934.

Mannequin. Dir. Frank Borzage. Perf. Joan Crawford. MGM. 1938.

Marie Antoinette. Dir. W. S. Van Dyke II. Perf. Norma Shearer. MGM. 1938.

Marked Woman. Dir. Lloyd Bacon. Perf. Bette Davis. Warner Bros. 1937.

Mary of Scotland. Dir. John Ford. Perf. Katharine Hepburn. RKO. 1936.

Mata Hari. Dir. George Fitzmaurice. Perf. Greta Garbo. MGM. 1931.

Midnight. Dir. Joseph Kane. Perf. Claudette Colbert. Paramount. 1939.

A Midsummer Night's Dream. Dir. Max Reinhardt, William Dieterle. Perf. Jean Muir, Olivia de Havilland. Warner Bros. 1935.

More Than a Secretary. Dir. Alfred E. Green. Perf. Jean Arthur. Columbia. 1936.

Morocco. Dir. Josef von Sternberg. Perf. Marlene Dietrich. Paramount. 1930.

Moulin Rouge. Dir. Sidney Lanfield. Perf. Constance Bennett. United Artists. 1934.

Mr. Deeds Goes to Town. Dir. Frank Capra. Perf. Jean Arthur. Columbia. 1936.

Mr. Smith Goes to Washington. Dir. Frank Capra. Perf. Jean Arthur. Columbia. 1939.

My Man Godfrey. Dir. Gregory La Cava. Perf. Carole Lombard. Universal. 1936.

Ninotchka. Dir. Ernst Lubitsch. Perf. Greta Garbo. MGM. 1939.

Nothing Sacred. Dir. William Wellman. Perf. Carole Lombard. Selznick. 1937.

On Your Back. Dir. Guthrie McClintic. Perf. Irene Rich. Fox. 1930.

Our Blushing Brides. Dir. Harry Beaumont. Perf. Joan Crawford. MGM/Cosmopolitan. 1930.

Our Daily Bread. Dir. Charles Vidor. Perf. Karen Morley. United Artists/Viking. 1934.

Our Dancing Daughters. Dir. Harry Beaumont. Perf. Joan Crawford. MGM/Cosmopolitan. 1928.

The Painted Veil. Dir. Richard Boleslawski. Perf. Greta Garbo. MGM. 1934.

Personal Property. Dir. W. S. Van Dyke. Perf. Jean Harlow. MGM. 1937.

The Philadelphia Story. Dir. George Cukor. Perf. Katharine Hepburn, Ruth Hussey. MGM. 1940.

Platinum Blonde. Dir. Frank Capra. Perf. Loretta Young. Columbia. 1931.

Possessed. Dir. Clarence Brown. Perf. Joan Crawford. MGM. 1931.

The Princess Comes Across. Dir. William K. Howard. Perf. Carole Lombard. Paramount. 1936.

Private Lives. Dir. Sidney Franklin. Perf. Norma Shearer. MGM. 1931.

The Private Lives of Elizabeth and Essex. Dir. Michael Curtiz. Perf. Bette Davis. Warner Bros. 1939.

The Purchase Price. Dir. William Wellman. Perf. Barbara Stanwyck. Warner Bros. 1932.

Queen Christina. Dir. Rouben Mamoulian. Perf. Greta Garbo. MGM. 1933.

Rain. Dir. Lewis Milestone. Perf. Joan Crawford. United Artists. 1932.

Ramona. Dir. Henry King. Perf. Loretta Young. 20th Century Fox. 1936.

Red Headed Woman. Dir. Jack Conway. Perf. Jean Harlow. MGM. 1932.

Resurrection. Dir. Edwin Carewe. Perf. Lupe Velez. Universal. 1931.

Road to Singapore. Dir. V. Schertzinger. Perf. Dorothy Lamour. Paramount. 1940.

Roberta. Dir. William A. Seiter. Perf. Irene Dunne, Ginger Rogers. RKO. 1935.

Romance. Dir. Clarence Brown. Perf. Greta Garbo. MGM. 1933.

Romeo and Juliet. Dir. George Cukor. Perf. Norma Shearer. MGM. 1936.

Sadie Mckee. Dir. Clarence Brown. Perf. Joan Crawford. MGM. 1934.

The Scarlet Empress. Dir. Josef von Sternberg. Perf. Marlene Dietrich. Paramount. 1934.

Shanghai Express. Dir. Josef von Sternberg. Perf. Marlene Dietrich. Paramount. 1932.

She Done Him Wrong. Dir. Lowell Sherman. Perf. Mae West. Paramount. 1933.

She Loves Me Not. Dir. Elliott Nugent. Perf. Miriam Hopkins, Kitty Carlisle. Paramount. 1934.

The Sheik. Dir. George Melford. Perf. Rudolph Valentino. Famous Players-Lasky. 1921.

The Shining Hour. Dir. Frank Borzage. Perf. Joan Crawford. MGM. 1938.

Show Boat. Dir. James Whale. Perf. Irene Dunne, Helen Morgan. Universal. 1936.

The Sign of the Cross. Dir. Cecil B. De Mille. Perf. Elissa Landi, Claudette Colbert. Paramount. 1932.

Skyscraper Souls. Dir. Edgar Selwyn. Perf. Maureen O'Sullivan, Verree Teasdale. Warner Bros. 1932.

Smilin' Through. Dir. Sidney Franklin. Perf. Norma Shearer. MGM. 1932.

The Squaw Man. Dir. Cecil B. De Mille. Perf. Lupe Velez. MGM. 1931.

St Louis Blues. Dir. Raoul Walsh. Perf. Dorothy Lamour. Paramount. 1939.

Stage Door. Dir. Gregory LaCava. Perf. Katharine Hepburn, Ginger Rogers. RKO. 1937.

A Star Is Born. Dir. William Wellman. Perf. Janet Gaynor. Selznick IP. 1937.

Stella Dallas. Dir. King Vidor. Perf. Barbara Stanwyck. Goldwyn. 1937.

Stolen Holiday. Dir. Michael Curtiz. Perf. Kay Francis. Warner Bros. 1937.

The Story of Vernon and Irene Castle. Dir. H. Potter/G. Haight. Perf. Ginger Rogers. RKO. 1939.

Street of Women. Dir. Archie Mayo. Perf. Kay Francis. Warner Bros. 1932.

Sullivan's Travels. Dir. Preston Sturges. Perf. Veronica Lake. Paramount. 1940.

Sylvia Scarlett. Dir. George Cukor. Perf. Katharine Hepburn. RKO. 1935.

Too Hot to Handle. Dir. Jack Conway. Perf. Myrna Loy. MGM. 1938.

Top Hat. Dir. Mark Sandrich. Perf. Ginger Rogers, Fred Astaire. RKO. 1935.

Topper. Dir. Norman McLeod. Perf. Constance Bennett. MGM. 1937.

Tropic Holiday. Dir. Theodore Reed. Perf. Dorothy Lamour. Paramount. 1938.

Trouble in Paradise. Dir. Ernst Lubitsch. Perf. Miriam Hopkins, Kay Francis. Paramount. 1932.

Union Pacific. Dir. Cecil B. De Mille. Perf. Barbara Stanwyck. Paramount. 1939.

Vogues of 1938. Dir. Irving Cummings. Perf. Joan Bennett. Walter Wanger. 1937.

What Price Hollywood? Dir. George Cukor. Perf. Constance
Bennett. RKO. 1932.

Wife vs. Secretary. Dir. Clarence Brown. Perf. Myrna Loy,
Jean Harlow. MGM. 1936.

The Wizard of Oz. Dir. Victor Fleming. Perf. Judy Garland.
MGM. 1939.

The Women. Dir. George Cukor. Perf. Norma Shearer,
Joan Crawford, Rosalind Russell, Paulette Goddard,
Joan Fontaine. MGM. 1939.

Wuthering Heights. Dir. William Wyler. Perf. Merle Oberon.
Goldwyn. 1939.

You and Me. Dir. Fritz Lang. Perf. Sylvia Sidney. Paramount.
1938.

INDEX

Sarah Berry is assistant professor of film and media studies and production at the College of Staten Island, City University of New York.